monsoonbooks

IN LUST WE TRUST

Gerrie Lim is a former Los Angeles music critic who was writing for *Billboard*, *Playboy*, *L.A. Style*, and *L.A. Weekly* when he found himself sidetracked into reporting about the adult entertainment industry in America. He wrote the popular "Cinema Blue" column for *Penthouse Variations* magazine (under the pseudonym Drew McKenzie) from 1999 to 2002, and then reported on the adult Internet industry as the International Correspondent for the trade journal *AVN Online*.

He is the bestselling author of three previous books: *Invisible Trade: High-class Sex for Sale in Singapore* (Monsoon Books, 2004), *Idol to Icon: The Creation of Celebrity Brands* (Cyan Books/Marshall Cavendish, 2005) and *Inside The Outsider: A Decade of Shooting the Pop Culture Breeze* (BigO Books, 2001). He spends his time in Los Angeles, London, and Singapore.

ALSO BY GERRIE LIM

Invisible Trade:
High-class sex for sale in Singapore

Idol to Icon:
The Creation of Celebrity Brands

Inside The Outsider:
A Decade of Shooting the Pop Culture Breeze

IN LU$T WE TRUST

WE TRUST

Adventures in adult cinema

GERRIE LIM

monsoon

monsoonbooks

Published in 2006
by Monsoon Books Pte Ltd
106 Jalan Hang Jebat #02–14
Singapore 139527
www.monsoonbooks.com.sg

ISBN-10: 981-05-5302-1
ISBN-13: 978-981-05-5302-9

Cover photograph of Asia Carrera©James Hundhausen
Author photograph©Russel Wong

Printed in Singapore

10 09 08 07 06   2 3 4 5 6 7 8 9

For P.H.
"Beware the naked concierge!"

Her body was a mirror that reflected back not only her feelings about the world, but her feelings about herself.

Wei Hui, *Marrying Buddha*

Contents

Part Three

Naked Hollywood

Foreplay

"Porn stars have issues like Kleenex has tissues." Annabel Chong said that to me one afternoon as we were having drinks on a balcony overlooking the pool at the Regent Beverly Wilshire, the very same hotel in Beverly Hills where, aptly, Julia Roberts played the naïve hooker and Richard Gere her suave client in their Hollywood hit movie *Pretty Woman*. (Not all porn stars were hookers, of course, though I knew some who were. Annabel wasn't one of them.)

This book, which began in Los Angeles and ended in London, was initially built around that idea, the strange nexus of innocence and commerce reflected by the "personalities" that these girls projected, as part of their "celebrity branding."

I was curious to explore the difference between the illusion and the reality. However, as time went by, the book morphed into something different, for which I am strangely indebted to the late Spalding Gray, whose monologue *Swimming to Cambodia* (about the filming of the Roland Joffé film *The Killing Fields*) first planted the seed. I first read it in July 2001, on board an Amtrak train from Los Angeles to Santa Barbara, and it was then that the idea of my own extended first-person account of the adult film industry in America began to take shape.

I wanted the book to be both a memoir and a travelogue, in which I could communicate my perspectives on the adult film industry, a business colossus that once evoked nervous mirth but now arouses genuine curiosity in so many people, to the point where it has become a mainstream staple of pop culture today. At the end of 2005, the American adult film industry generated an unprecedented US$12.6 billion, in a year in which a record-high 13,588 hardcore titles were issued by the various production companies. Such numbers were surely countervailing forces against the conservative views of the George W. Bush administration.

This was suddenly the tenor of our times, wrought of the winds of change that reflected new realities. Not everyone has to like what the adult entertainment industry produces, and perhaps understandably so, but everyone has to now confront its obvious existence. Because Jenna Jameson had become a household name. And so I asked Jenna about what fame had done for her, and her views were quoted in *Penthouse* in her Pet of the Month layout. Because Asia Carrera was a genius at the stock market. And so I wrote a story about Asia, commissioned by and published in *The Wall Street Journal*. I found myself in the position of explaining the inner workings of a whole industry to a mainstream audience that, until recent years, had little or no access to such arcane knowledge.

I then felt compelled to chronicle that journey, a ten-year cycle of events inspired and motivated by an astute observation I had first encountered in Joan Didion's *The White Album*, the very book that made me want to become a writer, in which she wrote: "We live entirely, especially if we are writers, by the imposition of a narrative line upon disparate images. By the 'ideas' with which we have learned to freeze the shifting phantasmagoria which is our actual experience."

This, then, is a book of my actual experiences.

Gerrie Lim
April 2006

Part One

Landing on Mars

Enter Drew McKenzie

Annabel Chong, over dinner one night, pointed out to me the fact that we were the only two people from Singapore involved in the adult film industry.

We ate out on a wooden deck with a panoramic view of Benedict Canyon, a setting so lush that we could've been in Tuscany but for the howling coyotes reminding us that we were still in Los Angeles. Perhaps it was the crisp autumn air, a nice if nippy chill we'd never get back home, but Annabel thought her observation really funny. From a country of four million people, there were just the two of us. From a country where porn is illegal, no less, which made us an even rarer pair. Double happiness. Or double trouble.

We laughed about this, as we watched the sporadic traffic below us taking those famous bends on Mulholland Drive. Maybe that car whizzing by was Jack Nicholson and Lara Flynn Boyle. Or maybe it was nobody. There were lots of nobodies in this town, enroute to becoming somebodies. A lot of them were aspiring actresses, some who transitioned from struggling in mainstream Hollywood to become porn stars. Annabel was one of them, but she now preferred to be known by her real name, Grace Quek, because she was about to retire from the business. She was tired of being the girl from Singapore—the tiny city-state in Southeast Asia—who had become a celebrity, literally overnight, thanks to one infamous gangbang.

The one significant difference between us, of course, is that I've neither disrobed in front of the camera nor participated in a gangbang. However, that's only because I'm always on the other side of the camera, as the ersatz scribe and enthusiastic chronicler of lust, the not-so-innocent bystander and, for better or for worse (usually worse), the only writer from Southeast Asia to land on Mars.

The red planet, figuratively speaking, happens to be the San Fernando Valley, annexed by Los Angeles in 1915 and still the epicenter of that ongoing earthquake called American porn. "Mars ain't no place to raise a kid," to quote Elton John from his song "Rocket Man." An anonymous urban sprawl north of Los Angeles, the Valley (as it is more popularly known, thanks to Moon Unit Zappa's hit song "Valley Girl") comprises 220 square miles of mostly residential homes, apartments and ugly strip malls. The physical area is about the same size as Singapore.

I have long harbored a personal theory as to why the San Fernando Valley is porn's Ground Zero. The sheer sameness of the place, with all the solidly middle-class houses with their identical meticulously mowed lawns and ultra-clean residential streets, offers the perfect anonymity for anyone wanting to shoot porn. Even *AVN* (*Adult Video News*, the trade journal of the industry) is headquartered here, on a small side street in quiet, suburban Chatsworth. A few blocks away, every few minutes or so, some director is calling "Cut" as a couple disengages after having rutted furiously. Condoms get discarded, vibrators stop buzzing, and baby wipes go around to dry off the nether regions, all in a day's work.

Sure, some sex-starved nosy neighbor might call the police if they peek over the hedge and spy naked people next door, but it really doesn't happen often. Everything is done with a modicum of secrecy. Both cast and crew are told to park their cars a discreet distance away from the house. But funny things do happen, like the time two girls, Gwen Summers and Jessica Drake, attracted police to the house because a neighbor had alerted them to screams. When the cops arrived, they discovered that it was Gwen who'd been screaming, in ecstasy.

"It was a movie for Legend Video, called *Sex Acts*," Jessica told me. "I was dressed like a fairy godmother and Gwen was a princess, and I was fucking her with a strap-on so hard that the police showed up. They thought it was domestic violence. So I'm walking around the set wearing a strap-on and we're taking a break and I didn't know the police were there yet. And I'm walking around pretending like I'm jacking off, and I ran right into the cops. I went, 'Holy shit!' I'm standing there naked wearing a strap-on!

"They said, 'We got a call for domestic violence and there has been some screaming and yelling.' And I pointed to Gwen and said, 'It's her! It's all her fault!' The cops were laughing, because I'm sure it's happened to them before, and they said, 'We're just going to go ahead and take a look around the premises, so that we can say we searched everything.'"

"I am a sex worker," Jessica cheerfully declared to me, having starred in such porn-fan favorites as *Blonde Brigade*, *High Infidelity*, *Trick Baby*, *Trailer Trash Nurses* (and, let's not forget, the sequel *Trailer Trash Nurses 2*), and the best-selling adult DVD of all time, the Jenna Jameson scorcher *Dream Quest*. "I got into this business to do that, so people could see me have sex on camera, for the attention. I want it. Everybody look at me! Me, me, me! And I like the fact that I inspire people. I realize that I provide a fantasy and I'm fine with that. I want to be everybody's fantasy."

We writers, ever on the lookout for the soundbite, love this kind of stuff. So many of us have penned pieces about porn, even literary lions like Martin Amis, and serious magazines like *The Economist* ("Branded Flesh," read its headline in the issue of August 14, 1999, a piece about porn's biggest studio, Vivid Video). The modern world had accommodated the preferences of those with non-vanilla sexual tastes—a trickle-down victory for the 60s counterculture and the 70s feminist movement. Libertarian democracy is about having freedom of choice and its proponents, people like me, were no longer shunned but now made to feel privileged. People I met at dinner parties would raise an eyebrow but also pepper me with questions galore. "Is there really such a thing as a fluffer?", "You actually had lunch with Asia Carrera at her house?", "Have you ever met Tera Patrick?" I have also lost count of the guys who beg for knowledge of their favorite stars from the past: porn queens like Kristara Barrington, Tori Welles, Rachel Ryan, and Tiffany Mynx. "So did you test-drive her?" a woman asked me with a knowing wink, when she found out that I knew *her* favorite porn star.

With such smartass *joie de vivre* was this book written, covering a ten-year cycle from 1995 (when I started out working for *Spice*, the adult cable channel) to my most recent journalistic outpost (as International Correspondent for *AVN Online*, the journal of the online adult business). The pinnacle of that decade was, undoubtedly, the four years I wrote the "Cinema Blue" column for *Penthouse Variations*, from the issues of October 1999 to that of April 2002, the very last one containing what many would surely consider my all-time professional highlight: my very own interview with queen bee Jenna Jameson herself. In such top-tier fashion did I leave Bob Guccione's then-ailing empire, with no small whimper but a nice, if non-coital, bodacious bang.

Two years later, Jenna published her autobiography, the coyly titled *How to Make Love Like a Porn Star: A Cautionary Tale*, which became a *New York Times* bestseller, the closest to mainstream success that anyone in the industry has attained. Good for her, I thought. "I made it one of my missions to get this industry accepted by the public," she told me. "And I think I have been pretty successful in doing that, especially in getting it accepted by women. They see my interviews and go, 'Wow, she's a real person! She's like me. She has a personality like me. And she has no inhibitions when it comes to her sexuality.' I think that has an impact on the way some women go about their sex lives." This quote was also used in the text accompanying Jenna's *Penthouse* Pet of the Month centerfold layout in 2004 (*Penthouse* owns the copyright to everything written by all its writers, hence they could use it without even notifying me; I never even knew about this till I saw the magazine itself, but I felt proud to be credited.)

That single utterance by Jenna, in my opinion, summarized the cult of the porn star in all its postmodern glory. Never underestimate the vicarious pleasure compelled by the image of the sexually available woman. How else could one explain why porn in America has become such a massive business?

In 1998 I began researching the stats and discovered that a whopping 686 million adult videos were rented in the United States. By 2001, out of US$63 billion earned in video rentals, US$23 billion came from adult films. Whenever the American economy seemed to career upon uncertainty, porn (both online and offline) seemed the only business growth area, with no end in sight. Indeed, at the time of writing, the American adult entertainment industry is at its strongest ever, having generated US$12.6 billion in the year 2005 alone. Of this, US$4.3 billion (or thirty-four percent) came from video sales and rentals and another US$2.5 billion (or twenty percent) came from adult Internet sales.

"Because the majority of companies are privately held, hard numbers are difficult to ascertain," noted Paul Fishbein, president of *AVN* Publications. "But when you add up all the segments, from videos and magazines to strip clubs and Internet, a number that approaches US$13 billion seems logical." The total number of hardcore titles released in 2005 was a record 13,588 (including new releases, features, and that ever-reliable money-spinner, those two- to four-hour "greatest hits" compilations). There were 957 million rentals of adult DVDs and VHS tapes in 2005, and the wholesale value of these sold throughout the year had topped the one-billion-dollar mark. (The study was culled from combined research done by *AVN*, *Forbes*, the *New York Times*, Kagan Research, Juniper Research, and an influential pro-porn advocacy group, the Free Speech Coalition.)

And some of this was the indirect result of people like me.

Why? Because I was commissioned by my editors to provide readers with provocative prose, since I was in the privileged position of getting to meet the lovely *Penthouse* Pets on their movie sets. "Did you ever have any formative moments when you realized that you were born to be a sex goddess? Were you always sexually exhibitionistic?" I asked the sultry brunette Devinn Lane, *Penthouse* Pet of the Month for October 1999 and contract girl since January 2000 with Wicked Pictures. Devinn had starred in teasingly titled films like *Bordello Blues* and *Working Girl* and would shortly go on to create and host the *Playboy TV* hit reality series *7 Lives Xposed*. (A holdover from the old Hollywood studio system, "contract girls" get paid massive amounts of money to work exclusively for a single company, for whom they are required to star in a set number of films each year.)

"I can remember," Devinn purred, "being very young and being excited by the fact that boys were interested in me, that they were watching me, that they would make comments about how my breasts bounced up and down whenever I walked down the hallway to my locker. There was a kid who would pull my skirt down in the middle of the quad at school, and it really wasn't that embarrassing to me. Those are the things you don't understand until you get older and you realize you are an exhibitionist. I actually enjoyed the fact that everybody saw that."

That sounded mildly tittilating, to be sure, but what was really interesting about that interview was that it could be seen in the full glory of widescreen DVD. Yes, sweet young Devinn was cheerfully topless, her 36D breasts bouncing away happily as she gleefully chatted with me on a couch backstage, making for my only appearance thus far in an adult DVD. (The viewer need only click on "Devinn Lane Interview" in the extra features section of her film *Jack and Jill*, produced in 2001 by Wicked Pictures.) Naturally, I can be seen keeping my composure throughout.

However, as often happened, the old excitement started to wane for young Devinn, and on November 14, 2005, she officially announced that she was parting ways with Wicked Pictures, her onscreen home for the past six years. Towards the later part of her contract, which expired in July 2005, she had moved to the other side of the camera and had directed and produced twenty-five films, including *Pillow Talk*, *Beautiful Nasty*, a three-part series called *Road Trixx,* and a talk-show series called *The Devinn Lane Show*, the latter in mock tribute to David Letterman—complete with zany "Top 6 or 9" lists ("Top 9 Reasons Why An Adult Film Star Should be President") and interview segments where her fellow porn star "guests" giggled away while she chatted with them and showed clips from their latest films (usually, and conveniently, those from Wicked Pictures). Truly, to see a gorgeous blond lass beaming ever so proudly following a ten-minute clip of her performing virtuoso oral and then vaginal sex, was something Letterman could never even dream of having on his show. Writing about adult film was a newfound challenge in my first forays, as I found myself professionally examining the genre. The very first "Cinema Blue" column, which I wrote in the spring of 1999, was a piece of live *reportage*—my first-person "fly on the wall" view of a porn shoot. The film was entitled, aptly, *Flesh for Fantasy*, and the venue was the Malibu beach house of the director, Nic Cramer. It featured a winsome threesome—Rebecca Lord, Linda Thoren, and Keri Windsor—three girls, sucking tit and licking clit, with colored vibrators and rubber toys to boot. My prose was naturally evocative of such nuances:

> Linda sat on Rebecca's bare thighs and promptly impaled
> herself with the rubber member. The camera followed it
> disappearing into her vagina ... After Linda cried out with
> one orgasm after another, it was time for another break.
> "Some producers here in L.A. call me Linda Decibel," she
> told me, sipping cold water from a tall glass. "It's a bit
> embarrassing. I'm actually very shy, but when I'm naked
> in front of a camera, it's totally different. I don't know
> what comes over me. I just become this sexual being, an

21

exhibitionist, a complete slut. I really like it when guys get to see a close-up of my pussy."

My editor at *Penthouse Variations* was V.K. McCarty, herself a whip-wielding demi-goddess (known as Mam'selle Victoire) in the New York S&M scene. In that story, the first of many I would write under the column "Cinema Blue" for her magazine, I was to play a role, "a film critic from a small Midwestern newspaper," an observer reporting back for the one-handed reading of our faithful subscribers. I was told to conjure my own *nom de plume*, and I chose Drew McKenzie, a zesty moniker bespeaking sexy, androgynous *frisson*. (For maybe two seconds, I thought of calling myself Norman Bates, from Hitchcock's *Psycho*, but it just didn't have the same ring.)

And so I navigated the world of gorgeous women with perfect hair and pendulous breasts, armed with the best disguise; I was a bespectacled Asian guy with a prep-school vocabulary and graying Bruce Lee hair, who carried around the film sets three vital things: a notebook, a tape recorder, and an attitude.

I copped the industry parlance. I could talk to directors like Andrew Blake, about directors like Paul Thomas; to A-list girls like Asia Carrera, about girls like Stephanie Swift. All it took was an uncanny ability to set them at ease, so they could feel like I was their confidante.

Sexual openness is also about sexual trust. Shayla LaVeaux, for instance, once stopped in mid-sentence to thank me: "You make me feel very comfortable, Gerrie, you're a great interviewer." She then continued telling me about the first time she ever masturbated in her family bathtub when she was twelve years old. Halli Aston gasped when she found out I was from *Penthouse Variations*. "That was the first porn I ever read!" she gushed, and told me she had learned to masturbate from perusing it after discovering her father's secret magazine stash. (I didn't need an ice-breaker with her after that, and we did a long three-hour interview.) And Jenna Jameson had no trouble telling me her pet stories about sex in public places (hers was in an open hallway at the Beverly Hills Hotel, with her then-boyfriend).

It was a favorite interview tactic of mine; if they were ever ill at ease to disclose raunchy details, I could first share my own (in a darkened corner of a disco, as I disclosed to Jenna, with a tall blonde I'd only just met; "That's so cool!" Jenna squealed). In such manner, they could somehow sense in me a kindred spirit and then trust me enough to tell all. You catch more flies with honey, as they say.

In some ways, it was meant to be my gig, because *Penthouse Variations* was America's digest-size journal of fetish and kink, with a 300,000 circulation mostly in the Midwest. Yes, in the quaint enclaves of the Bible Belt and the quiet suburbs of Stepford Wife country! What better, more perfect readership could there be? A survey of our subscribers in 1998 revealed that ninety-three percent preferred magazines as their main source of erotica, ninety-one percent indicated that they masturbate and enjoy it, fifty-three percent admitted they frequented sex shops, and thirty-sevem percent had been *Penthouse Variations* readers for more than ten years.

I think that V.K. might have factored into the equation the implications of my coming from Singapore, a country where *Penthouse* cannot be bought legally and porn is still banned. I think she saw in me someone who could revel in my mission, to invade all those impressionable minds, all those places where seemingly staid people did delightfully nasty things behind closed doors, things they wouldn't dare tell their conservative neighbors at the local church fair. She liked the fact, I'm sure, that I did not fit the stereotype of the goofy, buck-toothed, short-haired, nebbish Asian man at all, but rather seemed like someone these people could actually hang out with. I was going to be, as she put it, "our man in the San Fernando Valley."

I remember my first Drew McKenzie fan letter. Some guy wrote me from Ohio, telling me how much he enjoyed reading my interviews with these girls and asking me for recommendations on porn movies to rent. He also wanted to know if the girls had real orgasms on screen. He must have liked my movie tips, for he never wrote back. Who knows how much I may have changed his life?

I remember how mine was changed.

In 1986, I was living *la vida loca*, the acceptably mad life of a rock critic in Los Angeles, writing about music for stylish magazines like *L.A. Style*, *L.A. Weekly*, and *Playboy*, and interviewing the likes of Tina Turner, David Bowie, and Pete Townshend. One night, I'd arrived late at a music industry function and took the very last seat available, which found me next to an elfin blonde lass. Her name was Karen and she spent most of the evening telling me about how she had moved from her small town in West Virginia, expressly to become a rock star. She sang in a band, one of many gigging the L.A. club circuit in hopes of snagging that big-time record contract.

Maybe she thought I could help her career. Or maybe she was too drunk. After the party, I walked her to her car and leaned in to kiss her goodnight, and she responded by promptly jamming her tongue down my throat.

Well, to paraphrase Bruce Springsteen's hit song of that day, you can't light a fire without a spark. Karen and I dated for about a year. She worked a secretarial job in downtown L.A., and I would meet her for dinner. We would return to her office later, to spend the rest of the night on the carpet, the table, the armchair. You name it, we did it. She would call me the next morning to tell me about the rug burns.

Karen's favorite thing to do on weekends was to smoke a bag of pot, get totally stoned, pop in a tape and watch porn. I hadn't been watching much porn at all, at that point, and was only vaguely interested in it, but now I had somehow chosen to exchange bodily fluids with a porn fan. Good golly Miss Molly, what was I thinking? Karen's finest long-term contribution to my life, however, outlasted our relationship; she subscribed to the

Adam & Eve mailing list, and put me on the list too.

Adam & Eve, the largest adult entertainment mail-order company in America, fine purveyors of everything from videos to vibrators, was based in the unlikely outback town of Carrboro, North Carolina. Like many mail-order companies, it often urged its subscribers to refer friends. Thanks to Karen's generous initiative, those mail-order catalogs continued to arrive in my mailbox month after month, long after we broke up. I began to peruse them with newfound wonder.

The osmosis was taking effect, immeasurably, the seed firmly planted. I had discovered porn. It always happens when you're not looking. Especially when a woman you're actually having sex with turns out to be the wicked messenger.

Something else transpired, just before Karen and I split up at the end of 1987. One sunny afternoon, in a public parking lot, Karen was giving me a blowjob in my car. She was an exquisite deep-throater. I could actually feel the very back of her throat; a mildly strange but not entirely unpleasant sensation which aroused me even more. So I was a bit perturbed when she suddenly stopped.

"There's a security guard watching us," she whispered, looking out the window of my car, a sporty Volkswagen Scirocco painted gold with a handsome maroon trim—a likely target for parking-lot voyeurs on any given day but, surely, more so with a blonde inside visibly bobbing her head up and down.

She looked at me, I looked at her, and we burst into giggles. "Why not?" she shrugged. "Let him watch." And with that, she immediately put my cock back in her mouth.

Thanks to this moment of telepathy, leading to sheer spontaneity, we were performing in our very own porn movie, sans camera. We did have one viewer, so I guess that counted.

Years later, I would interview porn stars who would tell me what a rush it was for them, knowing people were watching them do the same on camera. The more people watching, the better— that's what they always told me. Turning people on was what they did for a living, after all, or else what was the point of being a porn star?

"It's kind of a rush being paid to have sex," one girl told me. "Usually when I'm having sex, I'm thinking of the thousands of guys jerking off at home later, watching me have sex. That gets me off!"

"Yeah," I agreed, all too knowingly. "I can relate to that." To appreciate porn is to understand that level of vicarious pleasure, whichever side of the camera you happen to be on. If you don't understand that, you'll never get it.

I also remember another pivotal event, also in the mid-80s: the screening of the porn classic *Café Flesh*, at the famous art-house cinema in West Los Angeles, the Nuart Theatre. Two friends took me to see it one night. We'd smoked a bag of *sensamilla* in the car before going in, so I was mildly buzzed as I ogled the lead actress, Pia Snow, who'd also appeared in *Penthouse* under the name Michelle Bauer (and remains better known today as "the B-movie equivalent of Carole Lombard," as one critic put it, in such cult classics as *Vampire Vixens from Venus*, *Attack of the 60-foot Centerfold* and, under the name Michelle McClellan, that late-night cable collector's item, *Hollywood Chainsaw Hookers*.)

Something between my legs acknowledged her as the very kind of brunette I personally liked. But what really took me by surprise was the visual sensibility of *Café Flesh*—what film critics term the "look" of the film—which was stylish, futuristic and very sleek, with obvious nods to *film noir*. The story was about a post-nuclear milieu where highly-sexed people performed live sex shows (at a place called Café Flesh, of course) for the viewing pleasure of those rendered impotent by the bomb. I had never heard of Rinse Dream, the director (whose real name, I later learned, was Stephen Sayadian—whoa, porn people have fake names? What a revelation!), and I was amazed that someone would bother to put so much effort into something primarily meant for men to masturbate to. The art direction, the production values, the attention to detail ... all fascinated me.

I learned later that the script of *Café Flesh* was written by Jerry Stahl, under the pseudonym Herbert W. Day, before he became famous as the author of *Permanent Midnight*. And that the record producer Mitchell Froom, who had been responsible for so many albums by musicians I personally liked (from Los Lobos to Richard Thompson) had composed the music, before he became famous himself and married the singer Suzanne Vega. Hmm. There must be more to this, I thought. And I hadn't even discovered Andrew Blake yet.

Years later, in September 2003, I would find myself on the set of *Café Flesh 3* (the sequel to the sequel!) at *Hustler* Studios in Canoga Park, California—deep in the heart of the darkest Northwest San Fernando Valley—watching director Antonio Passolini put the delectable Sunset Thomas through her paces, as she took on three guys at once on the same bed. She played a surrogate First Lady, wearing only a Stars and Stripes bikini, and the three guys wore masks with the faces of three American presidents (Washington, Lincoln, and Nixon; why Clinton was missing was beyond me)

It was exhausting just watching her, as she sucked and fucked all three of them for what seemed an eternity. But I was enthralled, because Sunset was already a big star, even outside the adult film community. She was widely known as porn's most famous working whore, a blond beauty who spent her off-camera hours having sex with her fans out at Nevada's most famous legal brothel, the Moonlite Bunnyranch (where all good porn stars go to, well, moonlight) and she had also starred in *Cathouse*, the HBO series based on the same. During a break in filming, I met her and as we shook hands, I noticed she had the most perfect cheerleader smile. Gleaming white teeth contrasting with bright red lipstick. She casually strolled around backstage, wearing not a stitch, and glowed with a nonchalant confidence. I was quite taken by her naked charms.

Of course, I had previously seen her in Michael Ninn's *Sex* and its sequel, *Sex 2*, and Michael Raven's offbeat porn homage to the psychedelic age, *White Rabbit*, named after the Jefferson Airplane song, no less. (The term "Jefferson airplane," by the way, is slang for a used match bent to hold a marijuana cigarette that's been smoked too short to hold without burning the hands, something I've never done myself since I unselfishly don't bogart joints, but, ahem, that's another story.) I had also just seen the ad in *AVN* for Sunset's latest film, *Truck Stop Trixie*. On the box cover, Sunset is dressed as roadhouse diner waitress, licking dripping soda from a straw. (You get the picture.)

Now, here she was, completely naked and casually chatting with me, as I made a mental note to hold still my beating heart.

Suddenly I understood why Samson was a sucker for Delilah, (especially in the screen version with Hedy Lamarr, whom I consider a dark-haired version of Sunset Thomas). Unlike some other guys that evening, I wasn't about to rush back to watch *Survivor* on TV. I was more interested to see if I would survive this. The three guys were breathing hard and we hadn't even finished the scene yet. Kelly Holland and Jake Jacobs, the cinematographers, were talking about shooting the next position. Kelly had her camera over her shoulder and Jake was working the crane overhead, its rotating jib hovering above the circular bed.

And Sunset Thomas looked as fresh as a football cheerleader, all five feet five inches and 36-24-36 of her ready for more. Sex, she has always told anyone who cared to know, was like food to her. And she was always hungry.

It was going to be a long night.

How did this happen to a guy from a squeaky-clean country like Singapore? Well, there was a tall blond hippie chick I saw one afternoon as I was leaving school when I was fourteen, walking out of the gates of Saint Joseph's Institution in Singapore only to be confronted by the sight of her strolling down Bras Basah Road. Her nipples visible, her braless breasts doing a carefree jiggle under her brown cotton top. It resulted in my first memorable erection of note. (What can I say? I was a late bloomer.)

I don't think she even noticed the bespectacled schoolboy she'd unknowingly stopped dead in his tracks. But it was her air of insouciance that stayed with me, much more than the delectable roundness of her movable feasts under the fabric, the sort of haughty detachment I would later see over and over again, in all the adult film actresses I met. It was exhibitionism with an unspoken culpability, of the kind that tacitly addressed only an unseen voyeuristic audience.

I liked that look, the Brigitte Bardot pout, which all good strippers and porn stars have emulated since, especially after it had single-handedly (pardon the pun) put Saint-Tropez on the pop culture map. That, coupled with the fact that she resembled Linda Thoren, a coincidence I would also realize as relevant only many years later. But mostly, methinks, it happened because of a certain security guard, whom I still have yet to thank.

The Weird Turn Pro

As the late Hunter S. Thompson so famously quipped, "When the going gets weird, the weird turn pro." I never fully understood that now-famous gonzo-defining maxim until I made the career move from music critic to porn pundit. It was a slow transition, but one that began with a single innocent phone call.

Looking back, I had no inkling at all as to how things would eventually transpire when, on January 26, 1995, my friend Christine Fugate called to ask if I would be interested in working with her on a new CD-ROM project for *Spice Interactive*. I didn't even have cable television in my apartment at the time and only knew of *Spice* because a friend's father subscribed to it. This friend often went into graphic detail about the adult movies her father watched openly in the family home, which I found amusing to hear. (What a healthy upbringing this girl had, I thought! This must be the 90s equivalent of how, in the 70s, hippie parents would walk naked around the house in front of the kids.)

Sure, I told Christine, I had some time between projects. I was writing for *Billboard* at the time, penning long conceptual pieces about film soundtracks and independent record labels, and saw her offer as another way to leverage upon my industry contacts and work for a new media outlet. Christine would eventually go on to direct *The Girl Next Door*, an insightful documentary film about the life of Stacy Valentine, the Tulsa Oklahoma housewife who became a porn star, which became a left-field hit at the

1999 Sundance Film Festival. But this was four years before that happened, and she was asking me if I would serve as music editor for her new CD-ROM magazine.

Spice was then attempting to cash in on the CR-ROM format, since "multimedia" was the buzzword of the day. They had already planned thirty new releases for 1995, including interactive games, MPEG-compatible movies and CD-ROMs utilizing the then-trendy Quicktime video software for both Windows and Macintosh users. Of course nobody foresaw that in just a few more years the Internet would render the CD-ROM format obsolete. Back then we all thought we were hot shit. (This predated by a mere few years the now infamous Internet gold rush, which would eventually bomb as well. What we never learn, as they say, we are all doomed to repeat.)

At that juncture, the multimedia arm of the company, *Spice Interactive,* was selling new CD-ROM discs with corny titles like *Interactive Sex Therapy* and *The Treasures of Spice.* Our newly planned magazine was going to be called *Surge* (a somewhat more subtle title, to be sure). It was going to be a softcore magazine like *Playboy,* but only accessed via a computer disc, and we'd have an "interactive centerfold" as well as cutting-edge interviews with the likes of William Gibson, thanks to the wonderment of video-compression technology.

For the premiere edition of *Surge,* I extolled the virtues of two acts that had just released their first albums, the Orange County punk-pop band Sugar Ray and the Alaskan-born, San Diego folkie songbird Jewel Kilcher (known today just as Jewel). At that time, I had never worked with any kind of hardcore porn and thought that working with Spice would merely be an adjunct to *Playboy* on my resumé, fusing my passion for current music trends with an editorially hip men's magazine.

However, we only lasted one issue. The powers-that-be at Spice pulled the plug, after it became evident that *Surge* just didn't have the eye-candy pull of the other racier titles. (The sales must have been appalling for that first issue, but in mitigation I must say it was tough sharing shelf space with typical Spice titles like *Angel of Passion, Lap Dancer, Flesh Tones,* and *Erotic Dreams*). Nevertheless, in the summer of 1995, our editorial and sales teams were assembled to promote the disc at the upcoming "E3 show" (the famous Electronic Entertainment Expo) held at the Los Angeles Convention Center.

This could even be fun, I thought, as I drove down Pico Boulevard from my apartment in Santa Monica for the first of the three days I had agreed to volunteer for. I could have cruised down the Santa Monica Freeway and then changed to the Harbor Freeway and made my way towards downtown Los Angeles, but I deliberately took Pico despite all the traffic lights, simply because I wanted time to think. Los Angeles is a decentralized landscape, a hundred suburbs in search of a city, connected by a massive system of six-lane freeways with cars speeding over the usual sixty-five miles an hour limit, but you could also navigate your way on what we called surface streets, particularly if you needed to ruminate. Looking back, I believe I had intuited that I was about to behold something cataclysmic and tumultuous, possibly even life-changing, and so I wanted to stay centered. I had then belonged to a Buddhist *vipassana* meditation group for five years, and I wanted to slow my mind down, breathe deeply, and Zen-out the half-hour drive.

I also wanted to read the funny billboards and, with the neighborhoods turning gradually Latino as one went east towards downtown, check out the semi-rundown *bodegas* and the drug-dealing *cholos* along the way. I wanted to think about entropy and the need for rejuvenation.

When I got there, it took me forever to find the booth. It wasn't in the main halls at all, but tucked away in a far corner under a large green tent with an over-18 age restriction sign outside.

We were in the porn section!

We were all there under the aegis of *Spice*, so our booth was right there with all the big porn companies that were promoting their newly concocted CD-ROM projects too. VCA Pictures, for instance, had its girls signing their interactive discs at its booth, and so I got to meet the irresistible Juli Ashton, star of *New Wave Hookers 4* and *Butt Detective*, who would go on to fame and acclaim as the host of Playboy TV's *Night Calls* and, in 2000, land a historic US$25,000-a-movie contract-girl deal. I remember getting very turned on when I read an interview with Juli, a former junior-high-school teacher, in which she revealed that she had screwed half the guys in her college dorm, at Colorado State University. (Sad to say, I'd only slept with one girl throughout my undergraduate years, so I was duly impressed.)

But what really sent me over the edge was meeting a sweet young thing named Taylor Hayes, who was also signing autographs for VCA, standing next to Juli, and who would later become one of porn's biggest stars too. She was a newbie then, and told me she had only been in the business for two months and had only done four films. Fame was only starting to knock on her door, since she had just been in a *Penthouse* magazine layout, under the name Taylor Lynn, "a 22 year-old Virgo" and "a make-up artist" who was "in constant demand working for advertising companies and film shoots." I asked her for an autograph each time I went over to see her, and she obliged each time, pulling from the stack of glossy black-and-white VCA Platinum promotional photos, in which she stood wearing very little, in a pose leaving no room for doubt.

"Gerrie—All my hot, wet, sex! Love, Taylor Hayes."

Followed by "Gerrie—Thanks for all those multiple orgasms! Keep them cumming!"

She signed with a zesty flourish and much giggling, every bit the porn ingénue enjoying the attention. I was completely swept away by her natural ease, at the obvious way she embraced being a celebrity. I had an inkling that this girl was going to go far. When I asked if she liked having sex with girls, she just nodded and said: "Yum!"

Five years later, I ran into her again, at a Vivid Video shoot.

(She would outgrow VCA and eventually sign on to become one of the fabulous Vivid Girls.) I reminded her of our first meeting back in 1995. She gasped. "Wow, that was such a long, long time ago!" She said she was pleased that she had helped inspire me to continue exploring porn.

Sometimes it takes only one girl, the right girl, with the right attitude, to take you to the next level. Windows open, vistas are revealed, and no recovery is in sight.

Taylor Hayes was a trip, but I was never to recover after I met Sara St James, who added something truly potent to the mix. I'd spent quite a bit of time talking to her at her booth. Dirty-blond and foxy, a California girl to the bone, she was there under the auspices of a B-movie studio for which she performed schlock-horror fare in various states of undress, under the name Jacqueline Lovell. She'd also posed nude for men's magazines like *Hustler* and *Mayfair*, as Sara St James. "I'm sure you've seen me," she said. "I'm everywhere." But she hadn't done a true-blue porn movie, hadn't gone all the way, and told me she wasn't ever going to. She'd had sex with lots of guys, but never on film.

Well, actually, she conceded, there was this one thing.

"I have a masturbation video," she whispered. She looked at me with her piercing green eyes, and I knew we were in the zone; she was sharing a secret of sorts with me.

She told me to call her agency, Pretty Girl International, and wrote the number on a card, along with the name of her agent. "Call him if you want to get it," she said. "Tell him I sent you."

I was stunned. I wasn't used to this yet. Here was a girl telling me I could watch her masturbating and she was even telling me how to get it?

Of course, I did call her agency and I did get the video. And it was a revelation. After frigging herself into screaming oblivion, Sara lay back smiling as the camera zoomed down, to offer close-ups of her still-throbbing, very swollen clitoris.

There was no turning back now. I needed to know how all

this happened, how a whole industry even existed that made such visual phenomena possible. And thanks to Sara St James, I was on my way.

The Japanese call it *mizu-shobai*, the "water trade," sometimes also called the "floating world." The liquid analogy is rather apt, since it refers to the various subcultures of the sex industry—the brothels, hostess bars, massage parlors, strip clubs, and the like. The taxonomy of commodified sex fascinated me. Where did the line blur, from glamour models who merely posed nude to porn models who actually performed sex? There were so many areas of overlap in between, and I liked the armchair philosophy I could deploy in delineating the differences.

Much of this derived from a bizarre time in my life, when I made the fatal mistake of dating a stripper. Truly, I must have been out of my mind. (To those of you fantasizing about falling in love with sex workers, I only have one word of advice for you: "Don't!") She was a lovely girl, tall, big-boned and blonde, and hailing from deepest New Jersey. We defused our illusion (or at least my illusion, since I stupidly initiated the supposed relationship) quite acrimoniously, while attempting to vacation together in New York in the fall of 1994, during which time we hardly spoke to one another while sharing a room at the ultra-swank Paramount Hotel, on West 46th Street in mid-town Manhattan. I spent most of those evenings drinking alone at the famous Whiskey Bar next door, a famous supermodel hangout owned by Cindy Crawford's husband, Rande Gerber, but the only people I remember meeting there were the members of the band Arrested Development. I thought my own emotional development definitely arrested.

Two days after I'd returned to Los Angeles, assuming we'd never meet again, she called me to apologize. And to say she'd just had "a dream about you and me and a dead rat."

Charming. We would not speak again for another eight years.

However, in happier times, we would actually discuss our favorite porn stars. I had never done this with a woman before, so it was quite fun. I was particularly intrigued by her insistence that she did not want to be a porn star herself. She wasn't into anonymous men enjoying her from the privacy of their homes. As a working stripper, she needed to see the men she was disrobing for, to look into their eyes and confront the blind lust she inspired. Sexual empowerment for her, as a "self-actualized, sex-positive feminist," as she called herself, meant spreading her thighs and "showing pink." But, she averred, "Guys I can't see renting videos to watch me at home, that's just not my trip."

I was fascinated with these kinds of metaphysical boundaries, born of variations of the proverbial forbidden fruit.

Long before the dead rat appeared to darken her dreams and spook the hell out of me, I'd spent a day with her in a jacuzzi at a house belonging to one of her friends, a bucolic retreat full of S&M paraphernalia, high up in the Hollywood Hills. We soaked in the warmth of the sunny day, both of us naked (we'd had sex the night before, so this was literally the morning after) and we talked about who we liked seeing on video. She had a thing for Tiffany Million, but she didn't know much about Nikki Dial, my favorite porn star at the time. But we both agreed that Traci Lords was, objectively, the best.

In a surreal turn of events, I actually met and interviewed Traci herself some months later. It was my first full-on interview with a celebrity porn star. I talked to her for a whole hour, and remember her being extremely vivacious but pained about her past. She abhorred porn and told me she thought it was boring. But, when I probed further, she admitted that she was pissed off about not being paid for the two films of hers that were still circulating legally, since they were shot when she was over eighteen. (Actually, there is only one film—*Traci I Love You*, made in 1986, which also exists in a shorter, edited version under the title *A Taste of Traci*, hence the popular belief that two films were still out there.) Every other prior porn flick she had done had been pulled from the shelves, following police raids, and she had been accused by many people in the industry for lies and backstabbing and giving the industry a bad name since she was legally under-age for most of her career. (The legal age of entry for porn stars in the United States is eighteen.) She had started in porn at age fourteen and was done by age eighteen. Wow, what does one do for an encore?

In her 2003 autobiography *Underneath It All*, she dismissed *Traci I Love You* in a mere two pages, pleading the influence of vodka. However, she acknowledged that filming did take place in Paris the day after her eighteenth birthday. When I met her at the end of 1994, she told me it still bothered her that the film was still in circulation. "I feel like I'm extremely exploited by it. I'm just talking from a personal experience about the way that it's been handled and the people that distributed it and the way that I had been constantly fucked, which is the best word for it, financially, emotionally, in every possible way. I'm supposed to be making money out of it. I'm not, and I have yet to do anything about that, but that's a whole other issue.

"The reason that I hate that tape," she explained, "is because I feel I was not in a place to make that decision when I made it, and I regret the fact that I made that decision at a point in my life when I was too fucked-up to know what I was doing. That's why I regret it. I'm not trying to pretend that I wasn't a fourteen-year-old porn star. I'm not denying it. I'm not hiding it. I'm not ashamed of it. I'm not particularly proud of it all the time. I have really conflicting emotions with it." This, she added, was manifest in her fear of video stores, since she had been recognized in too many of them, thanks to her visage on so many porn titles. But "it's not about witnessing my own face on a box cover, which doesn't happen anyway because they're all off the market except for one. It's not about that. It's about my own head trip, of my own discomfort in my own skin, with fame. I have a hard time with that part of it."

However, that was the very part of it that most fascinated me. After all, we wouldn't have been sitting there talking in a private

37

room at a record company office on the Sunset Strip if she wasn't promoting her debut CD called *1000 Fires*, an electronic dance album that was, I thought, actually quite good. (Unfortunately for her, it would tank on the charts despite some favorable reviews.) On one song, she publicly admitted that she had been raped when she was eleven, and I talked to her about that—about the mechanics of making public one's private life for mass consumption.

I think in retrospect that I have always taken perverse pleasure in that supreme irony inherent in porn—that a porn star makes public her private parts yet keeps her private life personal. I somehow must have realized very early on that the commercial packaging of sexual expression entails some very deft strokes, pardon the pun, since it subverts the very notion we are all schooled to believe—that sexuality is an intensely private thing, almost something to be shunned in decent company. Yet the very *raison d'etre* of the water trade is the exact opposite—show everything, since all they have is your body and they can't touch your soul.

Theoretically, anyway.

Four years later, at the end of 1999, the best kind of Christmas present arrived for me. I received an email from Sweden telling me I had just been nominated for an *AVN* Internet Award. (*AVN* is the acronym for *Adult Video News*, the bible of the American adult film industry, and its Internet version *AVN Online* was the magazine I would eventually work for two years later.) To say that I was thrilled beyond belief was sheer understatement, much less the fact that it was for work done on the personal website of Linda Thoren, a relatively unknown Swedish porn star. The whole experience was a major watershed experience for me, and the beginning of my real induction into the world of adult cinema.

Linda had been the lynchpin that scored me my coveted gig as the "Cinema Blue" columnist for *Penthouse Variations* magazine, Her film *Flesh for Fantasy* was the very first one I ever wrote about for the column, and I essentially got the assignment because that film was directed by Nic Cramer, who had won "Best Director" at the *AVN* Awards for two years in a row. The magazine wanted me to capture his genius at work. I was already Linda's online editor, and that indirectly got the editors at *Penthouse* to take notice of me. Work begets work, even if it was work most people would scarely believe.

Linda's website was nominated in the "Best Personal Sites" category, and the culprits jointly sharing the credit were Linda, myself, and her fellow Swede, Bengt Gronkvist, our webmaster. As far as we were concerned, we were already winners in our own minds, since Linda was relatively unknown and a true-blue newcomer to the professional porn ranks, and all the other nominees were big-name porn stars: Jenna Jameson, Julia Ann, Lori Michaels, Alexandra Silk, to name a few. Neither Linda, Bengt nor and I attended the awards ceremony in Las Vegas, in part because we knew there was no way we could win. (The eventual winner, deservedly, was the hot favorite, Danni Ashe, for the second year running.) But we did toast our good fortune with a very nice bottle of wine on the deck of Nic Cramer's Malibu beach house, where Linda stayed whenever she stopped over in L.A., and as the waves lapped the shore we sipped and reminisced about the past year.

I wasn't fully aware of it at the time, but working with Linda had given me my first intimate glimpses into the inner workings of an industry that didn't ever open its doors readily to strangers. This, in turn, offered me all the insight I would need to cover the business itself. The real wonder of it all, though, was the fact that it exemplified how the Internet truly defied geographical borders. Linda had only been signed to a contract with the American studio Sin City since May and, at the time when we started working on the site together, she was still living in Stockholm, as was Bengt (who updated and maintained the site from her office there). I was, at the time, living and working in (of all places) Hong Kong. We were thousands of miles apart, but what we managed to do transcended time and distance.

All this was quite something to behold, for someone hailing from a country where porn is banned. My first actual exposure to porn was when I was fourteen, when someone sneaked an issue of *Penthouse* into school and we passed it around at the back of the classroom. This was a big deal when you're attending secondary school in Singapore, and even more so when you were like me, in St Joseph's Institution, one of the top schools in the country and a proud bastion of the Christian Brothers brand of Catholic education (where sex, basically, was simply assumed not to exist). *Penthouse* was banned in Singapore because the government authorities were like the Christian Brothers, but with less of a sense of humor.

But, really (and figuratively), who gave a toss? Not us. Not when someone's dad had obviously snuck one in past the airport customs folks, and his son was now everyone's new best friend. And in that issue of *Penthouse*, the US edition of July 1974, I discovered that there was a thing called "X-rated movies" from a pictorial featuring a gorgeous German girl, a redhead named Brigitte Maier. She was almost famous, since she would go on to star in *Sensations*, the porn classic directed by the Italian *auteur* Alberto Ferro (more famously known as Lasse Braun), which premiered to some controversy but also much acclaim at the 1975 Cannes Film Festival.

And so, my curiousity was piqued, thanks to the fact that I had actually bothered to read the text accompanying her photos. (Now, seriously, how weird was that?)

I think, in retrospect, that I always associated porn with a certain elegance, thanks to Brigitte Maier, and also with a certain European *je ne sais quoi*, whereby eroticism is more naturally and stylishly expressed (certainly more so than most American porn, a view I still hold today). In any case, whatever Brigitte Maier had, I saw the very same thing in Linda Thoren. Linda had won the "International Starlet of the Year" award at the 1997 Festival Erotica in Barcelona. I discovered that factoid from reading an interview with her, in the British magazine *Bizarre*. It was a short interview accompanied by a single topless photo of her, but I had an inkling this girl was bound for glory.

She had appeared in twenty-two porn films since her debut, *Private Triple X #10*, in which she had sex with three guys, shot in 1995 on her eighteenth birthday. She recalled it in her charmingly mangled English, on her personal website: "This was my first real pornshooting. I was barley legal and horney as a stray-cat. The shooting took place in Paris and I was banged by three guys in every hole I got—and I loved it. I think I came four times during one scene. Now, when I think back, I still think it's the best scene I ever done. At least, it's the most genuine. I didn't think for one second of camera-angles—I just fucked."

There was a naïve innocence to that which I must have liked, for I emailed her after an online search revealed that she was selling a home video of herself masturbating, for US$35 payable by international check, available by writing directly to her. Growing up in staid, strict Singapore had only made me develop a sense of rebellion, and I just loved this very kind of devil-may-care attitude, the kind that flips the birdy at tsk-tsk social judgement. I didn't ask Linda to sell me a copy of her video, but I did offer to copy-edit all the editorial areas on her site, mostly correcting her English.

She agreed and, in the course of our discussions, she also asked me to ghostwrite her monthly letter to her fans. Linda basically wanted someone to write as her, to express her thoughts in her own voice, but entirely in English for her American fans to enjoy; these guys were, after all, the very target audience for her website, a need made more pressing by her new contract signing to Sin City. We concocted this scheme: half of this would be free for everyone to read but the really sizzling stuff would be reserved only for her website members. (This is lesson number one for those interested in the editorial side of porn: most of the stuff you read is always made up or retold with the poetic license of the pornographic imagination, and don't let anyone tell you otherwise.)

In exchange, Linda offered me any number of videos of hers

that I wanted. She even sent me by airmail, as a token gesture to seal the deal, a videotape of three scenes she had shot but which were not yet released commercially. The tape made its way from Stockholm to Hong Kong. "To my hero Gerrie," she signed, on the glossy photo of her enclosed with the plain black video box.

Hero? I'd never been called that before. But, hey, to actually get to pretend to be a sexy Swedish porn star once every month, and with her cooperation too? Sure, I could do this. I knew I would spend the rest of my life regretting it if I turned it down.

Each month, Linda and I would email each other and we'd discuss what aspects of her life should be revealed to her fans. And then, after we agreed, I would craft her "Letter of the Month," as she called it. For instance, here's what I wrote for April 1999:

> *Hi everybody, I'm Linda Thoren, how are you doing? I'm now back in Sweden after a hectic month in Los Angeles, where I worked on several new movies (with Sin City, Pleasure Productions, Wicked Pictures, VCA, and Penthouse Video). Right now, I'm on my spring tour of Sweden. The schedule is listed on the homepage, so check it out and come see me strip! I had a really busy time in L.A. but working my ass off (so to speak) seems to be paying off. I have just been signed to a contract with Sin City, so you'll be seeing me in their films and videos exclusively later this year. You have no idea just how thrilled I am about this! Meantime, this summer, watch out for a new film I just did with director Nic Cramer, called* Flesh For Fantasy ...

This would be followed by an account of the shoot, and the sexual details would heat up with each progressive paragraph:

> *When you guys see the film, you'll see Rebecca shaving Lacey ... You'll also see the two of them thrusting on the floor with a two-headed dildo while I'm masturbating on*

the couch, first with my fingers and then with a cute pink vibrator! You should see the look on the guy holding the camera between my legs ...

And then, at the end of the page, there would be a teaser that I would also make up each month. *"Want to read more about the sexy things I did in L.A.? Click HERE to join and be a member!"* This would be followed by a "Continue" button, which sent the reader straight to the membership sign-up page.

I got the idea from having visited those tacky peep-show clubs on 42nd Street in New York, the ones with the automatic windows where the poor, pent-up patron has to fork out more money each time if he wanted to see more of the girl. It's the same principle. The guys have to join the site to read more, in order to get off. Porn, let it be said, isn't ultimately about sex. The sex is only the conduit. It's really always about money.

So, if the hot, bothered and bewildered reader decided to type in his credit card number and join the site, he could then read my next page:

Hi again! A few days before I did that shoot with Nic, I did an outdoor scene with two guys. It was actually a cold day for L.A. and I almost froze to death. I was naked the whole time. This is one of the work hazards of being a porn star (in case some of you were wondering), I love being seen naked and I love to suck and fuck two men at the same time, but I'm human too, you know. Boy, do I hate cold weather. On another shoot last month, I was really moaning and coming pretty fast when the director suddenly yelled, "Cut!" Ugh, some stupid production assistant walked into the camera or something. It's very frustrating when that happens. I can get horny down there, between my legs, but it's often harder to get turned on mentally, because of all the lights and equipment and people around you at the time. The last thing you want to think of is where the camera is, or how I'm pulling my stomach in, or putting my breasts out, or whatever ...

43

Membership, as they say, has its privileges. It confers the special insider's view, the "behind-the-scenes" aspects of the business and the private details of a porn star's life. I really think this was a unique strategy, and it was what gave us the edge that resulted in our *AVN* Internet Award nomination at the end of that year. Not many porn stars were using their personal sites to do this in such a brazenly calculated yet eloquent manner back in 1999, since most membership "extras" on most porn star sites usually took the form of additional picture galleries, JPEG files meant expressly for their members' wanking pleasure. The DVD revolution and all those behind-the-scenes interviews, in what we now know as the "Special Features" sections, hadn't quite happened yet.

It was really great fun working with Linda. Ironically, her star would be in decline just as mine was ascendent. In February 2000, I wrote the last of her "Letter of the Month" pages. Linda had that month decided she was going to retire. She had been having medical problems, apparently caused by anal sex. And, from what I was told, Sin City had used her refusal to perform anal as reason enough not to renew her contract. Bad press accordingly followed; she either refused to do interviews or had made a petulant show of doing them grudgingly (as the company's publicist at the time had informed me), and then broke up with her boyfriend and manager, Tomas Edberg, and finally quit the business for good.

In March 2000, Sin City released the last of Linda's films, *Linda Thoren's Gang Bang*, a messy "gonzo" tape which featured her in a free-for-all with six other performers (four men and two women), entirely set on a single soundstage functioning as a room and with absolutely no dialogue whatsoever. The video came with an equally sophisticated box cover (not!), a full-color close-up of Linda's face post-orgasm, eyes closed and cheeks splattered with semen, three still-erect penises dangling above her. It was a bit ugly, and almost as if Sin City was determined to get their money's worth out of whatever they'd paid her for her contract, which she had served out for exactly the requisite one year.

By that time, though, she was long gone back to Sweden and couldn't care less what Sin City was doing. Nic Cramer told me later that she was living in Stockholm, studying to be an accountant. One year later, Sin City was still mining the vaults and releasing old footage cobbled together as "new" material (such as *Linda Does Hollywood*, released in the summer of 2001 with an amusingly ridiculous box cover of her dressed as a Viking), and Nic himself would purchase old scenes shot in Sweden from her directly, to compile into "new" films (such as *Passion Tales #6*, released at the end of 2002!) "Linda Thoren is a find," raved *AVN* reviewer Dan Miller in his "Video of the Day" section, apparently not knowing she was long gone or, perhaps, playing along with the bluff. We insiders knew about girls coming and going all the time, and, sadly, many so-called "retirements" weren't always taken seriously. (Many girls staged "comebacks" after their drug money ran out or if they needed to sharpen their media image to help publicise their stripping at the clubs.)

I was only sad for Linda, though, because she had been responsible for getting me started in the business yet had fallen casualty to it. She was a girl who unabashedly loved sex but she had, as Nic told me, an inbuilt stubbornness typical of Northern Swedes—she wouldn't play politics or make nice in accordance with studio protocol. She'd made no bones about the fact that she was a nymphomaniac from a small town with a name few non-Nordics could pronounce (Ornskoldsvik, try saying that fast), who used her real given name to do porn (a rarity in the business), but she learned the hard way that while her unflagging honesty was a valuable asset in captivating the fans, her naivete had failed her. She simply didn't have the gumption for the game.

Linda was, for me, an object lesson in how sometimes, it's much better to save your insatiable love of sex for the privacy of your own bedroom. The difference between Linda and myself wasn't simply that she performed in front of the camera and I didn't. It was the fact that I have a perverse fascination for artifice. So what if the sex wasn't "real"?

I recall an argument I had once with someone who complained that "nobody ever sweats in Andrew Blake's films." Of course not, I said, that's the whole point! I actually asked Andrew Blake about this when I finally got to meet and interview him at the end of 2000. "Sweat will mess up their hair and their make-up will run," he agreed, chuckling. "This is not about reality. This has nothing to do with reality. It has to do with fantasy. It has to do with angles and positioning and women with their breasts hanging just right. I don't want to see the bad parts. I only want to see the good parts. If people want to watch amateur porn and gonzo porn, there's plenty of that out there."

So where, I asked him, was the fine line between erotica and pornography? "I don't think there is one," he replied. "I think it's the way it's packaged and the way it is presented, and in the sensibilities that you bring to it. You can have the most salacious-looking blowjobs and have it look quite beautiful and make it art, as opposed to making it have less than 100 percent visual style. I try to do pictures that have a lot of style to them. And the other stuff I see out there has no style. If they're both going to be called pornography, I would rather my work be called erotic pornography as opposed to sleazy pornography."

"I've said this for years," he concluded. "When people who are hungry want something to eat, they can go to different places. There are people who will go to a beautiful restaurant and have a three-hundred-dollar meal, and there are going to be the other people who are going to go to a McDonald's and have a couple of Big Macs. I'm the expensive restaurant."

I liked that analogy. I also liked the fact that in the hierarchy of sex workers, porn stars were at the very top of the totem pole. Unlike strippers, escorts and call girls (all beavering away, so to speak, a rung or two below on that same labor-intensive ladder), porn stars were the most glamorous and best paid, the metaphorical expensive restaurant dishes in the gastronomic universe of commercial sex.

However, writing about porn and cultivating the eloquence

to do so was one thing, but getting used to the company of these highly sexual women was another. The trick was to gradually imbibe them into one's cultural DNA. I found through the years that I really did like the company of these crazy girls. I just made sure that the relationships were personal but never actually sexual, and dating them was a total no-no, a Pandora's Box I veered away from like pestilence and plague.

My sanity, and theirs, was at stake.

Plot? What Plot?

"**Y**ou have to be crazy to be in this business," Andrew Blake once told me. "It's the kind of craziness that lets your inhibitions down, that enables you to do these things. I think there is a 'porn flaw'—the flaw in these girls that makes them work from their private parts rather than from their heads. Girls who should be on *Felicity* but instead they're in *California Blowjobs #15*. You know what I mean."

That was in April 2001, and by that time I certainly knew what he meant. I knew so little about the adult film industry going in but became more and more intrigued by it the deeper in I got, if you'll pardon the innuendo.

I remember, for instance, being on a set one afternoon and feeling completely flummoxed to learn that male porn stars were usually given flesh-colored condoms to wear so as to minimize visibility on film (Kimono Micro-Thin Plus, made in Japan for Mayer Laboratories in Oakland, California) or if they wore white condoms, they were the thinnest-possible (Crown Skin Less Skin, lightly lubricated, also made in Japan but for Okomoto USA, Inc. in Stratford, Connecticut). Sharon Mitchell, one of the great veterans of the blue screen, once gave me an all-American condom (from Ansell, Inc., in Dothan, Alabama), and she wrote her phone number on the package.

I never called her but ran into her some years later, at A.I.M. (Adult Industry Medical) Healthcare, the clinic she ran in the San

Fernando Valley suburb of Sherman Oaks, where all conscientious porn stars go for their AIDS tests and medical check-ups. I reminded her of the condom she'd given me, and we had a good laugh. "That was back in 1992, and you were the first porn star who ever gave me her phone number," I told her.

Next to us in the clinic reception room was Laurie Holmes, ex-wife of the late John Holmes—"Johnny Wadd" to those who remember him for his massive schlong that often got him into trouble, grimly but wonderfully played by Val Kilmer (sans visible schlong) in the film *Wonderland*. Laurie, a pixie-faced, curly-haired brunette formerly known as the porn star Misty Dawn, was actually there working the reception desk, doing her bit to help her fellow porn stars. She had met me once before, at the home of another porn legend, *Screw* magazine publisher Al Goldstein (another story entirely, as with everything Al Goldstein). Laurie was also a real working girl, putting in time at America's most famous legal brothel, the Moonlite Bunnyranch in Carson City, Nevada; I'd seen her in their print ads.

It was an eerie rendezvous. We bantered cheerfully as several girls strolled in and out getting their HIV tests done, but I was struck by the incipient tension of the moment—the realization that there was a time in my life when I couldn't even have imagined being in the same room with these two women, let alone any of the other legendary lasses. What was more palpable, and memorable, was the fact that I enjoyed their company greatly, even as I would be the last to surmise that we would stay, so to speak, bosom buddies. No, we had a business relationship, or we formed an alliance of sorts. The porn industry is very small and close-knit, and operates entirely on trust.

Even when it operates largely on money, it still operates sooner or later on trust.

I remember Nic Cramer, the director to whom I owed my own infamous entry into this industry, telling me about his protracted legal problems with the company he had signed himself to, after he had sworn on his mother's Swedish meatballs that he would never work for those scumbags again. "I'm back to work for Pleasure Productions, we settled my lawsuit against them on the eve of trial, July 31, with a go-back-to-work package and a stack of cash upfront. It entails eighteen movies—six films, twelve videos—to be shot over the next eighteen months, a bunch of bonuses and performance incentives, and a five-figure check as a 'signing bonus' to me, all under non-exclusive terms this time around. We start work September 2002."

A year later, he was complaining to me about how fed up he was with the business and how he was still planning to retire altogether and maybe even return to Stockholm, once he figured out how to pay off the mortgage on his Malibu beach house. I always liked Nic because he was different from the rest of them. He lived by the beach, instead of in the valley like everyone else, and he was often caustically opinionated about the people in the business.

I never had the balls that Nic had, though, to blast colleagues openly in public or in print. It was through him that I learned how the business functioned. For example, I was amazed to discover that porn directors usually get paid a flat fee for each film, unlike mainstream Hollywood where they usually get a cut of the film's proceeds and can earn residual income through percentage points off gross receipts. This is the main reason why the producers are the ones getting rich, and why directors are always constantly working, and why the amount of videos being churned out month after month is nothing short of staggering. Nic, after winning "Best Director" two years in a row at the *AVN* Awards (in 1998 and 1999), found himself still toiling in the salt mines like everyone else, and perhaps he took umbrage with this enough to speak candidly with me.

"I've talked to Linda a lot lately," he told me in August 2002 when I inquired about our mutual friend Linda Thoren, now retired and living back in her native Sweden. "Mostly because I bought some scenes from her and I'm still waiting for releases and I.D. shots a year later. She's as imbalanced and manic-depressive as

ever." Nic had weathered two bad relationships with porn stars—
he had previously dated Taylor Wane and Melissa Hill, both of
whom he had little good to speak of, and the only girl he said he
liked enough to even consider dating was Gwen Summers, a perky
part-Japanese sex kitten whom I was also friendly with. Gwen
and I had first met on the set of one of Nic's films, *Irresistible*, shot
not far from where Michael Jackson used to live, in the upscale
valley enclave of Encino.

Gwen was married, and in more ways than one (and perhaps
luckily for me) distinctly unavailable. She had told me a great deal
about how she got into porn, to get back at her abusive husband,
porn actor/director Johnny Toxic, only to discover that revenge is
a dish best served cold, not hot. She discovered that she actually
enjoyed having sex with other men and was stuck, and continued
to make movie after movie, returning home to look after their
young son before dashing out again for the next shoot.

"Another producer just bounced a check on me again,"
Gwen would sigh, whenever I ran into her again, on yet another
set somewhere deep in the Valley. "It would really suck if you
were young and starting out in the business and you were really
depending on that check." Every time I tried calling her, her cell
phone would remain unanswered and every time I asked her about
it, she would tell me that her son had been playing with her phone
and had "thrown it somewhere again." I found this egregious lie
somewhat amusing, since like most working actors porn stars live
and die by their cellphones and the callbacks they hope to get.

Well, illusion was their business and I could play the game too.
Whenever I went on-set to cover a shoot, I would always carry
a little blue notebook, the flip-open-and-jot variety; I must have
intuited that I would need to record the usable factoid or quotable
quote whenever I least expected it, since my tape recorder would
be deployed only for actual interviews. I could flip open to any
one of them at random today, to cast my mind adrift again to
another situation from another time.

I now have many of these little blue notebooks to refer back to. Before each shoot, I would annotate the pertinent information for my own reference. Here's one of them:

Naked Hollywood #5 "Twisted"
Starring Gwen Summers, Dru Berrymore, T.J. Hart

Naked Hollywood #6 "Money Can Buy Anything"
Starring John Decker, Dale DaBone, Inari Vachs, Dillon Day

Call Time: 8 am. Both films being shot back-to-back.

Director: Kelly Holland

6/19—1051A North Cole, Hollywood
(corner of Cole and Santa Monica)
Left of Studio space across from Gold's Gym

6/20—TBA

6/21—Studio 5533,
5533 Satsuma Avenue, North Hollywood
(Fashion-fetish show)

6/20, 6/21 and/or 6/22—interview Nina Hartley

Here's another one, less cryptic and infinitely funnier, documenting a shoot in elliptical fashion, written so that I would easily remember it later when penning the actual piece:

Metro Shoot, "Black Widow"
June 26, 2001
Bel-Air, California

Directed by Mike Quasar (a.k.a Quaserman)

Stills by Michael Bruno

Girl/Girl—Sisterhood/bonding scene.

Chandler plays "Nancy Pollard"
Stevie plays "Cindy Smith"

Quasarman: "You have to do this inane dialogue, after which you sample each other vaginas. I'll be in the bathroom, feverishly masturbating."

Stevie is to "cascade across the room." Stevie and Chandler kiss after dialogue. "Oh good, I'm going to cascade over and get a vibrator."

Metro publicist Harry Weiss: "Plot, what plot? Puh-leeze, we're just smut peddlers!"

Mike Adams, producer: "It's just porno, you know."

Chandler: "Is it Miss or Mrs Smith?"

Quasarman: "It doesn't matter. The home viewers are going to fast-forward through this scene until they see your breasts."

Green wall, beige carpeting, tan-brown couch, faux-Renoir on wall above them.

Stevie walks in with two wine glasses and keeps dripping water. "Lick it up like a good little whore," says Mike Adams.

A glass table is moved alongside Chandler, a purple vibrator on it.

Quasarman: "Do you like the economy with which I am shooting dialogue now? I realized editing my own stuff that 90 percent of what I shoot, I never use."

Quasarman does his own videography when he directs. "Okay you guys are kissing and it's all about vagina. Lots of nice softcore in the beginning, before you get down to jamming things into each others' colon."

Chandler wears red velvet top, grey skirt, black heels.

Stevie begins by getting between Chandler's legs and eats her. As Chandler luxuriates, her grey skirt is pulled up.

Chandler is completely naked. Stevie wears a red dress pulled down to her midriff, to expose her breasts, back and butt. Her vagina is in my line of sight. She has an all-over tan, contrasts with Chandler's pale, sallow skin.

Stevie has only been in the biz since last October, she has done only five girl/girl scenes before.

Quasarman crouches three feet away, shooting close-ups of Chandler's pussy being eaten, then moves behind Stevie to get POV shot of her butt with cheeks open, vulva exposed. He keeps pulling Stevie's dress up further, to get more of her naked butt.

Chandler starts whimpering, and moaning softly, and then her cellphone rings. Next to Mike Adams, who doesn't know how to turn it off. Chandler has to teach him how to turn it off. She apologizes to the crew and we're all laughing. Stevie pauses, lifts her head off Chandler's crotch.

Quasarman moves camera high, shoots from above, swoops down to capture Chandler's near-orgasmic frenzy. Then accidentally kicks Stevie in the foot. They have to stop.

Quasarman: "I was so close to shooting a sex scene and the moment has passed from me."

Cut to stills. Chandler stares off into the middle distance, absent-mindedly, with a blissful smile, as Stevie eats her, and the still cameraman shoots.

Quasarman starts singing some power ballad.

Chandler: "Is that Winger or Warrant? I know it's one of those long-haired gay boy bands."

Quasarman: "Witty Banter is my cousin. We had a band called The Banter Brothers. And we had a hit called 'Shuckin' Oysters'."

Chandler: "I need candy chews. They make gummy vibrators."

Stevie comes back. Quasarman: "Ok, she's back and she'll be licking your vagina now."

Stevie's chewing candy too. Quasarman calls for the C-light. Stevie kisses and pulls, puckers lips on Chandler's vulva opening, pulls skin back, inserts index finger into Chandler's vagina and plays with it, exploring. Moments earlier, she'd told me she'd done only five girl/girl scenes and had trouble finding other girls' clits. "Mine sticks out so it's easy to find my own. But it's hard sometimes to find the other girls'—some of them look at me and ask if I've ever done it before!"

1.35 pm—Endless index-finger probing. Chandler goes, "Ahh," whimpers softly, mewing like a cat.

Chandler has her legs lifted high in the air. She hangs on to the heel of her shoes, then props up on both elbows, palms on the undersides of her calves, so that her open thighs are clearly seen.

Quasarman: "We can swap now. Switcheroo, and swap the shuckin'"

Chandler pulls Stevie's dress down. Then Stevie steps out of it and reclines on the couch. Chandler leans in between her legs and starts chewing on her pussy.

Stevie uses her bare feet to play with Chandler's butt while she's being eaten. Chandler uses both hands and spreads her thighs wide open and eats.

Stevie now has both legs in the air, and she arches her back. "Oh gosh, yes, mmmm, yes."

The line is very nice. Visual juxtaposition of her brunette and Chandler's blond hair. She pulls on Chandler's hair as Chandler uses her mouth on Stevie's erect nipples. Chandler masturbates Stevie with her hand between her legs.

Chandler stops suddenly. She picks her teeth—she pulls pubic hair from between her teeth!

"I hate it when that happens," she says. "That's why I like a girl who's shaved."

In between takes, I chatted with Chandler. She's a blue-eyed blonde, five feet three inches, 110 pounds, a nice 34B-23-24, and has a readily identifiable diamond-shaped tattoo etched around her navel. On one occasion, we sat by the pool and she was completely naked, one of those girls who liked to walk around on set totally nude, oblivious to the fact that everyone around her was fully clothed. Later, we sat inside her car and talked while smoking a joint together.

Chandler was born in Seattle but grew up in Florida, where she'd started out as a stripper. Her parents divorced when she was six. She had, as she put it, "the typical porn star background, I was really bitter and decided to be rebellious, I got into a lot of trouble and was grounded most of my childhood, so my only social life was sneaking out a night. And, of course when you're sneaking out at night, the people you're hanging out with aren't usually the best sort of friends to be with."

Inspired by seeing other feature dancers like Teri Weigel and Janine Lindemulder, porn stars who made their real money on the dance floor, she moved to Los Angeles and met producer Patrick Collins, signing a contract with his company Elegant Angel. "The money was a big bonus surprise," she said, and started work under the name Chandler Steele; she'd entered the business with her real-life husband, Christian Steele, by screwing him in amateur porn videos. When they parted ways, she dropped the last name. "He had a really small penis, he could never get it hard," she told me, laughing. "It's not a lie, everybody knows it. I met him on ecstasy, and so, I mean, anything felt good at the time."

"The small penis thing isn't a big deal," she added. "I've had sex with guys that had small penises, and also with guys who were average and also guys who are really super-big. And sometimes the guys that are smaller actually feel better." In conversation, she is actually a lot quieter and often given to pregnant pauses and abject modesty whenever she is complimented on her very taut and toned, athletic-looking body. She told me she enjoyed mountain-biking and snowboarding, and showed me her scars, one attained from impulsively riding a dune buggy over a cliff. Her favorite exercise, however, is masturbation.

"All day!" she replied, when I asked her how often she self-pleasured. "Oh my God, that's so bad. My hands are always down my pants. It doesn't matter where I'm at. And I don't know that I do it. They just go down my pants. My friends are always going, 'Get your hands out of your pants,' and I don't realize it. I keep a bottle of lube in my car, and a little vibrator. When I'm at home, I'm constantly going off to my bedroom to play with my toys!

"It's the weirdest thing. When I do it, I fantasize about guys. It's never about girls. And the guys never fuck me. I only fantasize about them eating my pussy. I fantasize about dirty, dirty, dirty things and coming really hard, that's the way I like it. I get myself off. I learned about sex by watching porn and reading dirty magazines. I ended up finding a porno when I was babysitting this girl. The house had a stack of movies and I grabbed the one that was up the highest, I figured that would be the scariest movie, and it turned out to be a porno. *Babylon Pink*, directed by Henri Pachard, the first one I ever saw, made in 1974, the year that I was born. I remember I was so turned on by it. Even at that very young age, I wanted to be the girl in the movie.

"I think that this was meant to be. Completely and totally. There is nothing else in the world, there is no other job for me. I really enjoy being bad. Not in a bad way but in a good way, and it just makes it become a little more dirty, and it turns me on. I've been doing this for five years but I just now, about two weeks ago, decided this is what I'm going to do, that I can go the distance. I was thinking and meditating, and came to the conclusion that this is definitely the right career for me. A lot of girls walk around going, 'I fucking hate my job, I don't want to do this anymore,' and I say if you don't like it then fucking go elsewhere. I love my job. I've discovered I'm a raging nympho and a chronic masturbator, mostly because I don't have sex much outside the business, which makes it better for work."

Does sex on camera ever get old? "For a little while, it started to, when I was just doing girls. I love girls and I love fucking girls. But most of the girls in the business suck at it. And girls bore me. I just want to fuck 'em. I don't want conversation. I have a guy's mentality, I guess, when it comes to sex. Personally, myself, if I'm watching a porno to get off, I'd rather watch a comp tape, where it's just sex and there's no talking. I don't like a lot of dialogue."

I would run into Chandler again in February 2001, on the set of a Jill Kelly produced film, directed by Michael Zen, called *Perfect Pink #7: Sink the Pink*, which featured her in an all-girl feast of muff-diving and rug-munching. However, that orgy wasn't the most memorable scene for me. The one that really, truly, sent me featured a dark-haired frisky pixie from Salt Lake City, Utah, named Belladonna, now a legendary director in her own right but then an ingénue just called Bella.

She exhibited the least inhibition of any porn star I'd met. And she was actually the daughter of a Mormon bishop, which threw me for a loop.

In her dressing room before her scene, she made no bones right away about her penchant for raunchy rough sex: "I want every hole in my body filled. I just did a movie for Anabolic called *Five on One*, in which I did five guys all at once." The scene she was about to do, then, was a mere walk in the park. She would be having sex with only two guys, Bobby Vitale and Pat Myne, and it would end with a d.p. (double penetration).

I covered the shoot for the very hardcore *Fox* magazine, and here's how that scene appeared in its August 2001 issue:

Bella plays a nude model who seduces a photographer and his pal. She sucks and fucks them on a gray bench surrounded by pink balloons. (The color pink is a central theme in Jill's films.) Here's a girl who knows her Kegel exercises; Bella barely breaks a sweat while the two studs plunge their penises inside her until both men were dripping. Bobby Vitale, in particular, seems to have quite a thing for Bella and she reciprocates, and the two of them really go to town. Poor Pat Myne gets nominal attention and resembles a stage prop, as Jill Kelly herself looks on. She smiles and turns to me, as Bobby and Bella grope each other frantically. "They're in love," Jill says with a sigh. "Porno love."

I suppose it must be nice to be that young and that fresh, to be filled to the brim with exuberance and propelled by manifest destiny to display yourself so openly. The business never seemed to attract enough of them, and they usually stayed a few years before vanishing into obscurity. In September 2003, I watched Sunset Thomas starring in *Café Flesh 3*, directed by Antonio Passolini, who had written and produced the Michael Ninn classics *Latex* and *Shock*, and had also directed the previous *Café Flesh 2* sequel to the cult classic. I really went because I hadn't seen Sunset do her thing live before, but my big surprise was discovering an amazing new girl named Aria. She had been in the business for three years but had lately changed her name. Formerly billed as Marie Silva, she was twenty-six years old, and she would eventually retire from the business in May 2005.

Here was what I wrote in my notebook, scrawled during breaks in shooting:

LFP Studios
20932 Osborne, Chatsworth
(Off De Soto, south of Nordhoff)

Studio #1—Cafe Flesh #3
Antonio Passolini, director
Kelly Holland, Jake Jacobs, cinematographers
Patti Rhodes, production manager

Scene started before I arrived, day 2 of 3-day shoot
First 2 days at LFP, third day at a meat-packing plant in downtown L.A.

Apparently, they'd started shooting at 10.30 am. When I got to the set, Patti Rhodes told me to wait outside the studio until there was a break. I finally went in and saw Kelly looking very pensive. She told me: "Wait over at craft services, things are kind of tense on the set right now."

I couldn't understand what was going on.

I saw Joel Lawrence on a bed, jerking himself off lazily just to keep himself hard. Behind the bed, I saw a barrier, behind which a naked couple was kissing. Unknown to me at the time, this was Aria trying to keep Kurt Lockwood stimulated.

I went outside and talked to the crew. The grip truck guy was loading equipment onto his truck. He said one of the male talent had never done features before, only gonzo, and he didn't understand the stop/start nature of feature shoots. They were having some real problems with this guy.

When they broke again, I was hanging out in the craft services room, and Aria comes out to get an ice cream. She walked in totally naked. She saw a couple of guys staring at her—the male talent for the next scene, actually—and she says, "Don't worry, guys, I'm just more comfortable in the nude."

I talked to her in the hallway. She told me Kurt Lockwood, whom she had just fucked, had double-booked. He had another shoot to go to at 1 pm, and he wanted to get done with this scene. "He should know better than to double-book when you're doing a feature. I've worked with him before and he's been fine till now. I don't know why he's doing this. The scene was fine but he had a lot of attitude,

61

and was taking it out on Kelly, which is unprofessional."

She also told someone that she had been sick all morning. Woke up with 100-plus degree temperature and took eight Advils. And yet she was still working. True enough, she went in right after the break and did a d.p. and I interviewed her after that and she seemed back to normal. The sex had cured her fever!

Anyway, they broke for lunch after that and it was all anyone could talk about. How Kurt had thrown a tantrum on set and wanted things done his way. He had told the director, Antonio Passolini, that he wanted to "go to sex now or I go home."

Antonio: "So I told him, we are not going to go to sex now. We have two more scenes to shoot before we go to sex. And I guess he didn't understand that."

Kelly: "He was flipping out and yelling, and I have never ever seen a male talent flip out like that before. And then, when we did the d.p. he lost wood and started getting mad and really lost it. I've seen that before. Usually when that happens, the guy who's lost wood blames the girl. But this time, he blamed me!"

Kelly and Antonio agreed that they would spread the word to other people not to hire this guy.

During the post-mortem, I took the opportunity to sneak off and do a one-on-one interview with Aria. Lovely girl, one of the most amazing girls I've ever interviewed. It's very rare that I get turned on when I'm doing an interview but I did. She wasn't wearing panties and sat on the couch—we shared a couch in the LFP front room/

reception area, which was deserted. She put her legs up so I could see her bare crotch. She had no problem with it, and told me she never wears underwear when she wears skirts. She was wearing a white t-shirt and a denim-blue skirt—VERY short.

The interview is on tape. Her big thrill and major reason for doing porn: "It's not the money. I can make money doing other things. It's the thought of thousands of guys jacking off at home to my videos."

She loves facials, says it's a control thing for her—it's about her controlling the guy's pleasure. Good point. "But I won't do bukkake. That's not even an enjoyment. You're not doing anything to get the guys off. I do have my 'crewkake' fantasy, though."

What's that, I asked. "My 'crewkake' fantasy—all the crew know about it, you can ask most of them and they'll go, 'Ah, Aria's fantasy!' I have this fantasy about doing a scene, getting my facial, whatever, and after the camera shuts off, the entire crew stands around my body and jacks off on my body. Not my face, just on my body. From, like, the neck down."

Has she ever done it? "No. It's just something I fantasize about. I almost got them to do it yesterday. There's always somebody that chickens out. The rest of the crew was going, 'C'mon, dude!' And I don't want a gonzo crew. That's like, two people. It's got to be a big crew. Like ten or fifteen people."

She has great etiquette—she came onto the set while the next scene was being shot to thank the crew personally, before leaving the studio for a hairdresser's appointment.

A couple of years later, I found myself entranced by a passage from *The Sexual Life of Catherine M.*, the memoir of the French art critic Catherine Millet, in which she documented her own true-life sexual escapades. She'd started out participating in group sex in various Parisian locales, and concluded that "what paradoxically gave me pleasure was identifying familiar feelings in unusual circumstances."

Voila! I think I was drawn towards porn because it made for the most compelling kind of mental disconnect. After all, I was actually being paid to watch people have sex, often with multiple partners, but the point was not the scene *per se* but its context, based entirely on my perception. Porn is recreational sex in a protected space, which I was made privy to. And in the free-for-all nexus of connections that was the city of Los Angeles, the garden of Eden that was the San Fernando Valley provided the best kind of enclave for such complicity. The area was large enough to be anonymous, yet small enough for kindred spirits to congregate in the secret places only they knew about.

And I had access to it.

Beyond that privilege, though, it was hard work. I was always interested in detecting what commonality might exist in a host of questions: did this scene remind me of something else I'd earlier witnessed? Was I getting turned on or bored? Was that blowjob better than what I'd seen this girl do previously on film? How adept was she at taking such a big cock in her mouth? What was she doing with her hands on his shaft to make it more visually appealing to the camera? I thought about these kinds of things every time I'd walk to where the director was sitting, to stare into the little monitor that was recording what the camera was shooting. Vaginal close-ups and insertion shots never lost their fascination for me somehow, though I remembered sets where I saw clear signs of workday ennui—grips and gaffers reading paperback novels, some even sleeping and snoring away whenever the cameras weren't on. Some people had become so desensitized.

But not me. Perhaps because I kept in mind two things.

The real objective of porn, as my friend Lily Burana (the author of the brilliant stripper memoir *Strip City*) told me back when she was the editor of the short-lived magazine *Future Sex*, is that "it should make people really want to masturbate. Because that's where the rubber meets the road in this industry, and we can't ever forget that."

And, as Nina Hartley told me when I interviewed her in June 2001 for *Penthouse Variations*: "I think a lot of people should understand that porno movies are live-action sex cartoons. Just because a person likes a certain kind of pornography doesn't mean he actually lives it out ... You watch movies to see things you would never actually do in person."

Sometimes, however, I spied a spectacular blowjob being enacted and was immediately led back to my own such experiences. I remembered the first time I ever came in a girl's mouth, how she urged me onward and paused to coo with a musical timbre still resonant in my head today: "Come in my mouth, mmm, yes, mmm, I want you to come in my mouth!"

I'd seen that done on video too, countless times, but there was always something of a rush in hearing such spontaneous supplication. The New Age man in me wanted to validate her vulnerability, knowing that it took a leap of blind trust to say those words—especially to a complete stranger, even when you knew you were just playing a part for the camera. Reality existed in the form of a silky film of semen shooting down your throat, so don't ask to shoot if you can't stand to swallow.

Whoever said that porn degrades women has, obviously, never met that girl.

And I had met too many; all of them, ironically, in the days before I started covering adult entertainment. Were it not for them, I later realized, I could never have survived my time in the porn trenches, for they had taught me what I most needed to know. To be able to write about a genre like porn without metaphysically importing your own sexual past could only result in empty prose and, as Andrew Blake always reminded me, real erotica existed only in terms of the real sensibilities that one brought to it. In short, I was putting my cards on the table every time I visited a film set and committed my views to the printed page. There was just no other way.

Part Two

Damsels in Undress

Jammin' with the Jennarator

That mythical beast called mainstream celebrityhood had somehow eluded the majority of porn stars, with the notable exception of one. People who never even watched porn asked me about her, with a curiosity bordering on admiration. They liked the fact, I think, that someone could possess her combination of guts and guile enough to make the usually unmoved masses pay her due attention.

For sure, there was only one Jenna Jameson. But who really knew why?

In the book she wrote about her life, she confessed to so many things thought unspeakable. She had transcended a screwed-up childhood, and had come to terms with having been raped when she was young. She had made good on all her promises to make a better life for herself, to the point where she has become the human interest story of our time.

In real life, however, she was actually much more interesting than her legend writ large. Sure, she did have two bodyguards, four dogs, and a revolving door of both friend and foe. And, yes, lots of girls in the business also had her assets—if surgically-enhanced, double-D breasts are any reflection of success—but few had the kind of work schedule that would leave most celebrities running ragged. Consider, for instance, how her Club Jenna website (*www.*

clubjenna.com) posted her media schedule for the week in August 2004, celebrating the release of her infamous autobiography *How to Make Love Like a Porn Star: A Cautionary Tale.*

On Friday, August 13, a feature story on her in *Rolling Stone* magazine hit the stands. On Monday, August 16, a VH-1 special aired, called *Inside Out—Jenna Jameson.* On Tuesday, August 17, the book came out in New York, and she did an 8.30 a.m. interview with Howard Stern and a 7 p.m. book signing at the Virgin Megastore in Times Square. On Thursday, August 19, another book signing at another Virgin Megastore, this time in Miami, Florida. The next day she found herself in Cleveland, Ohio, and the following day in Lexington, Kentucky, both book signings at Joseph-Beth Booksellers stores.

Two days later, on Monday, August 23, it's Chicago, Illinois, and a radio interview and a book signing, then the following day in San Francisco, a book signing at the Virgin Megastore. Then two days later the much anticipated book signing in Los Angeles at the famous Book Soup on the Sunset Strip. The *L.A. Weekly* reported the event. "Not only was she incredibly sexy, wearing a low-cut pink blouse, but she was also incredibly nice and forthcoming," noted the writer, Benjamin Silverton-Peel, who'd waited two and a half hours to get inside, like the rest of the crowd.

"These weren't your stereotypical porno fans waiting for Jenna," he added. "Far from it—consider all the young, relatively attractive women in line. In fact, we were well over 200 people, gay and straight, extreme and moderate, waiting an average of two hours ... Along with most everyone else, I purchased the 592-page book. I'm sure many of the people waiting in line for an autograph silently thought, 'I've never read a book this big before.'"

It was particularly intriguing to me to see that three years after we'd first met—I'd interviewed Jenna in July 2001, a meeting that took three years to happen—she'd become a major star and the first from the porn world to crack the mainstream in a serious way. I remember first hearing about her in 1996, following her first year on the scene, as a contract girl with Wicked Pictures, for which she became the first newcomer to win all the top three rookie awards in the same year: "Best New Starlet" at the *AVN* Awards, "Starlet of the Year" from the XRCO (X-Rated Critics Organization) Awards and the "Video Vixen" award from FOXE (Fans of X-Rated Entertainment).

Additionally, she also won the *AVN* awards for "Best Actress" and "Best Couples Sex Scene" (with the popular male stud T.T. Boy in Michael Zen's *Blue Movie*, which also won for that year's "Best Film"). Not a bad sweep at all. In point of fact, the very first piece of press I ever read about her was in *Adam Film World*, a report about her XRCO "Starlet of the Year" victory. She was shown posing with her trophy, shaped like a wooden heart (nicknamed the "heart-on") and, she "just about flew onto the stage in her eagerness to claim it." She mugged for the cameras with the rapper Ice-T, looking every bit the newly arrived porn princess in a body-clinging silver jumpsuit.

I remember thinking she wasn't at all bad to look at in that va-va-voom, cager-beaver kind of way. She exuded the necessarily exuberant, porn-perfect, photogenic pulchritude attitude. I'd seen it before, and so I honestly didn't pay her that much mind, despite her slew of awards, until her legend grew.

And grew, and grew. Bigger than anyone had expected. I began hearing many stories, from many girls. Jenna had been thrown out and banned from yet another hotel room, in yet another city. For drunken behavior. For trashing her hotel room like a petulant rock star. She had a problem with vodka. She had a problem with pills. She had a problem with punctuality.

The last was an understatement. My first interview with her didn't happen, because she simply failed to show up. And it wasn't just me she had stood up, either—it was an entire film crew. I was scheduled to interview her on location. Seth McCoy, her Wicked Pictures publicist, called just as I was about to get in my car, and told me Jenna wasn't even in Los Angeles; she was in New Orleans and was refusing to get on the plane. They cancelled the shoot that day, of course. The fact that the director was Brad Armstrong, Jenna's ex-husband, might well have been a factor. (I actually met and asked Brad about this incident some years later, and he simply nodded and shrugged. "Well, that's Jenna," he said.)

So, yes, yadda yadda, Jenna this, Jenna that. But where in the world was Jenna herself?

Was I sick of her yet? My editors at *Penthouse Variations* wanted the interview badly, since she was, after six years in the business, considered The Chosen One—queen of the prom, pageant winner incarnate, the industry's most charming ambassasor to the outside world. Many people were asking me, when they found out about my "Cinema Blue" column, when I would be interviewing her.

Were they kidding? I myself had no idea.

There was yet another aborted attempt by Seth McCoy, this time a scheduling snafu (Jenna was in Los Angeles and suddenly available but I was not, having left town only that very week), but I was determined to get her somehow. And then, on September 26, 2000, I suddenly had a breakthrough. She'd just left Wicked Pictures and I'd managed to get her email address and wrote her, asking that we try yet again to connect, and to my amazement she emailed me back.

"Hi sweetie! Please call my assistant Linda. She will set everything up. Much easier to get things done now that I'm independent! Thanks again! Jenna."

I nearly fell off my chair.

And that's how I started talking to her assistant, Linda Johnson, at her new company Club Jenna, trying to get the ball rolling again.

One of the tricks to interviewing porn stars who were famous was to get them when they were newly off-contract, something that happened more often than one might expect. Many contract girls went "independent" after having been fired or having failed somehow to get their contracts renewed. Typically, most contract girls were blessed with short attention spans undercutting their disproportionatly bigger ambitions, and they usually had no loyalty to anything other their own bank accounts. Sad perhaps, but very much true. But I had timed this right, and Linda Johnson was smart, personable and helpful.

Linda warned me, however, that Jenna was one busy bee. She was furiously ramping up her new company and shooting scenes for the company website, from her new vantage point as a director. Linda hadn't let on that, unknown to me and the rest of the adult film world, Jenna was also on the verge of a major career victory—she was about to sign a big deal with the biggest studio, Vivid Video. Jenna also scored a seven-year contract, calling for her to star in fifteen Vivid titles and to also direct others, some of which would feature herself as well. And Vivid would be the sole distributor all Club Jenna products. A win-win situation. But much of all this was under wraps.

Luckily for me her superstar status did not preclude the complete abandonment of her best known skill—performing sex in front of the camera   or else my interview with her would never have happened at all. For that's how I eventually met her, by sheer accident.

On the morning of June 12, 2001, I showed up at The Faultline, a gay men's leather dive in East Hollywood, where the gay director Chi Chi LaRue (of infamous drag queen fame and acclaim) was directing a Vivid movie, *Where The Boys Aren't #14*, an all-girl slurpfest featuring nine Vivid girls and one "surprise guest." That particular mystery performer was none other than Jenna, making her first appearance in a Vivid film in five years.

"Who's the girl in the cowboy hat?" I asked my friend Melissa Monet, former porn star turned *AVN* reporter, who was also covering the shoot.

"That's Jenna," she replied.

I was stunned. Jenna Jameson, porn queen immaculate, was hardly the woman I imagined from her movies. She was tiny, and were it not for the cowboy hat I might have completely blinked and missed her. And, with my usual unblinking honesty, I told her so.

"Oh, everybody says that!" she laughed. "I photograph really tall, like a big girl. I have long limbs, for my size. I'm long-waisted and have really long arms and legs—they're just shrunken! My measurements are 32D-22-33. I've gone down from a size 34. I've found that as I've grown older, I've slimmed down a bit. I've lost my baby fat.

"My boobs are big but my rib cage is really small. My boobs are so much bigger than they really are—they're huge on my frame! I tour so much that I get to meet a lot of my fans in person and many of them say, 'Oh my gosh, I thought you'd be bigger!' They expect me to be six feet tall, when I'm only five-three. I thank the heavens above that I photograph bigger than I am, because I think that's sexier, that kind of 'model' look."

She completely disarmed me with her goofy, offbeat personality and boundless energy, all jam-packed into this petite elf with the perpetual troublemaker grin. I caught her joking with the cast and crew, jostling for position like one of the boys. At one point, she posed for a photo next to a mural on the wall, a caricature of a muscled leatherman, resembling Freddie Mercury in bondage gear. She stuck her tongue out lewdly, right against his crotch, and then gently stroked his apparent pelvic bulge with her hand. And then giggled, clearly pleased with the image she was creating. For Jenna, public visibility was *numero uno*, and she was going to appear as scandalous as possible.

She might've also thought I was going to write about that in my piece. (And, of course, I did.) Later, I watched her work. One scene from that film forever burned itself into my brain. It paired Jenna with Dasha, a tall, green-eyed, twenty-four-year-old blonde from the Czech Republic with the most awesome 34C-25-36 body. At five feet eight inches, she towered over Jenna but nobody watching at home would ever notice the height difference, not when Jenna engaged in some very hot and heavy petting with her while perched on a bar stool. Dasha crouched and performed cunnilingus on Jenna, and the final result on DVD was actually more engaging, particularly the final moments as the camera zoomed in on Jenna as she lay on her back on top of the bar counter, thighs open wide and neck nicely arched. Dasha, almost kneeling and with her eyes level with Jenna's pubis, used her fingers to send Jenna into orbit.

For all the hard, fast sex she enacted, though, Jenna could get all misty-eyed, as she did during our interview when I took her down memory lane.

"My mother was a Las Vegas showgirl," she told me, "with all the feathers. She died when I was young and from the time I was small, I wanted to be a showgirl. And so I studied dance for twelve years, and when I turned seventeen I became a showgirl. That was the highlight of my life. I was at Vegas World, at the Stratosphere Tower."

She said that with a believable sincerity, in a tone of voice that dared anyone to doubt the romance implicit in such an ambition. In that, she was always consistent. "I wanted to get away from the craziness of L.A.," she explained, when I asked her why she chose to live in Scottsdale, Arizona, right outside Phoenix. "Did you know that Scottsdale is ranked number one as the cleanest city in America? Here I am, Jenna Jameson, the dirtiest girl in the world living in the cleanest city in America!" She laughed maniacally.

There was a factoid I'd always wanted to confirm. Yes, Jenna nodded, she still checked into hotels under the name Savannah, her personal idol, the porn superstar who had famously committed suicide. At the height of her fame, the former Shannon Wilsey from Orange County, California, had earned US$4,000 per sex scene and US$1,000 per box cover and starred in sevety-eight movies in just four years, before putting a gun to her head in 1993. She had cut up her face quite badly in a car accident, apparently driving under the influence of something or other.

"Savannah was the reason why I got into the industry," Jenna explained. "I saw her. Before I knew of this industry, I always thought oh, it's seedy and the girls are gross, and this and that, and then I saw Savannah. And I thought, this girl is unbelievable. She's so beautiful. And I said, I guess it's alright for girls to get into this industry, you know, and to be a model. And that's the reason I got in."

But didn't most people know Savannah was dead and so it must be an alias?

"Yeah, but I don't think they ever put two and two together," Jenna replied. "They don't ever really think about it. A lot of people know my real name because it's printed on the Internet everywhere, so they usually try my real name. They don't figure that I'll check in under another star's name."

The story of how Jenna Massoli became Jenna Jameson, a name she picked to honor the famous Irish whiskey, is, of course, now the stuff of legend. The accolades tell only half the story. In July 2005, she topped the list as the most popular celebrity in a poll conducted by the website *WomenCelebs.com*, which measured popularity in terms of frequency of visits to websites dedicated to famous people, no mean feat given that the site offered links to 7,496 female celebrities. Jenna had outranked the likes of Paris Hilton, Angelina Jolie, Pamela Anderson, and Hillary Duff. This was five months after *Playboy* magazine had named Jenna one of the world's "25 Sexiest Celebrities" in its March issue; she was the only adult film star on the list.

And, to top it off, she even made the Forbes "Celebrity 100" list in June 2005, which included female luminaries like Madonna and Oprah Winfrey. Her company Club Jenna, the *Forbes* article noted, "will hit revenues of US$30 million this year, up 30 percent in a year," and "her fans can rent her digital moan as the ringer on their cell phones and buy Jenna sex toys, action figures, and even a piece of herself, molded in soft plastic, anatomically accurate and priced to move at US$200."

That price point was a revelation to me, since it represented a very unique value proposition. Wicked Pictures had been selling plastic replica vaginas of its contract girls starting at around US$30 each, encased in velvety-matte, attractively designed boxes with text printed and penned to tease: "ultra-real, super stretchy" and also "succently soft" with "invitingly tight, textured sleeve." Clearly, now that she was no longer with Wicked, Jenna had clearly upped the ante and turned the tables on her former paymaster.

But enough of celebrity cheerleading; what about some of the sordid stories I had heard? Were any of them true? No, Jenna insisted, she was not habitually prone to smashing up hotel rooms, but yes, she used to have a horrendous drinking problem. She now allowed herself a glass of Merlot to calm her nerves before a shoot, but nothing stronger. If there was one thing she would like to change about herself, she told me, it would be her bad temper. Some of the legendary stories about her blowing up were true.

"I have a really bad temper," she admitted. "I've always had it. It runs in my family. My father's like that, my brother's like that. I'm actually reading a book right now that is called *Awakening the Mind*, it's Buddhist meditation and it's really helping me." Maybe with time, she hoped, some of the people she had pissed off would forgive her. I'd heard the complaints from an array of first-hand sources.

"Jenna was always such a bitch to me when I was never anything but nice to her," one girl told me. "I remember one movie I did with her when she threw a fit and announced that a certain male star was not allowed to have a pop shot in a scene with her. Everyone was, like, 'What the fuck?' and the director argued with her about it until she finally stormed off the set because she didn't get her way. Nobody knew why she was being such a brat."

Teri Weigel, a former *Playboy* Playmate turned porn star, documented one memorable encounter with Jenna in her "Totally Teri" column, on the industry tell-all website, *AVN Insider* (*www. avninsider.com*). She recalled an evening at a strip club where she was appearing, slotted to open for Jenna, who was headlining. "I started my show with Jenna and the club owner sitting at the front of the stage. I was halfway through my first song when I took off both of my shoes, which was a trademark of my routine at the time. I thought I heard cheering coming from the front

79

of the stage, but I was wrong—it was Jenna screaming. Then, inexplicably, she picked up a glass and shattered it on the stage, sending shards everywhere."

Nursing a cut leg, Weigel completed her set but then found Jenna refusing to go on stage, very much in the throes of a "childish tantrum ... It must be true you can take the girl out of the trailer but you can't take the trailer out of the girl. She was a heartless diva then, and she's a heartless diva now."

However, people who succeed seldom scaled the ladder in order to win popularity contests. "The thing is, you can't get to where I am and not be a smart person," Jenna told me. "It's impossible." So what if people hated her for being such a drama queen? She had a solid fan base and enough media coverage to offset the naysayers. The critics still loved her. At the 21st XRCO Awards show in June 2005, she was given the "Mainstream Adult Media Favorite" trophy and inducted into the XRCO Hall of Fame. ("I've been in this industry for about twelve years now and that's a long time," Jenna purred in her acceptance speech. "I feel very humbled. This has been a long wild ride for me." She added that she was "concentrating on building an empire for women in general in the business.")

Earlier in the year, at the *AVN* Awards, the Club Jenna/Vivid co-production *Bella Loves Jenna* was voted "Best Video Feature," and the "Best Couples Sex Scene" award went to Jenna and her husband Justin, for their scorching performance in the Vivid movie, *The Masseuse*. She had just released *Virtually Jenna: The Official Video Game of Jenna Jameson* (available for download at *www.virtuallyjenna.com*), developed for Club Jenna, Inc. by the Vancouver-based company xStream3D Multimedia, Inc., whose spokesperson Brad Abram told *AVN* that players "can pose her like a centerfold, dress and undress Jenna and her friends and let their imaginations control the outcome." The company had "devised a way to simulate control of her sexual activity and even decide when she reaches a state of bliss."

Jenna added herself: "What I like about it is that everything within the game is completely user-controllable. It's amazingly realistic and the player gets to manage every scene change, every camera angle, every zoom, pan, or tilt of the freestyle cameras. Plus, the player gets to decide how excited I get, and can direct the action in every scene."

That reminded me of the time I'd spoken to her in 2001, just as her interactive DVD, *My Plaything: Jenna Jameson*, had only been released. "Every man who sees this DVD is going to want to fuck me," she told me proudly. "If I were a man watching it, it would be the ultimate jack-off."

Her seven-year Vivid contract would not expire till 2007. I asked if she had ever felt overwhelmed by the mass adulation. "Yeah, I've won every award you can win," she replied. "The word would have to be overwhelmed. I never expected it to take off the way that it did. When everything started to snowball, I kind of freaked out. I had mainstream offers coming in left and right. I was hosting a show for the *E! Channel*. I had a thousand things on my plate. And, you know, I handled it all in my stride. I tried to keep a level head and everything. You would think that it would all start settling down now, but it's not. I kept expecting to get a break, and it just keeps getting bigger and bigger.

"I've slowed down and moved behind the camera a lot, and I've cut down on my feature dancing, because that takes a huge chunk of my time. Now I'm concentrating on my productions and my website. I'm shooting at least three times a week and my number one worry is to keep my content current. I have live sex streaming on it, twenty-four hours, and I also do bi-weekly live chats. It's different from doing movies because it's for a targeted audience. I know who I'm playing to. And it's cool, because all my members are like a club. I know every one of them, pretty much, I talk to them twice a week. So it's really satisfying for me, because I know it's my project. As long as there's a demand I'm going to stay. I'm not one of those people that are going to want to leave while everybody's wanting more."

For every anecdote told about what a shrew she could be in

public, there was always the perfect public face that she was very good at presenting to journalists—which might well be, of course, why she was so nice to me. In all the hours I spent with Jenna, on the set and later several times over the phone (she had given me her personal cellphone number to call), there was never once the slightest hint of the surly girl I'd heard about. "My favorite thing in the world to do is to go do interviews," she gushed. "'Cos it's me being me. It's a lot easier than, you know, playing a part. I've done *Nash Bridges*, I was in three episodes, I had a lot of scenes with Don Johnson, and I've done a lot of acting in the mainstream, but doing interviews is my favorite. Because then it's like I'm getting my point to people about who I am and what I represent."

I also recall telling her that one reason why my editor had asked me to chase her down was the fact that at the time she'd come out with her own pin-up calendar, a sixteen-month bikini-and-beachwear keepsake, shot in Saint Barthelemy in the French West Indies by photographer Brad Willis. Wicked Pictures had sent my editor the calendar and she had sent it on to me.

"The reason why I did the calendar? Well, I never really thought of doing a calendar," Jenna explained to me. "And then there was a publication that comes out—about calendars, I can't remember the name of it—and they had a list of the top fifty calendar girls. Number one was Cindy Crawford and then there was, like, Christy Turlington and you know, all the main *Sports Illustrated* girls. I was number nine. And I didn't even have a calendar out! And I was, like, 'Oh my gosh, I've got to do a calendar!!! How can I let this opportunity pass me by?!!'"

She went to Steve Orenstein, her Wicked Pictures boss, and he agreed to let her do it. "So he flew me off to St Barts and they shot me for two weeks," she recalled. "It was such a great experience. It was totally different from anything I had done before. And it was really, really well received by everyone. Except I had trouble getting it into big mainstream stores like Wal-Mart and stuff, you know. They don't want to have anything to do with a porn star."

The City of Houston, Texas, certainly didn't either, at least not initially, when her autobiography came out. The city fathers had demanded that all copies of the book be removed from public library shelves after a complaint had been made about Jenna's nude photos inside. In February 2005, however, the Houston authorities capitulated to the protests of the American Civil Liberties Union, after its Houston chapter argued that removal of all twelve copies of the book in the library system violated the First Amendment's free speech guarantee and breached due process of law.

Immediately after the book was reinstated, all twelve copies were checked out and there was a forty-person waiting list.

How amusing, I thought, especially since the coy title *How to Make Love Like a Porn Star* didn't tell you much about making love at all. My favorite part of the book was the section where Jenna recalled attending the red-carpet premiere of the film she'd been in, Howard Stern's *Private Parts*: "Billy Corgan, Flea, Angus Young, Sting, Bon Jovi, LL Cool J, Rob Zombie, Joey Ramone—everyone I idolized was there. I was a little porn girl thrust into this world of rock superstardom ... Until then, I had come to believe that I was a star. But when I met all these people, I realized I was just a niche icon, not a real celebrity. I had sex onscreen; I did some perfunctory acting. These people moved and inspired millions of people with their music. All I did was contribute to Kleenex sales."

I liked that because it reflected my own observation that, in person, Jenna was always full of surprises. She might have done "some perfunctory acting," but she had a knack for answering questions that was far from perfunctory. Like the obligatory porn-star views about sex positions. "My favorite position? Wow. I'm kinda weird," Jenna replied. "I like, if you can imagine this, laying on my back with my legs together, and the guy's legs are on either side of me. So my legs are like squished together. It's just a lot of friction." Uh, I asked, wasn't that kind of difficult? No, she casually replied, "as long as he has a big dick, it doesn't matter. As along as it's, like, about eight inches."

I can also still watch one of my favorite Jenna films, *Wicked Weapon*, and grin knowingly about the subtext in scene two, in which Jenna gave Brad Armstrong, her real-life husband at the time, a superb blowjob. It ended with him shooting his load on her face, his sperm jetting a nice white line across her upper lip. Jenna's response was sudden anger, with pure fire in her eyes. "Why did you come on my face?" she snarled. "Why the fuck did you come on my face?!!" She pushed his cock away like a useless toy. That, I thought, might not have been in the script at all. At the time, they were already having offscreen trouble. "We were married only two months," Jenna giggled, when I asked her about the divorce. "Can I say 'mistake'?"

In *Wicked Weapon*, Jenna played a vigilante crimebuster called The Jennarator, spoofing Arnold Schwarzenegger's *Terminator* while upstaging Pamela Anderson's *Barb Wire*—Jenna's costume actually resembled Pambo's kickass getup, but with an overall slicker tone and very badass helmet to boot. In her autobiography, Jenna revealed that the whole costume was her idea; she had fantasized about appearing on stage at strip clubs attired in such a jaw-dropping outfit. The film was, in my own view, essentially a B-movie spoofing itself, an act of demented genius. It had lots of zany dialogue and gave the viewer enough to focus on without detracting from the sex, especially during a spectacular orgy in a palatial mansion that most critics singled out as one of the best group scenes ever shot.

In some ways, though, I liked Jenna's previous film *Dangerous Tides* better, mainly because the sex was more intense and terrifically torrid, even as the story went somewhat awry (who could believe such a contrived tale, about swingers on a ship invaded by terrorists?). I didn't really care for the much-hyped *Flashpoint*, the *AVN* "Editor's Choice" for June 1998, a film that lost itself amid firemen and arson, drownings and suicides, ax fights and car explosions. The real pyromania, for me, was a sizzling bathroom scene in which Jenna took on the equally wild

Brittany Andrews. (And, to be sure, it must be a bad movie if a lesbian scene was the only thing I remember about it.)

Wicked Pictures cannily packaged these films as blatant vehicles for Jenna (or rather, for the more important "Jenna Jameson legend"), and in all fairness they did it very well. It was easy to understand why *Dream Quest*, Jenna's last film for them, was the biggest seller ever, after they'd marketed the hell out of it. However, in an exposé of her falling out with Wicked, in the December 2000 issue of *AVN*, Jenna revealed why they had parted company right after *Dream Quest*. Many saw it as an ironic move, since the reviews had raved about how the film had successfully fused science fiction and medieval fantasy with porn. But what they saw as a career peak, Jenna saw as merely another career move—and a way of turning crisis into opportunity.

For this was the big turning point, it would turn out, marking her unequivocal transition from contract girl to diva superstar.

She was incensed because Wicked owner Steve Orenstein had sold and licensed JennaVision, an Internet entity she'd helped set up, to various third parties behind her back. He was, she alleged, "selling it to everyone who wants it, so they're going to be flooding the market with me and making the money and I'm getting absolutely nothing. The biggest thing is not even the money. It's just the fact that I feel like they betrayed me ... I called him and left him a message about this, saying you want me to bend over for you to fuck me a little harder?"

What Orenstein clearly underestimated was Jenna's ability to control her career. In an interview she did at around the same time, quoted in the now-defunct *XPlicit* magazine, she summarized her celebrity ethos: "I realized early on that the more you keep yourself in demand, the more famous you'll get. If you flood the market with yourself, people get sick of you." Ever so brilliantly then, she decided not to get mad but to get even. She created her own company Club Jenna and used it as leverage to structure a deal with Wicked's biggest competitor, Vivid. Just so she could stick it to them real good. She wasn't going to bend over and keel like a whimpering slut. Real life wasn't the movies.

And, to add insult to injury, she also signed a contract with Elite Model Management in September 2004, for "fashion endorsements, appearances, and editorial." Conor Kennedy, Elite's creative director, proclaimed that "the era of the supermodel is over. Photographers are looking for stars with personality and charisma, and Jenna is an icon."

A porn star as an Elite model? There was a time when such a thing would be laughed at. I recall talking to the person who had first "discovered" Jenna—the director Andrew Blake, who had shot Jenna's first feature: *Fantasy Woman*, which he directed in 1994 for Adam & Eve (now a collector's item, since it was never widely released on video). "Jenna was just a centerfold model, a print magazine model, at the time," Blake had told me. "She was pretty much the girl next door. I didn't look at her and think she would be a big star someday. She was the one who reinvented herself. I can't take any credit for that."

Jenna laughed when I told her that. "He must have thought I was this meek little mouse. I didn't say two words that whole time. I was just so shy. I'm sure he was probably thinking, 'Who is this girl?!!' And I remember there was a girl there, her name was Seana Ryan, a *Penthouse* Pet. I was eighteen years old. She looked at me with this weird face and said, 'Are you old enough to be here?!!' I looked like a baby at that time! That totally stuck in my head and I was so intimidated by all these girls, you know. I had no idea what I was doing."

She was twenty when she fatefully met Steve Orenstein and signed with Wicked Pictures, and so much had happened since then. Her massive 592-page autobiography consigned her period with Wicked Pictures to merely the last quarter of the book. She'd also glossed over her sexual skirmishes with other celebrities, implying that Cindy Crawford had made a pass at her (which, after the book's publication, caused Crawford to threaten a defamation suit). She got hit-on by Wesley Snipes (she merely wrote that she was actually offended by his boldness) and then recalled that

Sylvester Stallone impressed her at first by *not* paying her much attention at all when they'd first met, at the opening of the Planet Hollywood restaurant in Bangkok, Thailand (though they met again later and he couldn't stop staring at her breasts). Maynard James Keenan, lead singer of the rock band Tool, was apparently a huge fan—he even had a picture of her on his road case—but nothing ever transpired between them. (Jenna didn't know who Tool were, and so turned down an opportunity to meet him.)

But, really, what strange elements persisted, that caused one person to be so impressed with another? "Why on earth is Jenna Jameson such a big star?" I've been asked that by so many people, who don't understand it at all. I always explained patiently that the answer, if there even is one, is complex. It wasn't that she was the most beautiful girl in the business or even the best sex performer. (As blondes went, I personally preferred Silvia Saint, Ava Vincent, and Janine Lindemulder.) Jenna had, simply put, the best "branding" in the business. She knew she was a commodity and applied every muscle in her lusty body towards milking that cash cow, stomping her stiletto heels on lesser minnows to achieve her goals.

But she had always been nice to me, so I put in a good word for her with our Pet Promotions office, when she asked me for help in making her a *Penthouse* Pet. (Jenna asked *me* for help? No way! I had that conversation on tape, though, and occasionally replayed it to convince myself it actually happened.) But she taught me something—to her credit, she was never ashamed to ask the right people for help, even lesser mortals like me, if it meant achieving her end-goal of superstardom. I was, subsequently, so proud of her when I saw her on the cover and centerfold of *Penthouse* in early 2004, the accompanying text even quoting from my own interview with her: "I made it one of my missions to get this industry accepted by the public, and I think I have been pretty successful in doing that, especially in getting it accepted by women." Some good karma had rebounded, not that she ever needed my two cents (or, in industry terms, two fingers).

She had paved the way herself. "I have always had strong ideas about creative issues, but it was difficult to get people to listen to me when I was just an actress," she wrote (in her own biographical sketch, in *XXX: 30 Porn-Star Portraits*, by the portrait photographer Timothy Greenfield-Sanders). In the giant crap shoot of the glamour game, being able to give the perfect blowjob wasn't ever enough, and she'd known that all along. That was why, as I'd always said, I've seen the movies and I've met the girl. And the girl was infinitely and undoubtedly much more interesting.

The Ballad of Ava Vincent

So there we all were, huddled in yet another Romanesque mansion somewhere in the hills above Los Angeles. Another house with a long driveway, hidden from prying eyes, but another chance for me to ask existential question #1: How does one perform for a camera crew, jettisoning reservations about the naked body and putting genitalia not only on display but happily to work? I received an object lesson in this, on that lovely spring morning in May 2001, while covering a shoot for *Fox* magazine, a New York hardcore jack-off journal that paid me four figures each time I scribed "live" reportage from actual film sets.

The magnificent opus was entitled *Dripping Wet #4* (initially *Dripping Fucking Wet #4* but truncated to soothe the delicate sensibilities of the hotel pay-per-view market). Despite the lowbrow title, it was helmed by two of the industry's more famous females—star-turned-producer Jill Kelly and star-turned-director Tabitha Stevens. The zany title indicated a "gonzo" flick—"reality" porn with the emphasis on sex, lots and lots of it, with what lame excuse for dialogue improvised.

The view outside was to die for, a breathtaking sweep of the San Fernando Valley below. Lush foliage, more coyotes, the occasional hawk swooping down to smash and mangle a hapless squirrel. But who's looking at the landscape? We were filming Ava Vincent, a radiantly beautiful, alabaster-skinned blonde formerly named Jewel Valmont, now at the height of her earning powers. I chatted with her before we began shooting and she disclosed that she was going to be *Penthouse* magazine's Pet of the Month in the upcoming August 2001 issue, so her rates would soon be going up. The layout, by photographer Carl Wachter, had already been shot; entitled "The Best of Both Worlds," it made much of the fact that she is proudly bisexual, and the *Penthouse* stamp of approval was in sync with her newfound sense of personal branding. People would think of Ava Gardner when they saw her name, and she loved that kind of old Hollywood glamour.

She'd made a name for herself already, with sizzling performances in such diverse titles as *Adrenaline*, *Jade Goddess*, *Babes Illustrated #9: Cyber Sluts*, *Cumback Pussy #17: The Lingerie Edition*, and *Perfect Pink #8: Red Hot*. More notably, her attractive, five-feet-five-inch, 120-pound bisexual self had snagged her the "Best All-Girl Sex Scene" trophy at the 2001 *AVN* Awards in Las Vegas, the "Oscars of Adult," for her incisor-sharp starring role in director James Avalon's acclaimed horror-porn film, *Les Vampyres*. Her performance elicited rave notices. *AVN*'s elder statesman Gene Ross described her as "the stunning Ava Vincent ... although stunning doesn't even begin to describe Vincent, who sets the screen ablaze with her ethereal beauty in this modern Gothic masterpiece."

Ethereal beauty, that was about right. I was talking to her as she stood posing for still photos—what we call "pretty girl"—to be circulated and sold to the men's magazines or used on video box cover art. I was some ten feet away from her, with a full-frontal view of her open vagina. She stood and preened behind a fountain of water by the swimming pool, clad only in high heels. With exquisitely manicured fingers, she parted her pert pink lips, her labial folds all wet and glistening.

Heaven in a wild flower, eternity in an hour, to quote the poet William Blake.

The still photographer, Scott Wallach, kept clicking and his motor drive hummed away as Ava changed poses without being instructed. She'd obviously done this before. This was the foreplay part of the day, a little bit of peek-a-boo before we segued to live-action camerawork inside. I love exhibitionism, so this was sometimes more interesting to me than the actual shoot to follow.

Today, however, was not going to be one of those.

Because Ava Vincent, unlike me, wasn't contemplating William Blake. She was, a few minutes later, reclining in my favorite on-camera position: "reverse cowgirl"—porn biz jargon for "girl on top" but one where the girl straddles the guy with her back to him, thus displaying to the camera her flushed face, bare breasts and open thighs. I love seeing this sort of extroverted eroticism, especially if the girl arches her back just enough, so that her partner's erection is penetrating her to its full length, and she maintains the intensity by humping him from up high.

"Cowgirl" itself is when the girl is on top but facing the guy, the direct opposite of conventional "missionary." The lucky guy being straddled was Vincent's real-life beau, John Decker. He lay on his back and mugged ecstasy for the camera, as Ava rocked her hips in tandem to his upward thrusts. Very nice.

However, most adult film actresses, if they're honest, will confess that "reverse cowgirl" is their least favorite position to perform. It is physically very demanding—it kills your calves and murders your lower thighs, and your hands have to grip on something. It helps if there's a table or a nightstand or something to hold onto, especially if you're performing on a soft bed wearing high heels. The laws of physics are not negotiable when your center of gravity is at stake. In Ava Vincent's case, she was on top of John on the very edge of the bed, her feet on the floor. She had absolutely nothing to hold. Her hands were on both sides of him, her fingers clawing the bed sheets. She was really starting to tire quickly.

I distinctly remember two things from that scene.

The first was how her green eyes smoldered, as she looked at me while she was riding him, oozing lust incarnate. We'd just moved from new acquaintances mere minutes earlier to participants in a voyeuristic encounter. By sheer coincidence, my favorite film of hers, *Hung Wankerstein*, was just about to be released on May 15, 2001 (five days away; this shoot took place on May 10). It was a tribute to the B-movie genre, a porn *comedy* spoofing the Frankenstein legend. Ava played Inga, the oversexed Swiss milkmaid-turned-lab assistant, all Germanic vowels and Botticelli curls, who naturally got to make whoopee with the big green monster. (I kid you not, it's the only porn movie that had me rewinding just to listen to the *dialogue*.)

Ava, in real life, is a 34-24-34 blonde from Northern California, a theatre arts graduate from San Joaquin Delta College who'd chucked in her US$375-a-week job managing an adult book store in Stockton after she realized how much more porn stars could earn—at least US$500 for every sex scene (each movie usually contains five or six), and US$1,000 if there's anal sex involved, so it doesn't take a genius to do the math. Girls like her, always in demand, will do several shoots each month and appear in several hundred videos each year. It beats flipping dead cows at McDonald's.

The second thing I remember about that day was how the scene abruptly ended.

The main prerequisite for this profession is that you really (and they mean really) have to love sex. Because there's going to be a lot of it, more than most people can reasonably handle, and more than most girls need if, like a surprisingly high proportion of them, they actually can't orgasm all that easily. Faking with grimaces and groans is easy, but you also need to possess a pretty high threshold for pain.

Ava Vincent, her eyes pleading for mercy, her fingers straining to clutch the bed sheets, was on that very threshold. She gasped and moaned as John continued to thrust and the camera captured the "insertion shot"—her wet pussy clutching his cock as it slid in and out. This usually goes on for some interminable length, until the "pop shot"—when, theoretically, John slides out of her and blasts his semen into the air and onto her pubic area. Sometimes, the guy will pull out just before the magic moment and she'll turn around and catch it on her face. Sometimes she will quickly position herself, so that the guy can shoot straight into her mouth, or let some of it dribble down her cheek. The really good girls will resume sucking till the poor guy's been drained dry.

Ava, however, wasn't going to let John go all the way today. Hands grasping the sheets frantically, as her knees started to buckle in pain, she let out her last agonized gasp.

"That's it!" she screamed, to no one in particular, "I can't do this!"

She stood up, letting John's still-erect penis slide out of her, and promptly walked off the set. Nobody stopped her. They just shut down the cameras and lights. Tabitha called a break.

What I thought interesting was that nobody was shocked or surprised, and nobody complained. There have been shoots when a girl is a real princess and a total pain in the butt and gets told to "behave yourself like a good little whore," which usually makes things worse. Jenna Jameson famously stormed off a set, on Michael Zen's 1997 film *Satyr* (a legendary, embattled project which porn folks still discuss today with shared disbelief) when a production manager caught her sulking and told her off in such eloquent fashion; in her autobiography, Jenna remembers that she felt he had crossed the line by using the dreadful "W" word. But for the most part, these people had been on enough shoots to know when a girl's taken it to the limit.

Either that or nobody wanted to upset Ava Vincent, since she was now an A-list porn star. And the pain must've been intense. She looked like she could've clawed someone's eyes out.

Tabitha told me she understood, having had to perform the same kind of scene herself many times. Civilians who merely rent porn don't know the occupational hazards. Performing oral sex is easy, and so is having a guy splatter his come all over your face, but if it gets into your eyes it will truly hurt like hell. Tabitha's had that happen to her three times. "And two of those times," she told me, giggling, "were Ron Jeremy."

Jeremy, a.k.a. "The Hedgehog," is porn's most famous male star. I'd met and partied briefly with him, a nice-enough guy with an effusive passion for self-promotion. He was also a startling phenomenon, given the way he looks—way too fat and grotesquely hairy (hence the nickname)—and some girls also claimed him somewhat, ahem, hygiene-challenged. Not quite anyone's idea of a typical porn stud. Not Rocco Siffredi, not even John Decker.

But therein lies the legend, because Ronnie boy represents "everyman," a porn marketing notion writ large: if pudgy Ron Jeremy can get pussy, well, surely so can the average Joe Schmoe.

"He's a hero to regular guys everywhere," porn legend Nina Hartley once told me, having fucked him enough times to know. "A girl should not consider herself a porn actress if she's never done Ron Jeremy. You gotta do it. It's like paying your dues, it's like working your way up." So many stories have been spread that I had heard of how he prowls nightclubs after shoots just so she can score more pussy, as if "work" alone wasn't enough. One girl told me she "gave Ron a blowjob out of pity." Some guys have all the luck.

Tabitha Stevens, of course, wasn't legendary in the way of Jenna Jameson, but she was in so many ways the archetypal American porn star, having risen through the ranks as a Las Vegas stripper before performing sex on video in 1995. Ten years later, in May 2005, she would achieve a rare form of notoriety when the news broke that she was about to be seen in *Cathouse*, the HBO documentary series about the lives of the girls at Nevada's Moonlite Bunnyranch, no ordinary chicken shack thanks to its reputation for having porn stars on duty right in the house. Tabitha's role, however, was a highly unique one: as *AVN* reported, the show's new season "features Tabitha Stevens conducting a cock-sucking class for the Bunnyranch girls."

Blessed with a slight overbite, which made her fellatio skills visually pleasing on film, Tabitha was now being employed to teach the regular working girls how to blow. What greater validation than to be asked to teach what one does best? "I love doing oral," she told me, grinning. "I'm really awesome at it." No false modesty from this girl.

We had first met a few months earlier, on the set of a Michael Zen film called *Coming of Age*, in which she played a willowy blonde named Jennifer, who had "only been with one man before" and was about to change her life in one hot night of sexual experimentation. The role was an apt metaphor, since Tabitha had once been a working mainstream actress with a real SAG card. "I worked for a company called Capcom, I did a video called *Street Fighter* and I did SEGA TV commercials, and I toured the country for a year and a half, and then I did a bunch of features and it was wearing me out," she recalled. I was interviewing her while we waited for Ava to cool off outside.

"And I called Larry at *Hustler*. And from *Hustler*, I went to Vivid. I was married at the time and I wasn't happy in my relationship. There wasn't any sex and I wanted to see what it was like. I asked my husband if it was okay, and he said okay. And I called my parents the night before my first movie, and asked if they were going to have any problems with it. I asked my sister, I asked my grandmother, I asked my brother.

"And they said, 'It's your life, whatever you want to do,' they were very supportive about it. I come from a really good family. I wanted to try something for myself. I didn't want to be an extension of somebody else's life. That first movie was *Rolling Thunder*, with Racquel Darrian, a Vivid film directed by Paul Thomas. My first scene was with Bobby Vitale, and it was my first scene ever, a boy/girl, and it went fine. I did the scene and then right after that, I divorced my husband. I didn't think that it was fair to him, that I would be doing porn, because I'm having sex with all these people."

She was done with her third marriage now, having survived a recent tragedy. "I was pregnant with my last husband and we lost the child. After that, things just went downhill and we're divorced now." Her hair was also her natural brunette again after a peroxide-blond stage, and since she was also performing in her own film she wore only a short blue slip with nothing underneath. Sitting in the director's chair when the cameras were rolling, she liked to draw her knees upwards so she could curl her arms around them, seemingly oblivious to the fact that her wispy brown hairs and exposed vulva were open to view. Only on a porn set could such nonchalance seem so natural, though I couldn't help but ask if such exhibitionism came so easily to her.

"Oh totally," she replied, "I've been like this my whole life. Always, always. Even in the winter time, when I was younger, I'd walk around the house naked. Even now, I try not to wear underwear. I'll wear something see-through if I'm going to someplace nice. I don't want people to freak out too much. People know. People recognize me."

Then she told me her fondest memory of being spotted in public. "My sister and I went out, we took her kids with us, and we went to a Wendy's. She went up to order our drinks while I stayed at the table with her kids. And the guy says to her, 'Don't worry, I'll take care of it. Just tell Tabitha I said hi.'

"The guy at the Wendy's knew who I was!" She shook her head, giggling. So did she make conversation with the eagle-eyed waiter? "Yeah, it was funny. I went and said hello and told him, 'Next time I come in, I'll bring you one of my movies or something.' And he was, like, 'Oh my God!' He was pretty happy."

Tabitha had courted immense notoriety following appearances on everything from *Howard Stern* (several appearances, to nobody's surprise, since Howard loves her type) to *The Tonight Show With Jay Leno* (the latter particularly memorable for me, since she was on Leno's 'Street Jams' segment and I'd recognized her immediately!) and two *Entertainment Tonight* stories, one about the adult film industry and the other about cosmetic enhancements (she admitted to being a "plastic surgery junkie," having spent up to US$200,000 on everything from botox, rhinoplasty, liposuction, and several revisions of her 34DD boobs).

But mainstream fame wasn't her game. Having previously

been a B-movie sex-and-gore scream queen with Troma Films, the New York cult company (*Eve's Beach Fantasy* was the one most people remembered her in), she seemed to mirror her penchant for perversely lowbrow fare even in the adult world. She had been in such titles as *Blonde Brigade*, *Booby Call*, *Babes Illustrated #9: Cyber Sluts*, *Take 69*, *Texas Dildo Masquerade* and that less infamous but infinitely more frightening, Ron Jeremy-directed, John Wayne Bobbitt vehicle (read: disaster) called *Frankenpenis*.

And, lest we forget her return to her roots, the B-movie porn spoof *The Bride of Double Feature*, for which she was nominated for "Best Supporting Actress" at the 2001 *AVN* Awards. When I asked her if she had won any *AVN* Awards previously, she paused and didn't seem sure. "I think I have," she mused. "I wasn't there to collect it. It was years ago, or at least a few years ago. I did a series called *Fuck 'em All*, for All Good Video, which won 'Best New Series.' Which was very nice to have, it was cool to have it and everything, but I would rather my fans be happy, you know? I don't think the fans really give a shit about the awards. They're about liking you and liking your performance. I love the camera and I love my fans. And knowing that they're watching, that's what gets me going. I know I'm going to do the best that I can for them. I'm not getting any younger, I'm thirty-one years old. I was twenty-five when I got into this business. So as long as my body can hold out and I look good, I'm not ready to quit right now. Once people start not liking their job, then they should quit."

What does she tell the young girls entering the business? "My first thing is, warn anybody who might find out. They *will* find out. And then, make sure you can be comfortable with it, you know, because there are ups and downs. Don't come in because you need money. Don't come in because you need to do drugs, or because your boyfriend's making you do this. Come in with a strong, clear mind. Do this because you want to do it. There is such a thing as too much sex. You can get burned out. Sex is different when you're on a set, because you're stopping and you're cutting, you're doing this and you're doing that, and you're doing dialogue."

At that juncture, I spied John Decker still lubing and stroking himself, so that he could maintain his erection while Ava was resting outside, waiting to shoot again soon, most definitely in another position. I wondered how he managed to do this, day after day, week after week, without Viagra.

Nobody hires young women in this profession because they possess the range of Nicole Kidman or the versatility of Meryl Streep. For the most part, they need to look like Ava Vincent, but with stronger legs.

Four women in my own past sex life were blondes, and one of them somewhat resembled Ava (which might explain why I've always had a nostalgic thing for Ava, since porn stars often represent archetypes drawn from our own psychic baggage). But one look at John Decker, and I doubt I would ever want his job. Too much hard work, so to speak.

It was at times like these that I really started to question just how in the world I got here. Of course, growing up in Singapore during the repressive 1970s held all the answers. Everything about it has already been best summarized in that oft-quoted William Gibson magazine piece about Singapore, which begat the famous catch-phrase, "Disneyland with the Death Penalty," published in the September/October 1993 issue of *Wired* magazine. I always thought it interesting that so many outsiders armed with critical thinking could easily understand just why I spent so many years feeling frustrated when many at home didn't get it at all. Critical thinking was, I can attest, not part of the curriculum at school.

And so I spent my adolescence being forced to get my hair cut to a regulation length, simply because some know-it-all up high decided that that all male human beings in Singapore had to look one way and one way only. "Obsessed with short haircuts," the novelist Paul Theroux described the Singapore government of the time; Theroux left Singapore after three years of living there, vowing never to return (he still has not, for the past thirty years), but I bet he never had a Led Zeppelin poster on his bedroom wall, the one with the four guys standing in front of their private jet, which represented for me all that was important in life. Freedom of expression, libertarian democracy, I already knew what all that was at age fourteen. But I was told to not question authority and, as I was indeed brutally told, to "shut up." And so I decided I would leave Singapore the first chance I got and stayed away, with the odd visit back to see the folks, for a total of twenty years.

Of course, the anti-hippie hair rule doesn't apply anymore and rock bands with long hair play Singapore all the time now, the current administration seeking to project a more "hip" image of the country—loaded with electronic dance clubs galore, bar-top dancing in pubs, even a Crazy Horse burlesque revue, all aimed to impart some desperate sensation of "buzz"; and all this only after too many tourists had decided not to visit Singapore because it was, as most had described it, "boring." Even Joan Didion, whom I wrote my Master's thesis on, told me she had visited Singapore. "I found it a terribly empty place to live," she said.

And, according to the Singapore laws, anyone caught with a sizeable quantity of porn, even if you try to prove that it's for your own consumption (and not for sale), can be fined S$500 (US$300) per DVD or a maximum of S$20,000 (US$12,500), or six month's jail, or both. But you can still buy the bootleg stuff on the side streets around the city's main drag, Orchard Road, or up in Thailand, so I love what this says about progress (and I still stash my stuff safely away in Los Angeles). It was perhaps inevitable then that I would end up in Los Angeles, citadel of Southern California, the city where everyone came to reinvent their identity, to remake themselves anew.

I remember a music industry party, during the very moneyed early 90s, at Thunder Road, the famous Harley-Davidson biker café on the Sunset Strip. The music attorney friend who'd invited me told me that the porn star Lois Ayres would be there, and that he would introduce her to me. True enough, he did, and Lois became the first porn star I would actually meet in the flesh.

I remember she was invitingly friendly, in the way of

most celebrities, especially when they meet us media people at Hollywood parties. I had only seen her in one film—the Ginger Lynn classic *Blame It On Ginger*—and we had a pleasant enough conversation, of which I remember pretty much nothing. Later, I discovered that Lois had also been in *The Devil in Miss Jones III* and *IV*, *Every Woman Has a Fantasy 2*, and other self-explanatory titles like *Bi-Bi Love* and *Nightshift Nurses*, and had been written up by the adult entertainment journal *Adam Film World* in such glowing terms: "Originally known as Sondra Stillman, Lois changed more than her name in 1986 … Lois always looks like she just got fucked, and from what we hear, probably did. She comes across as a cock-crazed nymphomaniac who never gets enough. A sex performer par excellence, she virtually devours her partners." (Devours her partners? I remember reading that and thinking I was surely in the wrong business.)

There was another girl at the same party, though, who caught my attention. Her name was April, but she called herself Ivy. She told me she had moved to L.A. recently from the East Coast. "I want to be in porn," she told me matter-of-factly, and asked me to dance. She was slim and slender, with reddish-brown hair and a movie-starlet face, quite attractive and blessed with a vivacious personality. On the dance floor, she reached into my shirt and flirtatiously pinched my nipples, laughing gleefully and with a reckless abandon I found intoxicating.

She also told me she used to be the roommate of the porn star Madison, and had learned much from her when they both danced at the same strip clubs. But Madison was a big star now, and she wasn't. "Madison is always featuring," she moaned. "I want to do the same." I didn't know what "featuring" was but pretended I did, nodding ever so sagely, since I didn't want to risk losing her undivided attention. (She was pretty cute and, believe me, I can be as sex-brained a Neanderthal as the next guy.) Later, of course, I learned that strippers who become porn stars get to "feature"— they dance at the top of the bill for the night, and are announced as the club's showcase talent, which always brings in top dollars.

Ivy aspired to drag herself from the dungheap, following the stiletto heels of her former roommate, whom she confessed (after knowing me for all of ten minutes) she didn't much care for. "I don't like Madison, she's a very mean person," she whispered in my ear. Bitchy, bitchy.

From that party, I went to yet another party, where I met several people from a *Hustler* film crew and spent most of the evening talking to a very attractive brunette named Sara Lee, who told me she could be seen in that month's issue of *Chic* magazine, shot by photographer Matti Klatt. Sara was another Ivy, an aspiring porn starlet who hadn't done much yet except for a few magazine layouts. She liked the fact that I had been writing for *Playboy*, and this opened her up to me about getting her feet (and other body parts) wet.

"My parents would kill me if they knew," she said. "I'm just doing this for myself. To see what I can learn about myself." I was quite touched by her outward honesty, though I regrettably didn't ask for her phone number. I did procure that issue of *Chic,* though, and was slightly disappointed to see that her appearance was in a mere six-page "girl/girl" spread, in which she cavorted on the hood of a car with a blonde. Still, it was an awakening of sorts for me—the first time I was seeing someone I had actually met completely naked in a magazine, her thighs spread wide open, her vulva openly on display. (This was 1992, and Sara St James and her masturbation video were another three years away.)

Yes, Virginia, there is spiritual recompense. If I had stayed in Singapore, I would never have met girls like them. And my life would've been the poorer for it. I would not, for instance, have ever been to the *AVN* Awards in Las Vegas, which I attended in January 2001. It was Drew McKenzie at work, once more with feeling. I had flown up there because V.K. had asked me to pen a piece about what it was like to be there, at the infamous Oscars of porn.

The thing to remember about the *AVN* Awards, as anyone who has ever attended will tell you, is that it's never about the awards *per se*. Porn is about exhibitionistic sex, and the *AVN* Awards are really about putting porn as a genre on public display. The awards ceremony itself is usually an overly long, self-congratulatory affair. Too many people get too drunk to really care about who won what (unless you're one of those who really, sincerely wanted to win but tragically lost). The real action, and the focus of the story I eventually wrote, is the red carpet entry before the actual ceremony.

The Thai-British firecracker Tera Patrick ended up winning the Best New Starlet trophy that night, but most of the gawkers gathered outside the hall missed her completely since she was dressed far more conservatively than anyone would have expected, clad in a long-sleeved, black lace top with demurely see-through floral embroidery and simple beige slacks. The phalanx of photographers were aiming their lens at Nina Hartley, in an elegant red dress with black elbow-length gloves, looking like a bordello madam. Asia Carrera, in a yellow sequined Tadashi gown that she'd acquired from her neighborhood Topanga Mall boutique, came strolling in, one hand clutching her then-beau Clarke Irving, a tall and ruggedly handsome Englishman she would become engaged to but eventually not marry. And then there was Jessica Drake, wearing the outfit of the evening, a floor-length satin skirt cut dangerously low at the hip and, well, pretty much nothing else.

Across her bare chest were two white strips of cloth studded with rhinestones, draped in a V-shape but barely covering her nipples, leaving the rest of her breasts bare and pretty much all of her tanned torso open for public viewing. Eyes popped, jaws dropped. It was the closest thing to being completely naked.

Jessica told me later that she was nearly arrested for her outfit, or the lack thereof. "Hotel security did approach me and said that either I cover up or risk being arrested by vice, who apparently were in the hotel at the time. I politely told Mr Security that I was legally covered, because no nipples were visible. They were actually covered with make-up and taped. But he insisted.

So I covered up momentarily with a shawl but then after some thought, I imagined what a great time I would have without it and dropped the shawl for the rest of the evening. So there!" Jessica would win, appropriately, the "Best Tease Performance" trophy that night.

At 9.30 pm, with emcee Jenna Jameson still inside doing her thing, the first guests began their exodus out of the Venetian ballroom. A tall blonde I didn't recognize, wearing a cowboy hat and a backless black pantsuit, sashayed out onto the red carpet and was immediately accosted by a young photographer. "Do a fashion shoot?" he asked. She nodded, and pulled open her low-cut top. Out popped her bare breasts with their ripe, pink nipples. The young guy snapped away with his camera, grinning at his good luck. Freelancers live for moments like these, for shots they know will sell.

Another ripple surged through the crowd moments later. A tall brunette trumped that blonde by literally slithering out of her skimpy red dress. She untied her halter top and lowered it down to her navel, making unmistakeable the fact that she was wearing nothing underneath. She allowed the cameras to get as many angles on her naked breasts as possible, before bending down to aim her very round ass right into an outstretched zoom lens. The dress fell down low enough for me to get a glimpse of her brown pubic hair. She kept this position for what seemed like an eternity, before collecting herself and, still smiling, sauntering off before the cops could arrive.

But my own favorite moment would have to wait until the next day, when I attended the *AVN* Expo trade show at the adjacent Sands Expo Center. At the booth belonging to Extreme Associates, one of the more outrageous companies, was their girl—a pretty, strawberry-blonde nymphette named Keri Starr, who wore an outfit that threatened to beat Jessica Drake's from the night before—nothing at all except a makeshift thong comprised of stickers advertising the company's Internet search-engine site ("Search Extreme: The Joy of Search—*www.searchextreme.*

com"). The stickers were illustrated with pink lips emblazoned on a black background. She stood there signing autographs wearing two such stickers pasted over each nipple, and a bunch of the same stickers cobbled together as panties. She let the fans pat her otherwise bare derriere, grinning as the men stroked her bare skin with their palms. The crowd around her, predictably, was massive.

I decided to come back later when the lines were shorter. I'd touched a girl before, I knew what a bare butt felt like, and I didn't need to make a public spectacle of it. (I'm Drew McKenzie, you know.)

I strolled the massive hall, stopping to chat with other porn stars, and then headed back to her booth. This time, Keri was wearing a brown halter dress, her nipples straining against the very sheer fabric, making it obvious she was still naked underneath.

"The security people, they made me cover up," she sighed. "They said I couldn't sign wearing just the stickers." But she winked at me and grabbed one of the offending stickers. "This one came off one of my nipples," she said, "and you have to wear it." With that, she slapped the sticker on the lapel of my jacket, and then pulled out a glossy eight-by-ten photo of herself. "This is my last one and I'll sign it for you."

She smiled, grabbed a black marker, and wrote: "Gerrie— Next time you see me, you better cum on my face. Love, Keri Starr."

A few moments later, I was walking by the Wicked Pictures booth and ran into contract girl Stephanie Swift, a Eurasian beauty (one-quarter Filipino) who, in complete contrast to everyone around her, was completely dressed down in a simple cotton print dress and wore no make-up at all. She looked deceptively demure and quietly approachable, like a regular green-eyed brunette. "This has been my favorite year at the *AVN* convention," she told me. "It's the first time that I've really not been too nervous about everything. I've been doing this convention for seven years now, so it's like a second home to me. I'm basically showing the real me this year. I'm not covering myself with make-up or outfits or anything like that."

Several people interrupted us to ask her for autographs, and she cheerfully obliged. Did that make her feel like a celebrity, I asked? "I always feel weird when people say that," she replied, laughing. "I'm just used to writing my name. I'm really good at it."

Around the corner, at the Adam & Eve booth, Asia Carrera was doing the same, though her line was several times longer than Stephanie's and a few women stood among the mostly male throng, some actually getting autographs not for their boyfriends but for themselves. (Asian girls are often seen at Asia's signings, and many have told me what a role model she was to them.) At the awards ceremony the previous night, Asia had been inducted into the AVN Hall of Fame, that sacred place reserved for living porn legends. Her then-husband, the veteran director Bud Lee, was also inducted into the Hall of Fame. This was one for the record books—the first time a real-life couple had been ushered into the AVN Hall of Fame together, a rare achievement.

"Bud's pissed off because it took him twenty years to get his and it took me six to get mine," she quipped. Asia had made her porn debut in 1994.

Yes, I know, I said, "I just ran into Bud and he said, 'You tell Asia I did it with my brains but she did it with her tits.'"

"What, he said that? I'll kill him!" Asia squealed, and immediately dissolved into peals of laughter. She stared at the AVN Hall of Fame trophy sitting next to her at the booth. "It's nice to be appreciated for all the work I've put in but it also makes me feel old. Every time I look at it, I'm thinking it's time to retire. I'm always afraid of wearing out my welcome."

Adam & Eve was about to release for the first time on DVD her pet project, the film *Appassionata*, a classical-porn period piece set in the time of Mozart, for which she wrote, directed, produced, acted and even scored the music. (The film received seven nominations at the 1999 AVN Awards.) Asia even did the

DVD authoring herself. Computer geek, terminal overachiever, not to forget MENSA member, Asia is considered the smartest woman in porn with an I.Q. of 156. And one of the richest. I had written a now-famous piece on her, published in September 1999 in *The Wall Street Journal*, about her legendary stock-market prowess. ("If You Think Investment Gains Can Be Obscene," ran the headline.)

Well, why not? If the porn audience comprises a wider range of folks out there than most people might imagine, that's simply because porn is the most democratic of pop culture genres, with something for everyone. There's kitsch and camp as well as serious and ironic, and aesthetic details to suit every whim and fancy. How could it be otherwise, with the fake eyebrows and fake boobs galore, not forgetting fake names and sometimes even fake personalities to match?

In my reportage of the *AVN* Awards, I chose to close with an anecdote that illustrated this. On the Southwest Airlines flight back to Los Angeles from Las Vegas, Cassidey, the newest Vivid contract girl, best known outside porn for her appearance in the infamous Enrique Iglesias "Sad Eyes" video, found herself seated next to an average-looking, middle-aged couple. Making conversation as the plane took off, they asked the slender doe-eyed brunette what she did for a living.

"I'm a porn star," Cassidey replied.

Her flight companions had never seen her movies, not *Diary of Desire*, *Tonight*, *Marissa*, or *House Sitter*, not even the more prosaic, hyper-gonzo *Shane's World 21: Cliffhanger*. So, taken aback somewhat and perhaps not believing her, the couple asked her if she had any pictures of herself to show them.

"Sure," Cassidey complied, promptly pulling from her carry-on bag a hardcore magazine featuring her in a photo spread. She showed them pages and pages of her, buck-naked, legs spread-eagled, her pussy and asshole open for their visual assessment. Plus a few more, of her being penetrated by a rock-hard cock.

The wife looked amused. She asked Cassidey some questions

about what it was like to work as a porn star. The husband, however, looked completely out of sorts.

His eyes seemed about to pop out of their sockets as he perused the pages of the magazine, and his face visibly reddened. He had a sheepish expression, as if to say he wished his wife hadn't been there, for there was no doubt as to what he would really have liked to do with Cassidey.

I felt his pain. But I was always the sort of guy who could've spent a very pleasant flight seated next to Cassidey, checking out her layouts. I'd seen them before anyway, and, unlike that poor husband, I'd have no problem letting her know they turned me on. Porn stars love being told that. I know it would certainly make her happy.

She's a porn star, off-duty, on the plane heading home. What else did I think was going to happen?

Lust on the
Orient Express

A is for Asia

"Sometimes, I wake up in the middle of the night ... and I wonder: How the heck did all this happen?" So began the *AVN Online* cover story of January 2002, entitled "Deep Inside the Temple of the Geek Goddess: How a Mild-Mannered Porn Star Became the Master of her Virtual Domain," with the byline "by Asia Carrera."

It was a first-person memoir, detailing how she became known as not merely an A-list porn star but also an A-list Internet webmistress. What was really interesting about it, however, was the fact that she didn't actually write it.

I did.

It was the most interesting piece of ghostwriting I had done, and the result was so spectacular that Asia herself had the cover of that particular issue framed. She hung it up on the wall of her home's computer room (the actual physical domain of the webmistress herself, of course). I was commissioned by my then-editor Erik McFarland, who called me out of the blue one afternoon with the assignment.

Word had somehow gotten out that I was working with Asia on her autobiography, which my literary agent was then shopping to the publishing houses in New York, and so Erik hatched the brilliant idea to have me pen a piece "written" by her about her own life, with particular emphasis on her online presence.

This, of course, was an angle loaded with cultural relevance. The Internet revolution had been highly instrumental in making certain porn stars bigger than others and, arguably, the single biggest subset of adult entertainers to benefit from this were Asian porn stars.

Also, a lot of computer geeks happened to be Asian guys (or male Asian geeks who didn't have girlfriends), and there are some very telling statistics verifying this. Asia Carrera and Annabel Chong both told me that a very high percentage of their fans were Asian. At the strip clubs, Asian guys turned out in droves whenever Asian or Eurasian porn stars were feature-dancing.

In my own time in the porn trenches, I had come to meet and interview quite a few, most memorably Kira Kener (half-Vietnamese), Gwen Summers (part-Japanese) and Stephanie Swift (part-Filipino). The most popular of them all, whom I did not meet, was Tera Patrick (half-Thai); I did see her walk by not ten feet away from me at the 2001 *AVN* Awards, the year she won the "Starlet of the Year" trophy, almost unnoticed "because she was dressed much more conservatively that the other attendees," as I wrote in my *Penthouse Variations* piece on the big event, published in February 2002. (The reason we didn't meet was that I didn't recognize her myself, not until after she had walked by!)

Of course, Tera never had to flaunt her assets in public all that much, given her wild reputation. A former mainstream model with a nursing degree, she surrendered a degree in microbiology to become a porn star. Tera truly exemplified the sexually adventurous persona of the Thai sex kitten. My favorite quote of hers came from the July 2000 issue of *AVN*, in which she said: "A lot of girls tell me I don't understand because I've always had big breasts. I mean, I woke up at thirteen with 36DDs, okay?" She paused for effect and cupped them with her palms. "I walk around, and I hold these, and say 'Thank you, God.'"

Mind you, most Asian women who aren't in the business possessed neither those kinds of assets nor the glamour-puss veneer of Tera Patrick and Asia Carrera. I had spent a lot of time talking with Asia about this, mostly over drinks by her pool at her house in Woodland Hills (before she married and moved to Hawaii and then Utah). Asia was unconventional in that she had a lot of female fans, simply because of who she was, proving that there were indeed women out there who aspired to be both smart and sexy. I knew Asian women who were totally in awe of her legend. June Wang, a Chinese-American film producer I knew, actually made a documentary about Asia (the film, unfortunately, was never finished).

The mini-memoir in *AVN Online* that we were to collaborate on was a brilliant idea, since I probably knew more about Asia and had spent more time with her than any other writer she knew. I'd done several pieces on her already, including a long profile in my February 2000 "Cinema Blue" column in *Penthouse Variations* and the more famous *Wall Street Journal* piece of September 1999, which discussed her prowess at the stock market and the fact that she was a very popular porn star with a keen sense of humor, having written porn scripts under the pen name Dow Jones.

This led many people to ask me if our relationship had been entirely platonic. Some seemed shocked, even disappointed, to know that it was. In fact, Asia was sometimes surprisingly shy whenever I was on a set to watch her work. "That was the first time you've actually watched me have sex, wasn't it?" she'd said to me, after I'd seen her "live" for the first time. "I'm so embarrassed!"

I was somewhat astonished but also touched to hear that. "Because I consider you a friend, not just a colleague," she explained. "You even look like my father." She was serious about the resemblence and it became a running joke between us. "I can't date Asian guys," she'd told me, "because I would always be thinking that I was dating my dad."

In point of fact, she'd never had a good relationship with

her Japanese father (to this day, she remains estranged from both her parents) and she often confided in me many intimate details of the years of abuse at the hands of her overly strict parents, despite having been the straight-A student who would later go on to become a high-I.Q. MENSA member, a scholarship student at Rutgers University, and a piano prodigy who played at Carnegie Hall—twice!

The fact that I had lots of dysfunctional family issues myself was probably the main reason why I had a special fondness for porn stars and my friendship with Asia brought these memories and their attendent emotions up to the surface. I had always liked strong-willed, assertive women and there was no more powerful paragon of assertive womanhood than the female porn star, the archetype of the sexually strong female, who disdained both conventional norms and societal judgement.

Asia was a sexually assertive woman, but with a distinctly Asian twist—she was very soft-spoken and very shy, preferring her actions in front of the camera to do the talking, and her real-life reputation to do the rest. "Asia Carrera defied many porn star stereotypes," wrote Anne Semans and Cathy Winks, in their book *The Woman's Guide to Sex on the Web*, published in 1999. "She's Asian (half Japanese, half German) in an industry dominated by the California blonde. She's ambitious and multitalented, and she's an unrepentant computer nerd."

Most Asian computer nerds, of course, weren't her size— 5 feet 8 1/2 inches, 36C-25-36, and 110 pounds (at least, until her pregnancy and delivery; her daughter Catalina was born on March 4, 2005)—and fewer still owned pierced labia and a talent for vaginal as opposed to merely clitoral orgasms, a proclivity limited to some twenty percent of women in the world. "I come quickly, easily, and multiple times, so basically a guy has to be pretty darned lousy not to make me come," she told an interviewer once.

She told me she was proud to be Asian, since she had many of the good Asian traits—the hardworking and diligent work ethic

111

that careened towards perfectionism, clearly the Japanese side of her. Her mother's German heritage boosted her perfectionism even more. No wonder she considered her best professional achievement to be her film *Appassionata*, a classical music tale set in the time of Mozart, made in August 1997, for which she wrote, directed, produced, starred in, and scored the music, even playing the piano herself. It received a record seven *AVN* Award nominations in a field of 7,000 new releases, and in 2000 she even wrote and programmed the digital authoring for the DVD version.

In the course of preparing the book proposal for my literary agent (basically her autobiography, co-written by me), Asia did a truly phenomenal thing—she gave me access to her personal journals, and also gave me permission to quote from them. No one else had ever seen them before, and she entrusted me with the "whole lot.

They came in several spiral-ring notebooks, with entries that I found highly poignant and often painful. Many of these came from her late teen years, when she was suicidal. Like this one:

February 21, 1991

Man, what a fucked up childhood. Fucked me up. The household did it. Pressure, stress, how much could I be expected to take? I was an alcoholic, I remembered today, and a druggie. I smoked. I was suicidal an awful fucking lot. Without my friends I would have been dead long ago. Remember how my parents hated me? Told me I was worthless, a disgrace, a whore, lazy, good for nothing? My mother said please leave and my father said please kill yourself. Oh, it's all coming back. I remember many nights in desperate loneliness, lying on hard ground with slashed wrists, crying with a tearstained face for God to please, please kill me, put me out of my misery. I was alone so much, my parents grounded me always and took

my phone and answering machine. Dad would send my
friends away. I never talked to my brothers or sisters. I
was so alone. I was glad for my parents' hatred because I
needed attention so desperately. I just wanted someone to
care about me a little. I didn't even know what love was. I
thought it didn't really exist, because no one loved me and
I loved no one. I couldn't. My parents were supposed to
love me but they didn't, so how could I believe in trust and
love? I felt so worthless ... I was starved for attention.

In a weird way, I liked that particular diary entry, because
we had talked a lot about how many porn stars came into the
business because of screwed-up childhoods, how the desperate
need for attention led to extreme sexual exhibitionism, and how
teenagers in such dire emotional straits usually confused sex with
love and ended up in the adult entertainment industry.

Without realizing, of course, that it often offered no panacea.
Even scoring a studio contract wasn't always a career pinnacle, as
Asia noted in some of her other journal entries, in the years after
she became a Vivid Girl:

September 15, 1995

Hi, it's me, except it's not really me, because I'm not
Jessica now. I'm Asia. As I have been for two years now.
I miss my diaries, so I'm gonna write again. I'm married,
as of February 27, 1995, and still working as a porn star.
I was a Vivid Girl for a year, but I left now, and Steve
Hirsch is trying to keep me from working. He has gotten
me knocked off an R-movie and a non-sex role, but I just
shot a commercial for Playboy and I'm doing a video
vignette for Playboy next week. I also appeared in their
"Book of Lingerie" this month. I auditioned to be VJ
for the Spice Channel, but I didn't get it. That made me
sad. At least I made it to the finals. I won the "Performer

of the Year" at the AVN Awards show in front of 2,000 people and that makes me very proud and happy. I'll be sad when my year is up. Money is tight, because Bud has borrowed $5,000 from me. I hate having no money. I hate not having enough work. I feel like a has-been and I fear getting older. Time is so limited. My death draws nearer and nearer. My name must get bigger before I die. I hope someone will collect my diaries and tell my story when I am gone. That's why I've kept them! I have a great story and I'll tell the young and beautiful and hopefully famous. 3–5 more years. Sleeping pills. I hate my fucking life and I'm extremely depressed. Not much has changed in 8 years!

The centerpiece of her turbulent marriage to director Bud Lee was none other than Bud's chronic drinking problem, which came to a head one night when he beat her up and then woke up the next morning in an alcoholic stupor and swore he couldn't remember a thing. It was the wake-up call he needed, which led to him quitting the booze for good. Suffice to say, large portions of Asia's diaries would not have materialized were it not for the co-dependent nature of their dysfunctional marriage (and eventual divorce). One week after the aforementioned entry, for instance, she wrote:

September 23, 1995

I don't feel like living. Every day, I wonder why I'm here, why I bother. I'm tired of this, of fucking and stripping to make a living. And now I'm not even making a living because I have this husband who is an endless money pit. I can't keep treading water for the two of us. I can't sink any lower to make more money. There is no lower. I CAN'T GET ANY LOWER. I'M A SLUT, A WHORE, AND I HATE MY LIFE. I CAN'T DO THIS ANYMORE. I

CAN'T. I CAN'T! I'm going to take these here sleeping
pills and maybe I won't have to wake up anymore because
I don't love me or value me. All I want to do is destroy me.
SLUT. WHORE.

And yet, two months later, she created the first of her real crowning glories—her film *A Is For Asia*, which she wrote, directed and produced. It was made right after she'd left the security of her Vivid contract, and she was hellbent on a personal victory. What also made it work was the storyline—Asia played a porn star being directed by Bud in a movie that called for her to do her first facial cumshots and her first anal sex scenes, two work obligations that didn't sit at all well with her husband, a working porn stud played by Jonathan Morgan. The movie, in short, dealt with the distress experienced by couples working together in the business, and the jealousies that arose when one or the other had sex with total strangers. It was a grand visual depiction of how porn astutely separated love and sex.

There were other films in the Asia Carrera canon that I'd always liked—namely *Forever Young* (1994), *Intimate Strangers* (1998), and *Search for the Snow Leopard* (1998), as well as a highly compelling scene in Andrew Blake's *Unleashed* (1996), a three-way, boy/girl/girl with Vince Vouyer and Monique DeMoan. It was *Playboy* magazine's October 1997 "X-Rated Video of the Month," and one of my personal favorite Andrew Blake films.

But Asia told me she had no memory of it. "*Unleashed*? I don't remember which one that was," she said. "I did a couple of different movies for him, but they're always artsy-fartsy, they're all in a big glass mansion, they're always namby-pamby softcore stuff, and they never have dialogue. So it's hard to remember which one's which!"

Blake, for his part, told me his favorite memory of Asia was seeing her off-camera, sitting around and waiting for her scenes. Most girls smoked or read their scripts or gossiped. Asia killed time by reading *The Wall Street Journal* and checking her stocks.

I loved that observation, how it subverted the nose-to-the-grindstone, doggedly determined, mercantile Asian stereotype that we're known for the world over. Or perhaps it reflected my own paranoia, because I had issues with being Asian and, therefore, with being depicted in a particular light. And perhaps, in the end, that was why I chose to cover the adult film industry, to test to limits of social strictures, like any well-intentioned Asian porn star would proudly do.

A is for Annabel

I saw cultural subversion in its finest porn manifestation when I received an email from Annabel Chong, telling me that she was finally going to pull the plug on her website and retire completely from the business.

It was a serious undertaking, since killing your website meant killing your market value altogether. But Annabel did it in fine style, with typically anal-Asian panache. She left a snide note on her homepage, proclaiming her virtual death. "Annabel is dead," she wrote, "and is now replaced full-time by her Evil Doppelganger, who is incredibly bored with the entire concept of Annabel, and would prefer to do something else for a change … The ED is a diabolical yuppie who is working as a web designer and consultant. She specializes in .NET with C#, Database Development and also does web design."

Singapore's only real, internationally famous porn star had decided to quit, opting for a new life of relative obscurity. And who would miss her now?

We had met when I interviewed her for the April 1999 issue of *BigO*, the Singapore rock magazine that seemed to be the only media outlet back home that was on her side—a local tabloid, *The New Paper*, had vilified her quite unneccessarily—and so we stayed friends for a while, though I heard less and less from her as her post-porn years went by. Sometimes, I thought that appropriate. I was always less a fan of Annabel Chong and more a fan of Grace Quek (her real name), ever since I got the know her as a person. Her style of porn was never my taste—I was not a fan of hard, angry, fast fucking, and even less enamoured of that exalted genre she had become synonymous with, the gangbang.

In short, much as I believed that porn deserved its place in the democratic marketplace of ideas, using sex as a way to exact some kind of revenge just wasn't ever my trip. But I did like what Annabel stood for, even though no one got the joke. In retrospect, her "World's Largest Gangbang" of January 19, 1995, when she had sex with 251 men (recorded for posterity on home video as *The World's Biggest Gangbang*), was a tragic non-event, in the sense that she had set out with an agenda but most people never saw the humor in it.

They never grasped the post-modern notion inherent in her proclamation that "251 is just a number." It went right over everybody's heads, and the video made her famous for all the wrong reasons. I know this to be so because the industry immediately treated it as a watershed event, and bigger gangbangs were set up, resulting in Annabel's record being smashed later by Jasmine St Clair, Houston, and, finally, Sabrina Johnson.

Sabrina, a dark-haired lass from Manchester, England, ushered in the new millennium with 2,000 men, done over two days, and later said in an interview that she wished she'd never done it. At what point, she herself must have wondered, did pointlessness set in? Probably, I surmised, when the pain made her realize that the whole spectacle was built on repetition, which could certainly get boring. Worse still, the DVD version of the event, cleverly "divided" into two separate releases, *Gangbang 2000* and *Gangbang 2000 - Day 2*, received overwhelmingly poor reviews.

"Sabrina Johnson's big '2000-man' bang falls flat on every level," wrote Susie Ehrlich in *AVN*, July 2001. "Johnson is a beautiful girl who deserves better than getting fucked by a (pitifully small) group of guys who think that taking part in this event will make them full-fledged porn performers. She goes through all the 'passionate' reactions, moaning and writhing, but reality intrudes when one of the bangers actually believes she means it and starts smacking her ass. Watch her drop the act quickly."

In the second disc, Sabrina was seen "icing her swollen pussy sometime around 1,600," and the rules stipulated that "each guy gets a mere thirty seconds before being gonged, which signals the next fucker, but he can return with another number after a minimal passage of time." The questions one could conjure, surely, were all too obvious: Could a thirty-second penetration really count as sex? Wasn't this postmodern irony taken a tad too far?

In 2002, Sabrina decided to compensate for the public humiliation by directing her own gonzo series, cheekily entitled *Can I F*uck You ... Too?* in which she participated with total strangers she'd accosted on the streets of Europe. The first episode was shot in Antwerp, Belgium, where she lived (having moved there after her husband Graham had been busted in the UK and served a nine-month jail sentence for "living off immoral earnings") and it was generally well received by reviewers, though many preferred her in the likes of *Butt Banged Naughty Nurses*, made back in 1997, in which she took on six guys every which way and then drank all their sperm from a glass cup.

Annabel, however, was far more notorious. She had achieved the one thing that had eluded Jasmine, Houston and Sabrina: mainstream fame.

She'd made a big splash at the Sundance Film Festival with a documentary film about her life, *Sex: The Annabel Chong Story*, part of which dealt with the emotional fallout over her famous feat. The worst part of it wasn't the shock or horror of it all, or the reaction of her mother when she found out, but rather the way her fame tooks its toll on her adult film career. What most civilians don't know, and what adult film veterans know only too well, is that there is a pecking order to employment, and the worst thing a porn star can do is to gain a reputation as a gangbang girl. Annabel had made her name with such self-explanatory titles as

All I Want For Christmas is a Gangbang and *I Can't Believe I Did the Whole Team!*

It sounded strange indeed but the hierarchy of porn had inbuilt prejudices. A porn star who kept doing gangbangs soon found herself accorded pariah status, an outcast akin to say Chuck Norris in his laughable syndicated shows repeated constantly on daytime television. I had seen some of Annabel's films and thought they were generally one big yawn. But that wasn't the reason why I found her intriguing. I was much more interested in the emotional arc of her career, and in the way she saw porn as a sex-positive statement aimed at stoking the fires of philosophical debate.

She had a lot more than met the eye, an intellectual spark that few girls in the business even came close to possessing. And, like me, she had been away from Singapore long enough to see it with deserving amusement. After she was photographed in the *Los Angeles Times Magazine* of August 5, 2001, dressed in her golfing togs and brandishing her 7 iron, she told me with a laugh: "Golf is my way of keeping close to my Singapore roots. You can take the girl out of Singapore, but you can't take Singapore out of the girl!"

"I don't think Singapore is for everybody," she'd said when I interviewed her. "There are people who take well to the system and they seem to thrive on it. And, well, good for them. I do not intend to condemn anybody. I don't think it's my place to do so. But for me, personally, I don't think that it is a system that sits well with me politically." It was, she added, "the way the government posits itself as a father, like 'Father knows best.' A lot of people swallow that idea. Singaporeans are being subjected to a constant stream of propaganda. It's very insidious."

I asked her about her infamous gangbang. "After the first 100 men or so, you realize the number is just a concept," she said. "So it's not about sex *per se*, it's about exploring the concept of what sex is."

"Firstly, it's not sex as intimacy … it's sex as sports," she explained. "It's public sex. Sex is getting more and more public now. Look at, like, the Calvin Klein ads. More and more, in our society, sex is becoming a spectacle. And so how can we draw the line between what we do in private and what is otherwise? That sort of thing, it feeds into each other such that the private and the public no longer is important, and we're moving towards sex as 'information.' How many guys? 251. Or 300. Or 551, whatever, you know.

"And the other thing is the invention of this whole genre, this new genre of sex films that really does not come from the tradition of erotica or pornography but comes from somewhere else, like the *Guinness Book of World Records*, or sports. It's more like sports. There's a historical parallel between gangbangs and orgies and fertility-goddess rituals, but in our society our communal ritual is sports. It's football, soccer, whatever. It's really interesting, this playing out of our modern religion, which is sports."

One thing she wasn't going to do, she assured me, was attempt the "mainstream crossover." After hearing so many girls tell me of their deep yearning for recognition—the need to be a "real actress"—it was so refreshing to hear someone who had come to terms with her talents. "I cannot act," Annabel told me. "My parents were theatre pioneers in Singapore, back in the 50s and 60s, but I have no acting talent and I'm not about to kid myself. I have no aspirations to 'cross over' as a Hollywood actress.

"You have to understand that Annabel Chong is a persona, she's a character," she added. "I think the dichotomy is interesting. I think everybody puts on personas, although their personas may not necessarily have a different name."

How about being a role model for Asians in the adult entertainment industry? "I don't know about that," she mulled. "I don't know if Asians in the industry necessarily need a role model. I think most of the girls, the Asian girls in the industry, are pretty sussed. A lot of actresses are on drugs or whatever but the Asians are really together. Asia Carrera, for example, she's a really smart girl. She has her shit together and she's a really good businesswoman. Minka runs her own fan club. From my experience, the Asian actresses really have their shit together and they have a pretty good sense of where they want their careers to go within the adult industry.

"Also, the adult industry is so diverse, just like the rest of society, that the word 'role model' does not really apply. You know, people call me up to ask me for advice and I'm always happy to give them advice. If I feel they're not right for the adult industry, that they have certain things within their personality that will not fit well with the industry itself, I advise them: 'Don't do this. It's not what you really want to do.'"

After that interview, I managed to get her to write a couple of columns for *BigO* magazine, and to my fascination she kept dwelling on the idea of fame.

"Before I embarked on a career in stripping, an old stripper once offered me some useful advice," she wrote, in October 1999. "She took me aside before my first show, lit a Marlboro Red, and said to me, 'Look here, honey, show them only what you want them to see. You might be naked, but it ain't personal. They just want to see your pussy.' With that thought in mind, I hit the stage. At no point did I feel vulnerable about my own nudity. After all, I was putting on a show and my nudity was, in many ways, a costume."

The next column, in December 1999, was entitled: "Signing Autographs is Worse Than Doing a Gang Bang." She began with a description of her ordeal at the Fantasia Film Festival in Montreal, signing autographs for 300 waiting fans, with barely one minute to appease each individual before having to get to the next one as the festival organizers urged her to move on so the line could move.

"The thing I have learnt about celebrityhood," she concluded, was that "understanding does not grant immunity. You can deconstruct the entire process of fame until you are blue in the face, but that does not instantly take away its power to seduce. Take me, for example. I have been through the entire process from

121

the standpoint of the 'celebrity' and I know what an incredible sham it is."

Which was why, she giggled, she once satisfied a bizarre request from an obsessed fan in the best possible manner. "The guy wanted me to shit into a bag for US$150," she told me. "I went out and scooped up some dog shit and mailed it to him. He was completely ecstastic, thinking it was my shit. He wrote to me telling me he ate the shit and it was delicious."

What a brilliant response, I thought, to an absurd situation! In one fell scoop (sic!), she'd addressed the oft-forgotten truth that in the end, porn is merely a form of commodified sex whereby what people really pay for is the suspension of disbelief. Or, rather, the privilege of experiencing fantasy, often a manifestation of your own mind. There were no barriers to good taste.

A is for Asian

I remember buying *Porn to Rock*, a 1999 album pairing porn stars with rock music, which included one of porn's pioneering Asian stars, Suzi Suzuki. Her tantalizing bio inside the inner sleeve (my copy was on vinyl) read: "Suzi Suzuki was born in Tokyo, Japan, in 1972. As a child she lived in Germany and Japan and is fluent in both languages. She got her first job as a jazz vocalist in a Tokyo nightclub in her last year of high school. Now living in San Francisco, she appears in adult video and works as an exotic dancer."

It prompted in me that eternal question: What was this thing called "exotic," so commonly associated with Asian women, particularly in a sexual context? "Exotic," I have concluded, was the promise of something. But what exactly was that something?

I certainly understood the way many Asian girls in the business were quick off the mark to take advantage of their exalted status. For instance, I recall meeting a lovely Korean-German girl who called herself Jade, on the set of a movie she was appearing in.

I had a friend visiting from Hong Kong who had a penchant for Korean girls, and I casually told her that. "Cool," she said. "See me after the shoot and I'll give you my phone number."

She hurried off to get her hair and make-up done, and it took me a few seconds to realize that she wasn't asking for a date. She was setting up one. She was a hooker.

Asia Carrera once told me how incensed she was when she found herself on the cover of *L.A. X...Press*, a tabloid advertising incall and outcall services (specifically, the issue of February 10, 2000). "This prostitute magazine," she said, "used my photo without my permission!"

She had refused several offers in the past. A certain famous baseball player once promised her an insane amount of money to "go up to his hotel room." But could anyone blame that baseball star? He knew who she was, after all. Asia herself had emailed me the link to the "*AVN* Top 50 Porn Stars of All Time," compiled at the end of 2001, telling me she was voted in at number 22. (The top five: Ron Jeremy, Jenna Jameson, John Holmes, Traci Lords, and Linda Lovelace.) Annabel Chong, the only other Asian on the list, came in at number 40.

At the time of writing, the latest rising star in porn was also Asian, if somewhat unusually so—a Canadian lass named Sunny Leone, the 2003 *Penthouse* Pet of the Year, who'd signed exclusively to Vivid in May 2005. She was the company's "first performer of Indian descent," but her Punjabi parents weren't too happy; an *AVN* interview disclosed that when the Vivid contract was faxed to her parents' house, her mother asked: 'What's double penetration?'"

"She figured it out, and started crying," Sunny told the reporter, Peter Stokes. "I put them in their place, I told them I'm not stopping what I'm doing and it's only going to get wilder!"

That episode reminded me of the time I interviewed Kira Kener, another Vivid Girl, who told me her favorite thing in the world was to do a d.p.—"Because it makes your head spin," she quipped. She had been the *Penthouse* Pet for December 2002 and, at age twenty-eight, traded quite effectively on her 32DD-25-32 Vietnamese-Norwegian heritage. However, she was evasive when I asked her about being Asian and what it meant to her. Unlike Asia Carrera or Annabel Chong, who had no problems at all with the concept, Kira looked like she'd never thought of it before.

She told me she was born in San Jose, California, and had never been brought up in a typically Asian household. Her real cultural roots lay in rock music, particularly her favorite band, KISS. (Her *Penthouse* layout made special mention of how she had met the band's long-tongued bassist Gene Simmons and he had asked *her* for an autograph. That was the pinnacle of fame to her.) At the time we spoke, in November 1999, she had just re-signed for a second-year contract with Vivid.

"Last year I did six movies and this year I'll do eight," she told me. I asked her if she felt like she was carrying a torch for Asian girls, since she was only the third Asian girl ever signed to Vivid, after Asia Carrera and Kobe Tai.

"I suppose so, but I really don't think I look as Asian as they do. And, to a point, that kind of disappoints some fans. You know, it all depends on how I do my make-up. Most people can't figure out what my nationality is. I've heard it all, let me tell you. If they ask, I tell them the truth, which is that I'm Norwegian and Vietnamese."

She had spent eighteen years growing up in San Jose, and did not feel particularly Asian. "It's really strange," she told me. "Some of the stuff I follow traditions with, but most of the stuff I don't. My parents always worked. I only saw them when they left for work and when they got home from work, and once a year we went on vacation. That was it. They were both in the computer business. They wanted me to get into it too. And that made me want to keep getting away from it more and more."

It was easy then to see why she was a porn star: she was the typical neglected child who craved attention and so took to being a stripper and then to porn, in an attempt to erase her emptiness. I had seen this kind of defiance in so many girls; they all had different

124

versions of the same story. I tried a different tack: I reminded Kira of some of her scenes I'd seen, where she'd expressed a shyness in her eyes, very demure and very Asian, especially when giving a blowjob. Lots of white guys I knew were turned on by that sort of thing.

"Right," she agreed, "and that's what really amazes people once they meet me, because they totally think I'm one way and when they realize how I am, they're totally shocked. There's that 'shyness' side that I put out, and then there's this totally opposite side. And that blows everybody away. I am shy, but once you get to know me, the other side of me takes people by surprise. I'm wild and crazy, a lot of times."

Kira was the unapologetic party girl, who didn't care much for being stereotypically Asian in order to satisfy some fan's fascination for the jade-goddess archetype. She had made a valid point—about how one's ethnicity need not (or, perhaps more acutely, should not) become the focus of other people's expectations.

The best example of such vaunted panache, to my mind, is still the opening scene in that Christian Slater film *Very Bad Things*, in which Kobe Tai played a stripper who performed a bachelor party but came to a tragic end. It was an unusually long scene in a mainstream film featuring a porn star, and one which some people felt had helped adult performers gain visibility in Hollywood.

But, really, did it help advance the cause? Kobe Tai, the Asian-American Vivid Girl, playing a professional slut in a scene where she did the bump-and-grind before being killed off. Some would surely call that a cliché.

Kobe was only active in the adult film industry from 1996 to 2003. She'd starred in sixty-two movies before retiring. It was not a prolific output in porn terms, though her legend was secure among hardcore fans of Asian erotica. I remember her in Michael Zen's *Jade Princess*, a scene with the extremely well-endowed hunk Julian, which covered three positions—he started by taking her standing up, followed by missionary, and finally doggie—a scene obviously meant for the viewing pleasure of white guys who liked watching a big white guy take on a petite Asian girl.

That was the Kobe Tai "branding"—she was small, but was she ever mighty. I never met her personally but was intrigued by her legend. Vivid boss Steven Hirsch had given her the Japanese-sounding name Kobe Tai because he wanted "something that sounded Asian," never mind the fact that she was actually of Taiwanese heritage. In an industry where most people never used their real names, such poetic liberties were surely forgivable; what did it matter, anyway, since one always played a shadow of oneself—a sexual persona that, for all its impassioned elements, remained very much an illusion?

In her last film, the critically-acclaimed *Jenna Loves Kobe*, released by Vivid in 2003, she appeared in two sizzling scenes with Jenna Jameson, one shot Andrew Blake-style with European *haute*-glamour hats and corsets, the other shot in slick MTV-style in a jacuzzi with hot pink lights and soap bubbles drifting down. Kobe was then twenty-nine years old, and it was, however surprisingly, the very first time she had worked with Jenna, so it was actually a very good time to quit—the final scene ended with her applying some very serious tongue action on a writhing, moaning Jenna, so she was literally going out on top.

Strike one, then, for the yellow fever babes! The need to maintain appearances was what kept the industry going, and Asian girls knew how to play to fans of Asian porn. Including their fans in Asia—Asia Carrera told me that a lot of her website hits come from her fans in Japan as well as places like Singapore and Malaysia, where porn is illegal; Annabel Chong told me that, out on the road, the majority of her strip-club patrons were Asian and her best markets were Sacramento, San Francisco, Hawaii, and New York. Four out of ten emails she received were from either Jewish or Asian fans, on matters academic or philosophical and often unrelated to porn.

However, in the last interview I did with Annabel, for *AVN*

Online in July 2002, she told me she was "beginning to question the validity of the entire concept of empowerment within the adult industry. Even if one could be a successful entrepreneur, one is still subject to the whims and tastes of the fan base, which is rather limiting."

For people like Annabel and myself, who'd both left Singapore because, as Annabel herself so accurately put it, "we don't fit the one-look, one-style, one-choice nation," perhaps our own world views needed to be more open-minded than most. But it was hard to stay so receptive, when all people saw in you was a glorified geisha.

"What I really treasure right now is my privacy," she concluded, in that last interview. "I do not feel the need to rehash my life for profit. I now find satisfaction in being a non-famous, behind-the-scenes sort of person. Capitalizing on my notoriety holds little appeal for me. Pursuing fame is a double-edged sword. It may bring money and adulation but at the same time you are confining yourself to a public persona that you have created. I personally find that tiresome, having to play the same role after I have evolved into a totally different person. I've had my little ride, fame-wise, and it was interesting while it lasted. But now it's time for me to try something new."

"Something," she laughed, "where I get to use my brain for a change."

And that, ultimately, was why she quit.

Foreign Affairs

London Lust

I first went there on a cool, windswept afternoon in June 2005, when I was in London. I walked from my hotel on High Holborn to Oxford Street, and cut across to Charing Cross Road before wending my way right into Soho. There was a whip-smart sex shop called Swish, and the famous jazz club Ronnie Scott's was still there, but what really interested me lay a stone's throw from the gay bars of Old Compton Street: a modest flat in a nondescript building, right in the middle of the red-light district, where Anna Span appropriately kept her office.

"Back around 1988, when I was sixteen or seventeen, I was anti-porn and into women's rights," this most erudite of English porn directors, aged thirty-three, calmly told me. "Back in the 1980s, most people here were against porn if you were a feminist or had any sort of inkling that way, which was naively seen as the female voice. And I was walking down Old Compton Street one day—then it was full of sex shops, not like now—and I just realized that my anger was due to the fact that I was jealous. I was jealous because if you were a man you can go watch a sex show, you can buy a sex magazine, you can see a prostitute, or get a video albeit illegally, and this whole place was for men, for their fantasies and their sexuality to be catered for. There was nothing for women. There wasn't even a Chippendale's there, nothing on

RIGHT Well, I watched them have sex and then we went out for drinks. Tabitha Stevens (left) and Jill Kelly contract girl Haven, Deep nightclub, Hollywood, May 2001 *(Photo by Brian Gross)*

THE FIRST FILM TO SELL OUT ALL SIX SCREENINGS AT SUNDANCE!

"Jarringly provocative"
- ELLE

"Tightly composed and psychologically revealing"
- THE HOLLYWOOD REPORTER

"A really sophisticated psycological study that creeps up the back of your neck"
- GEOFFREY GILMORE CO-DIRECTOR, SUNDANCE FILM FESTIVAL

"First rate filmmaking. A moving and shocking porn film"
REBECCA YELDHAM SENIOR PROGRAMMER, SUNDANCE FILM FESTIVAL

"Fascinating, disturbing... The hottest ticket at the Sundance Film Festival"
- DETAILS MAGAZINE

SEX
THE ANNABEL CHONG STORY

A FILM BY
GOUGH LEWIS

SCREENINGS: SATURDAY, 15 MAY - 6:00PM - STAG
TUESDAY, 18 MAY - 1:30PM - PAL

LEFT Singapore girl Grace Quek, in her previous incarnation. Promotional postcard for the documentary *Sex: The Annabel Chong Story*, 1999 *(courtesy of David Whitten/Greycat Releasing)*.

BELOW "You're from *Penthouse*? Man, I have to talk to you!" Such was the general reaction to my press pass at the Webnoize convention, Century Plaza Hotel, Century City, November 1999.

Webnoize 99
NOVEMBER 15-17 Los
Century Plaza Hotel ANGELES

GERRIE
Gerrie Lim
Penthouse Magazine

www.webnoize.com

PRESS

ABOVE Asian faux-couple of the year.
With Asia Carrera at the *AVN* Expo,
Sands Expo & Convention Center,
Las Vegas, January 2001. *(Photo by
Clarke Irving)*

RIGHT "Look, mom, that's me!"
Asia Carrera, with our *AVN Online*
cover story on the wall, at home in
Chatsworth, California, September
2003. *(Photo by Gerrie Lim)*

BELOW *"Min mamma lagar de godaste köttbullarna i landet!"*
("My mother makes the best meatballs in the country!") says
Swedish-meatball expert Linda Thoren, at Barney's Beanery,
West Hollywood, October 1999. *(Photo by Leif Rock)*

Crystal Fantasies CoverGirl

Just before she gave me her masturbation video, she cooed ever so sweetly: "Let's rock the legs off my bed, baby!" Sara St James, signing as Jacqueline Lovell, Los Angeles, May 1995. *(Promotional poster from Crystal Fantasies)*

ABOVE She's dolled up in fetish gear and I'm wearing a Singapore Film Festival t-shirt! With Cheyenne Silver, on the set of Vivid's *Where The Boys Aren't #14*, The Faultline, East Hollywood, June 2001. *(Photo by Melissa Monet)*

BELOW LEFT A pornstar sandwich! Jill Kelly (left) and Shayla LaVeaux, Deep nightclub, Hollywood, May 2001. *(Photo by Brian Gross)*

BELOW RIGHT With Nina Hartley, on the set of *Naked Hollywood #6*, Tango Blues Studio, Hollywood, June 2001 *(Photo by Inari Vachs)*

television. It was that sort of climate.

"I just realized that I was jealous and, what's more, I was completely justified in being jealous. Because it is unfair. So from that point on, it seemed that it was completely logical. I was traveling and I was wondering what I wanted to do for a career. And I was a person who liked sex, I had gone traveling and had experiences, going to sex clubs, and I wanted to create something out there for women. I am the first woman to do it in England. I know that in America there have been girls from England but not directors, not in terms of having the power to do it and doing it properly. So I started the company in 1998, right after I graduated. I still shoot entirely in England, mainly in London."

Anna had graduated from the prestigious Central St Martin's School of Art with a B.A. Hons degree in Fine Art (Film and Video), with a dissertation entitled "Towards a New Pornography," about her female perspective on porn. She reexamined her feelings and, eventually, in early 2005, expressed them on her website (*www. annaspansdiary.com*), stating her beliefs that "to sexually objectify, that is to fleetingly view a person's sexual attractiveness separately from their personality/person, is a natural human experience, not just a male one, as traditionally depicted" and "censorship only proves to change direction of the censored thoughts, not eliminate them."

Seven years after her Soho epiphany, she started directing for Britain's Television X softcore cable channel, beginning with a show called *Eat Me/Keep Me*, shooting seventy-five episodes over three years. She was already working full-time at Television X as a film editor, watching thirty-five hours of porn a week and shooting on weekends, eventually writing her first book, *Erotic Home Video*, a handsomely illustrated coffee-table tome published in March 2003, based on her own experiences of making whoopee for the home video camera (aimed at helping couples do the same, which clearly worked since it sold 20,000 copies.)

Seven Anna Span features followed on DVD, all with amusingly British titles, like *A&O Department* (satirizing the medical profession, "A&O" connoting "Anal and Oral" as opposed to "A&E"—"Accidents and Emergencies"), *Good Service* (spoofing the oft-heard London Underground subway service announcements), and the more obviously entitled *Uniform Behaviour, Anna's Mates, Hoxton Honey, Pound a Punnet,* and *Toy With Me.* (*A&O Department* later received some unexpected publicity when its star and cover girl, McKenzie Lee, won the coveted "Best New Starlet" trophy at the 2006 *AVN* Awards; Lee had since become a contract girl with Jenna Jameson's company, Club Jenna, and received her award wearing a low-cut dress patriotically emblazoned with the Union Jack, reflecting her own wry sexy English manner, an onscreen tic that was now part of her "branding.")

At the time of writing, only the first three aforementioned titles were available in the United States, released by Union Jaxxx, the American arm of Anna's British distributor Rude Brittania. By the end of 2005, she had directed 165 scenes—a total of some thirty-three films—for the two biggest British cable entities, Television X and The Adult Channel, and also executive-produced *Women Love Porn*, a new DVD feature showcasing the work of five new British female directors.

"I started to watch porn with boyfriends in my late teens, but I didn't watch an awful lot," she remembered. "I did a lot of research for my dissertation at college and watched a lot there—Michael Ninn and Andrew Blake and Ben Dover and people like that—and then I worked at Television X where I was watching 350 films a year! I was full-time watching porn, basically, and shooting at weekends and just about keeping my sanity."

She started her own film line in February 2005, all the box covers proclaiming "Genuine Female Point of View," so that "women will buy it and men can buy it out of curiosity," as she posited it. Ann Summers, a chain of female-friendly sex shops in London, started selling her DVDs, though only in softcore versions. "Television X has at least seventy percent male buyers and sex shops are seventy-five percent male, so I'm selling to

130

men predominantly still," she noted. "I think the things I put in my work, there are deliberate aspects I will put in a porn film to attract women, which men really don't see or don't need to see them. They're looking at the models and the sex and whatever, but women notice them—eye contact, talking to each other, there's a storyline, there's comedy, all the underwear and the clothes I buy for the scene. I do the casting fairly carefully. I won't put a young twenty-one-year-old model to play the part of a forty-year-old businesswoman who's supposed to be really successful, because she wouldn't be at twenty-one. Little things like that."

"I have good-looking guys—I don't sell them by body parts, like blokes with nice butts," she added. "Because for a woman, that's not enough. You've got to have a nice face, a nice personality, you've got to make the girl feel comfortable in a scene and not make her look like she's being degraded. Also, I shoot female point-of-view camerawork, from the female eye, not just shooting at the woman from between her legs but looking at the woman with lots of shots of her face and also from the woman's point of view, looking at the guy. So I will have a penetration shot of the guy's dick the way a girl will see it. It's a much bigger picture, much more epic. It's 'couples friendly' but the sex doesn't err on the side of being plain."

She says she was greatly inspired by the French psychoanalyst Jacques Lacan, particularly his idea that "when you have access to what gives you pleausure, you have power. And if you are denied access to pleasure or you allow that to happen through your own lack of confidence or whatever, then you're disempowered." In such manner, she explained, a major American porn star like Chloe who has a reputation for getting pleasure from being choked while reaching orgasm is, in actuality, being empowered. Porn can, despite what its detractors say, be empowering.

"I mean, I shoot *bukkake* and double-penetration and anal and spitting and deep throat, stuff like that," Anna told me. "No pissing, though I wouldn't mind shooting that, but you can't sell it in England." Her film production budgets typically peaked at £6,500 (US$11,400) per movie (or £1,200/US$2,000 per sex scene, with usually five scenes to a film), excluding insurance and office overheads. Her girls got £250 (US$440) each for girl/girl, £300 (US$530) for boy/girl, £350 (US$600) for boy/girl anal, £400 (US$700) or a d.p. and £450 (US$790) for a gangbang. It was pretty much on par with most American productions, though in the UK this is more the exception than the rule. Most get paid considerably less than what Anna splurged out, though there were two significant ways in which remuneration for talent in the UK differed from America.

For boy/girl scenes, her guys were paid the same as the girls (whereas in the US, the girls were always paid double what the guys got). And nobody got paid extra for appearing on box covers ("because in England we don't shoot them separately"). For anal, d.p., and gangbang scenes, the men received £300 (US$530) each.

Some of her girls were certainly good-looking enough to work as high-class escorts. "Some of them are," Anna affirmed. "They can actually make more money doing that than working for me." So why do they even do it? "They think they will become immortalized by appearing on video." she replied, with a shrug. "There's so much shit porn out there, because everyone thinks it's easy."

Until recently, she informed me, there was no mandatory testing of performers for sexually transmitted diseases. British porn was now a newly rejuvenated industry; the sale of hardcore porn was declared legal only four years ago, and even then people were doing boy/girl scenes without HIV or STD certificates. The situation had improved, Anna grimly pointed out, but only within the last eighteen months. "I was one of the production companies that was right up there saying, 'We have got to get this down, we have to say: You have to be tested every thirty days or you don't work.' Previously, people had certificated but kind of irregular, like every six weeks or three months or something like that, with nothing organized. People would get the clap and all sorts of things because there was no testing for them."

"I was the only company, really, making girl/girl models go and get any sort of tests at all, and having to pay for them myself," she sighed. "The models would say, 'I'm not paying, I don't need this.' Part of the problem with the British industry is the attitude of the models. The hassle I get to look after the models' health and the risks they're willing to take, just because they're not thinking. I wrote a piece on *bgafd.co.uk* (British Girls Adult Film Database, covering 2,117 British porn stars), on advice to people getting into the industry, and one of the things I said was that British models need to up their standards so the performances will look good. They need to look after themselves, keep their nails good, go to the gym a couple of times a week. There's lots of people that aren't doing anything like that. They just turn up looking a real mess.

"I've been campaigning to get the money put up for models over here, because it's ridiculously low compared to the States. But then, we don't make as much money because we don't have as many customers on our doorstep as you obviously have in the States and we're not so established and don't have the massive distribution channels that people like Vivid have."

And then there was the statement made in a *Fox* magazine interview, by Sin City contract girl Hannah Harper, twenty-three, a perky lass with blue-green eyes hailing from a small fishing town in Devon. Anna had shot Hannah in some of her first-ever videos in 2000—one episode of a series called *Planet Nadia* and one episode of another series, *Majella Mates,* both for Television X. Succinctly explaining why she left England a mere four months after making her onscreen debut in the Ben Dover film *End Games,* Harper said: "The rates are so low. It's hard to get paid, to get travel expenses. Nothing is provided on set. No towels. It's like, we've got a room, two people, and a camera, let's go. The porn industry in England is still in the state where everyone thinks everyone in the industry is in trouble and needs saving."

Anna nodded in agreement. "Yes, there's still an underlying feeling of that. People ask me how I got into it, with questions like, 'Oh, did you have no other choice?' And I tell them it took me bloody ages to get into it and I had to work very hard. And I've got a bloody degree in porn, more or less, from the best art school in England. I'm now doing a Master's in philosophy, from the University of London." She felt encouraged, though, by the media attention that was almost non-existent four years ago. "There's a documentary now on porn or escorting or something like that every week. I've had two hour-long documentaries made of me, quite decent ones. The attitude has changed for sure, in the last four years. Now you have shops like Agent Provocateur doing expensive underwear, high-end shops like Myla doing sexy underwear with a bit of kink all the way through it, and websites selling sex toys."

But the industry in England still lags behind the United States in terms of production values, and Anna said she saw herself as a forerunner in the movement for change. "Most of what's out there now is fucking terrible," she observed. "We don't shoot in 16 mm like in America, and we don't do any film at all. It's just too expensive. We do DV cam—digital video camera—and a lot of them still shoot on mini DV. And you don't work with a proper crew, like having a lighting person come in. There just isn't enough money in England to do it. That's why England's kept at this sort of gonzo stage, this street-style. There's loads of problems, like getting insurance as a company—up until three years ago, I couldn't get insured because I was a porn company. I was asking for public liability insurance and employer insurance and they all said no. I had to go through my director's union to get it. Ninety percent of production companies here are uninsured."

"The British industry wants to have more freedom," she added. "It wants to be able to show female ejaculation, it wants to be able to do mail-order selling throuh the post." (Female ejaculation, or "squirting" as it's known in American porn, remained classified as an act of urination in the UK, even though biologically it wasn't.) And what of all those bad clichés associated with British porn, including the proverbial casting couch, which

134

usually meant girls giving free blowjobs before shooting? "Yes, that's all true, it does happen, but I would hasten to add that I am better than that—I certainly don't expect any sexual favors," Anna laughed. "I provide towels and baby wipes and stuff, the lubes and all that, and I shoot with an all-female crew, with two cameras. I find that this creates a relaxed atmosphere, and that to me is the key to getting a good performance out of people."

"The thing is, I like London," she said of her hometown. Originally from Bromley, in Kent (south of London), she noted in her online bio that her films pay tribute to the British comedies of the 1960s and 1970s—"very reality-based, like a soap opera, it's British people having sex in realistic settings." *Hoxton Honey*, for instance, is a send-up of London life (mildly lampooning the "scruffy, trendy media people living in Hoxton," as Anna put it), while *Good Service* and *Uniform Behaviour* take on the English workforce, featuring equal-opportunity sex from the cast in a variety of wacky roles (including policemen, firemen, waitresses, mechanics, soldiers, hairdressers, and, of course, gynaecologists).

My personal favorite was *Pound a Punnet*, a 2004 award winner at the 11th International Erotic Film Festival in Barcelona, which utilized various London settings (Holloway Road, Colombia Road Market, Deptford Market, and Soho's own red-light Berwick Street, where our interview took place). Its all girl/girl cast reenacted stories set in and around the open-air London markets (flower girl, fruit stall girl, fish market girl) with much expository dialogue, some of it *during* sex itself (which would be a no-no in American porn)—the kind of half-nervous banter that's so peculiar yet frightfully funny in that politely bumbling English way. All that was missing was Hugh Grant.

It made me realize that an Anna Span film worked on two simultaneous levels, both as dialectic and satire—her wry manner addressed the English social class system (or maybe just the English public school system), and so she had somehow created a porn vernacular all of her own. Less *Benny Hill* and more *Monty Python*, but only if you can imagine people from *Fawlty Towers* having sex, as only the English can do so well.

Or, maybe, you'd have to be English to understand. "In order to enjoy *The English Patient*, one has to be both English and patient," as the joke once went, of the Anthony Minghella film starring Ralph Fiennes, and the analogy wasn't entirely misplaced here. Anna Span's films were already being sold in America, in respectable numbers, though she had yet to do Vivid-style blockbuster business. Perhaps porn consumers in cities like Los Angeles lacked the jaundiced eye of smart Londoners like her, with her quirky views on things that turned well-educated people into well-intentioned perverts. I sensed I was in the minority too but with each Anna Span film I saw, I certainly felt counted in. Hers was, to me, such a fine madness.

Scorpio Rising

Europeans were more acutely attuned to the emotional nuances that separated love and sex, I'd always thought, since they lacked the ridiculous cultural baggage of most Americans. Erotica had been an integral part of their cultural DNA for so long. Catherine Deneuve could play a whore in *Belle du Jour* and remain a mainstream movie icon. Sharon Stone only became one with the help of a Dutch director named Paul Verhoeven, who convinced her to famously ditch her panties and wield an icepick in *Basic Instinct*, the film that made her a star overnight.

Kyla Cole, the *Penthouse* Pet for March 2000, didn't need any such persuading. Nor did she seek Hollywood stardom. She was happy enough, as a glamour model with a niche all her own.

The director Andrew Blake first urged me to look her up. We were shooting the breeze over the phone one afternoon in early 2001 when Andrew told me he had just shot "this beautiful girl from Slovakia named Martina, who calls herself Kyla Cole." She would go on to star in three of his films, most notably *The Villa*, for which she appeared totally nude on the DVD box cover, both front and back, and also performed in it one of my all-time favorite solo-girl masturbation scenes as well as some scorching girl-girl trysts with a Czech nymph named Nika Mamic. "When shooting, we didn't have to pose, we did everything so naturally," Kyla wrote on her website. "Believe me, she is one of the hottest girls I ever worked with ... She speaks perfect Czech, English, and French. She is every man's dream!"

Kyla herself, of course, was well aware of how she was every man's dream, too. When you worked mostly as a nude glamour model, who also did Andrew Blake movies, your main motivation was to be an object of fantasy and perfecting that became the ultimate goal. I had seen Kyla fleetingly, in numerous magazine layouts including *Guld Rapport*, a Swedish hardcore publication that I was also writing for. She'd appeared under her real name, Martina. I had actually first seen her in the December 1999 issue of *Genesis*, under the name Ester.

This, amazingly, made zero impression on me at the time, simply because I was about to interview Silvia Saint, who was on the cover. Silvia was the only reason I even bought that issue and so, at the time, I pretty much ignored the rest of the magazine. Only after I'd discovered Kyla did I realize who "Ester" was; the name wasn't Kyla's choice, it was, in the style of most nude photo layouts, conveniently invented by the magazine. She later chose the name Kyla Cole herself, though the text accompanying her American *Penthouse* debut was somewhat dubious—it stated that she was from Seattle, instead of Slovakia (she has since corrected this and issued a disclaimer on her website).

She worked only with girls or by herself in all her magazine layouts and movies, and firmly believed, as she declared to me, that "I am not a porn star." I thought that a refreshing distinction, if slightly disingenuous, but I was keen to explore the topic with her. When she visited me in Singapore in April 2005, she was wryly amused by my bestselling book about the escort business, *Invisible Trade*, and told me that she had turned down many such offers. She was once asked to spend a week with some guy in

Hawaii, for which she would be paid US$150,000.

"To me, that's just being meat," she told me. "It's a decision I made for myself. I mean, what is the difference between a prostitute and a porn star? They both fuck for money. I choose not to be either one, even though I was offered many opportunities. I want to leave something for privacy. Why spoil sex by having it as a job?

"And why not leave something to the viewer's imagination?" she added, though some of her layouts hadn't left much to mine. "If I was doing hardcore porn movies, I cannot imagine coming home to sleep with my boyfriend, because I would be thinking of it as work, that I would be working at home. So that's why I don't do hardcore."

Working with girls was "different," she insisted. "We're not really doing anything." She liked girl/girl shoots because they helped her indulge her own bisexual appetites, and as long as there were no men with erect penises in sight, it wasn't porn to her.

I didn't buy this distinction, and told her so.

There was a famous girl/girl layout in *Club* magazine called "The Road to Lezzieville," for instance, in which Kyla was seen with two of the most gorgeous girls in the industry, Tera Patrick and Bunny Luv, and to me it was hotter than many boy/girl layouts I'd seen. I liked it immensely and it sure was porn to me.

Kyla laughed, and said her memories of that shoot might well be tainted by the actual experience. "I didn't like Bunny Luv," she said. "She was sort of the jealous type, you know. And Tera Patrick, I don't know her at all. I just worked with her."

Well, making whoopee with Tera, or at least appearing to do so, wasn't quite "working" in the manner of office colleagues huddled around the water cooler. Regardless of the methodology, though, I was quite charmed by Kyla. Perhaps it was her small-town roots—she was born and raised in Eastern Slovakia—but she struck me as exceptionally grounded. "You could say I am photogenic, you can say that it's a gift, or whatever," she told me. "Maybe I am just lucky. I didn't expect to be famous in this business. It just came, so I am just living with it. I don't have to be any more famous than I already am. This is good enough for me."

How winsomely humble, I thought, for one with a natural talent for exhibitionism. The official story had always been that she got into nude modeling because of a boyfriend who had nude photos of other women adorning his walls. "Yes," she sighed. "I was dating one guy who liked to have those pictures of naked women. And, of course, you know, every girl wants to be like one of them. I first started to pose for fashion agencies and I got mainly offers to do *Playboy* stuff, blah blah blah, and so one day I decided to try it. And I found I could do it quite naturally. I don't think I am any different from other women. I take my clothes off because for me it is natural."

But some people, I told her, might find it a bit unnatural to see explicit photography featuring a ravishing beauty like her, her glamourous looks going somewhat against the grain. In Andrew Blake's films, for instance, she can be seen simulating masturbation for the camera. Members of her personal website (*www.kylacole. net*) can gain access to her extensive photo galleries, including numerous of her own vaginal and anal close-ups.

What did she think of anti-porn activists wagging the finger while her eager fans wanked happily away? Was there not a cognitive disconnect?

"I think they can think whatever they want," she told me. "I don't care if they masturbate on my picture. I mean, it's normal. Everybody masturbates. I am glad I can help them with their fantasies. Because not everybody has a woman. If I can help them with that, why not? Everybody knows that everybody is masturbating, so why not? If one of my fans doesn't want to admit it, he doesn't have to tell me, you know. I can imagine it. And he doesn't have to masturbate by looking at my pictures. He can masturbate by looking at other girls, you know. Because everybody wants to see something different.

"Basically, I don't care what people think. They can think whatever they want. For me, it is important that I know what I am doing, and that people know exactly what I am doing. Whatever other people may think, I will never, never, ever change just because it's their opinion." And what of those who put her on a pedestal, who see her as a living goddess or the embodiment of their dreams? "I don't think too much about that," she laughed. "It's their life and how they see it. It's okay. If they want to see me as their sex icon, why not?"

Over the course of her week's stay in Singapore, I saw her nonchalantly test that maxim. One afternoon, we walked through Chinatown and several people stopped to stare at her. An old Chinese medicine shop proprietor, resembling Yoda, stopped reading his newspaper to ogle Kyla. She was wearing a blouse cut quite low, and it didn't help that the sweltering tropical heat kept her exposed valley covered in a film of sweat, the glistening moisture reflecting light quite sinfully.

Many Chinese men, wherever we went, immediately turned their heads. I stopped to ask Kyla if she was aware of their stares. "Yes," she replied, beaming. "I hope they got a good look."

The year before, I'd interviewed her for an *AVN Online* feature expressly about her, in which she'd said she saw no difference between her American and European fans, except "that Europeans are better at geography." Her tongue was invisibly in cheek, as always, and she knew what men wanted and was pleased to provide, so long as her own parameters were met. In the end, did it even matter whether people chose to call her a porn star or a glamour model, or whatever moniker best bespoke her kind of celebrity branding? Hanging out with Kyla helped me to reinvestigate such ideas in my head, setting into motion the process of questioning once more the very things I found erotic.

And, unquestionably, I liked her kind of eroticism. Maybe it was because she wasn't American, and living as she did in the Czech Republic had imprinted her with their ineffable romanticism, the kind marked by the quiet intensity of a Dvorak symphony. When she parted company with me in Singapore, I told her it was such a pleasure getting to actually meet her, because I'd previously only had certain images in my head from looking at her photos, like we all do with the celebrities we admire from afar. "Well, I am glad I have not disappointed you," she laughed. "You know, everybody has to decide for themselves if it is a good idea to meet the girl that you are seeing in the picture. Because sometimes you can get disappointed. And so, the question is always about how you look in those pictures."

I'd seen past her beguiling 36C-24-36 figure and I liked how she had the nerve to see herself as nothing special, even if it was really only a bluff. (As Paul McCartney once said of his own fame as a Beatle, "It's all a bluff, really. Muhammad Ali told everyone he was the greatest, but did he really believe it?".) Glamour can be such a con job, after all. For example, Kyla confided in me her own shock at being conferred the coveted status of *Penthouse* Pet. "When I appeared in *Penthouse*, I didn't even know I was on the cover. Nobody told me. I knew that I was shooting for them but I was expecting that they would call me, or somebody from the magazine would let me know and send me my *Penthouse* key, or something. They did nothing at all. I found out by myself—I was there and saw myself on the cover of *Penthouse* magazine! I called them and I got my key and everything. They didn't call me."

All *Penthouse* Pets are given pendants with the famous *Penthouse* key logo, as a keepsake, but imagine having to actually ask for yours. Was this the fault of the magazine? Perhaps she hadn't left her forwarding address? Or did they send her the *Penthouse* key but, in typical Eastern European fashion, it had somehow been "lost" (read stolen) in the mail?

Shortly after, she appeared in *Playboy* as well, in a pictorial saluting that year's Olympic games. "I had two pictures or something, there were a few models. If I had never started in this business, I would not have been able to get the work opportunities so that's why I am thankful for this. Not just doing the movies but traveling, doing commercials, meeting new people." In the

February 2006 issue of *FHM* (UK edition), she was voted the top adult entertainer. But she also told me she was reassessing her career; she had done so many photo shoots, they were all starting to blur. There wasn't even a single, particular favorite layout she could cite. "I know that I cannot be a fashion model, for sure, and I don't think that I can look like a fashion model. Fashion models are tiny and taller and they don't have breasts, so I never considered that I could be successful in the fashion business. So I am happy where I am. I am happy that I know where my work is. I will give modeling another year, and then decide what to do next."

So, the *Penthouse* key, the *Playboy* pictorials, the Andrew Blake movies, and a personal website blessed with regular membership renewals—weren't those real testimonies to achievement for any girl in the erotica arena? It may seem an unusual form of validation, but her fans still bought her used panties online, at US$50 a pop, and they also ordered customized videos of her posing or dancing only for them, at a minumum charge of US$200 for a ten-minute clip.

A French fan sent her an unusual birthday present in 2002, when she turned twenty-four, through the International Star Registry (the organization responsible for naming stars), he had an actual star named in her honor, located in the Scorpio constellation, her astrological sign. So that her name, as he told her, "will forever be engraved in the sky." Talk about star-gazing, and star-worship.

I'd always thought, however, that the real measure of a sex icon lay in the way she handled erotic fame, since, unlike normal people, her nudity was really a uniform she wore to work. "When I look at my photos, I see someone else, not me," Kyla said. "When I meet my fans, I find that there are so many of them and everybody is different. Some of them are nervous, some of them are okay, some of them are shaking and they don't know what to say. They are very shy.

"I am always laughing, because they don't have to be nervous, they don't have to be so shy." She looked me right in the eyes, half-winking, and smiled that lovely Slavic smile.

"I am just the girl next door."

International Relations

When you've watched too much American porn, you can forget that there are other ways, other perspectives, that can make the super-slick, mass-marketed products of American companies seem hollow. I once wrote a piece for *AVN Online*, which became the cover story of its April 2004 issue, called "Foreign Affair" which dealt with the porn industry's non-American girls (since "foreign" equates with non-American in America, however weird that sounds) and how they used their personal websites to further the cause of their own celebrity branding. The genesis of that project actually stemmed from an October 1999 interview I did with the French porn star Rebecca Lord, the long-term impact of which, of course, I had no inkling of at the time.

We met to talk at, of all places, a Starbucks in Encino, California, sitting outside in the sunshine because Rebecca, effusively Parisian, was a chain smoker. She told me her personal theory about the differences between Europeans and Americans. "We are less puritan in Europe and more open-minded. If you go to the beaches in Europe, everybody's topless and nobody's watching people's breasts. It's natural. Here in America, if you go topless you know that everybody will watch you and it's like a bad thing, like it's illegal. People are more against violence in Europe and more for the erotic. Look at Hollywood movies and how they will cut parts with nudity and yet they leave all the violent parts alone. In Europe, the same movie will come out and they will cut the violence and leave the nudity. I think that explains a lot.

"The industry is very small in Europe. Because there is less need for people. Because people are more open-minded, and so they have less need for porn. What people here go through is the opposite of Europe. There is more repression, so there is more need. The same situation applies to drugs. Because when you make drugs illegal, people will actually buy drugs and use them. If drugs were legal, there would be fewer people who would need them. It's exactly the same thing with sex. The industry is not working that well in Europe. Most of it is small amateur companies. In France, there are only three big professional companies, and that's it. I think that's why the porn industry in America works so well. Because more people are sexually frustrated."

One of my favorite examples of this was a box cover of Rebecca's, a four-hour compilation tape that Sin City strung together as a "greatest hits" showcase, called *French Kiss*. On the cover, Rebecca wore rubber fetish gloves and stockings, with the accompanying slogan: "French fries. French toast, French tart." On the back of the box were a dozen stills and only a one-sentence blurb: "Tastier than a cream-filled croissant." Rebecca, like me, found it piquantly funny. Her chosen career was not merely a job to her, after all, but a vocation and she had a sense of humor to match its uniqueness. "I like to think of myself as the Mother Theresa for sex," she told me, deadpan serious. "I think being a porn actress is a great job, because we bring fantasies to people. We bring happiness to people, to couples as well as to lonely guys, to old guys, or handicapped people who can't have sex anymore, or to normal people like you and me."

However, she added, "I think there is a big difference between a porn star and a prostitute. The difference, to me, is that a porn star brings fantasies to the public. We have sex with people in the industry who are professionals and we sell videos to customers who like to watch us. Bring a prostitute is about having sex with customers, for physical pleasure. Not all jobs in the sex industry are the same, just because there is sex involved."

Five years later, when I started work on my *AVN Online* "foreign girls" project, Rebecca not only readily gave me a second interview but also volunteered to put me in email contact with her friend and fellow Las Vegas resident Olivia Del Rio, the

Brazilian porn star. Olivia had co-starred with Rebecca in *Pure Sex Vol.1*, the inaugural release from Rebecca's own company, Lolita Entertainment. Back when that came out, in July 1999, I didn't really know Olivia at all (I knew only of Vanessa Del Rio, a porn star from an earlier generation), so I visited her website (*www.oliviadelrio.com*) and was fascinated by what I saw.

Rebecca used her site (*www.rebeccalord.com*) to entice members who wanted to know more about her as a person, writing lengthy, confessional thoughts, but Olivia was unabashedly different. She was into selling herself completely as a sex object, and her site even had a special section devoted to her escorting services; discerning gentlemen across the United States could book her online, at her regular rate—US$2,500 an hour.

Having been to Brazil myself, back in 1984, I'd already been seduced by the sexually-open lifestyle which now seemed well reflected by this woman from Belo Horizonte; Olivia was five feet seven inches, 34C-26-34, and had already starred in a slew of stuff—from edgy director Thomas Zupko's *Flesh Circus* to Joe D'Amato's more pedestrian *College Girl*, the latter shot in Budapest and Prague, and featuring her with three studs who popped simultaneously on her face. "The fans tell me what they think of my sex performances, often in great detail," Olivia told me of her often voluminous email inbox. "These guys ask me many questions and provide me with many suggestions. I can relax and enjoy chats with them and get wild. I'm not that different from other adult stars, but who else could murmur some Portuguese words while having sex? After meeting lots of fans at different conventions in the US, I have the feeling thet they come to my site to see something other than your usual California blondes."

Her unbridled energy is reflected on the site. As her "bio" page states, she likes "beautiful dicks, horny chicks, and bondage," and her favorite fantasy is "to fuck a man's ass." But she had to base herself in the United States in order to secure a fan base, because "the adult entertainment scene in Brazil is pretty small. Ninety-nine percent of the movies made there are gonzos, and they don't have really big budgets. Also, the Internet in Brazil is something for the rich people. Not many poor people can access the Internet."

Indeed, we sometimes forget that there are parts of the world where Internet penetration isn't high simply because it isn't affordable to most people. For my *AVN Online* story, I looked at the case of Australia, culled from a 1998 Goldman Sachs Investment Research Study—unlike some other writers in this business, I never invented statistics to impart intellectual heft—which revealed that forty-two percent of Australia's 6.9 million households (as opposed to individuals) had computer access, and PC penetration alone stood at twenty-six percent. I was interested in Australia because I had once lived there myself, so I knew quite intimately the cultural context, and also for two other good reasons: Monica Mayhem and Jodie Moore, arguably the two most famous porn stars from Down Under. (Well, there was a third, actually—Monica and Jodie were, in my eyes, carrying the torch first lit by Cheryl Rixon, the 1979 *Penthouse* Pet of the Year, Australia's first adult entertainment sex goddess, but Cheryl was before the age of home video.)

I'd first met Monica in October 2001, in (of all places) a bowling alley in Tarzana, California, which was the location that day for a Toni English *Naked Hollywood* episode. The series starred Nina Hartley, Keri Windsor, Dee, and Asia Carrera, so I knew Monica was there to play a guest role. What was her part, I asked. "Well, I play a slut, basically," she giggled, nodding at the innuendo. "But I'm just doing dialogue today. I've done sex already." We hit it off immediately, and I sat down with her to do an impromptu interview which ended up as a personality profile ("Let's Get Ready to Rumble: Monica Mayhem Shakes Up the Net," *AVN Online*, April 2002).

Her life story was already very much the stuff of porn star dreams. Originally from Brisbane, Queensland, she'd been lured to the bright lights of big-city Sydney, with dreams of being an actress. But once there, as her online bio disclosed, she "got caught

146

up in the world of financial markets, foreign exchange tradings and futures broking." She started out working for Westpac, an Australian bank, before joining Lloyds Bank and Commonwealth Bank. This career path eventually took her to London, where she worked in futures brokering for Salomon Smith Barney. But the free spirit in her rebelled against the regimentation of the business suit.

"Bored to death of that world, I decided I needed to be in a job where I could choose my own hours and do what I wanted, when I wanted, and with whomever I wanted to work with," she recalled. "I answered an ad in a newspaper for glamour models. I checked it out, decided, yeah, I can be naked. I did quite a few softcore shoots in London."

The turning point came in December 2000, when she graduated from modeling to stripping, at the Spearmint Rhino club in London. "One night after work, we were all getting drunk and I met one of the owners, who was American, and I dared him to fly me back to the States with him," she told me. "Four hours later, we were on the plane to Texas—I'd gotten a free trip to America!

"So I left everything behind and came over, totally spontaneous. I had no money, nothing at all. So I danced for one night at the Spearmint Rhino in City of Industry, and made a lot of money there. After that, I kind of got hooked up with a photographer, Hank Londoner; he shot me for everyone and anyone, *Swank* and *Leg World* and elsewhere, and then he sent me to an agent who talked me into doing videos." Monica served her porn apprenticeship in decidedly downmarket fare—reflected in titles like *Fast Times at Deep Crack High #3*, *The Oral Adventures of Craven Moorhead #6*, and *The Blowjob Adventures of Dr. Fellatio #35*—before landing better parts in better films, most notably four VCA films: *Portrait of a Woman*, *The New Girls*, *The Stalker*, and *Hysteria*.

"I think *Hysteria* is my strangest film to date," she told me. "It's about aliens possessing me and I'm just going crazy, masturbating and having sex. Porn, to me, is an easy way to make money that's fun at the same time." It was better than having to monitor the Dow Jones Industrial Average, no doubt. Monica and I continued to keep in touch, long after the interview appeared in print, partly because of a watershed event that sealed our friendship.

It had to do with the story I'd written about her in *AVN Online*. The production of her personal website (*www.monicamayhem. com*) was done by a company called Pop Sex, Inc., the Internet arm of the gonzo porn production entity Shane Enterprises, which was in turn owned by my friend Jennie Grant. I'd first met Jennie when I interviewed the porn star Shane for *Penthouse Variations* three years earlier. Jennie was friendly enough with me to speak her mind about Monica's comments in that *AVN Online* interview; she'd winced when she read the final paragraphs, in which Monica had divulged something unbecoming of a true porn star, at least in Jennie's more business-minded view.

"I don't get any pleasure from penetration," Monica admitted to me. "That doesn't do anything for me. I'm not like most girls who say they love doggie style because they can feel it deeper. I can't climax vaginally and that's been my biggest trouble. Even clitorially, it's very, very hard. I orgasm only from oral sex, masturbation or vibrators."

"When I'm being penetraed by a guy on-camera, I find it very easy to fake," she added. "I get pleasure from whatever's on the outside, like skin contact. Nothing internal. I guess it's all part of the acting." Jennie, as a producer, understandably didn't like that but I found it refreshingly candid, since some porn stars tended to exaggerate their sexual attributes. Many of them bragged that they're built for the business because they're easily orgasmic, so Monica was being unusually honest.

"Don't worry about that whole thing with Jennie," she emailed me at the end of February 2002. "Some people are just touchy." By this time, Monica had won the XRCO (X-Rated Critics Organization) "Starlet of the Year" award. I congratulated her, but to my surprise she wasn't gushing with enthusiasm. "I

148

really don't think this award will take me anywhere," she told me. "I haven't had any new phone calls or anything yet, and I don't think that people take these things too seriously in the biz. But thanks, matey."

Three years later, I saw her in the July 2005 issue of *Genesis*, a nine-page layout with her blond hair gone, now dyed a deep red-brown. She also showed off her new tattoos—red flames on both wrists, plus a dragon on her left upper arm—none of which I'd seen before. "Yes, it is red," she emailed me when I asked about her new hair. "I got more tattoos. The writings on my wrists are all runestones—health, success, happiness, protection from enemies, love, wealth, divinity, my sign (Pisces), my planets (Neptune and Jupiter), and on the back of my neck, the protective eye of Horus. The dragon on my left arm is from the Welsh flag, as I'm part Welsh, and the right arm is just a Celtic link with snake heads. And the flames on my wrists, well, just cause I'm on fire!"

By that time, Monica had done more than 200 films and looked very, very hardcore after just four years in the business. Maybe it was the heavy eye make-up but there was a hardness in her eyes I hadn't seen before, a kind of pulchritude laced with pathos, noticeably different from the fresh-faced ingenue I'd met back in the bowling alley. Something had happened to her. A certain cynicism had possibly crept in. I found it savagely arresting, even sexy. In November 2005, she told me she was still working, having just been filmed having sex in productions from Metro, Naughty America, Playboy TV and by directors Nicholas Steele, Sean Michaels, and Suze Randall. "Just everyone," she quipped, with a sardonic shrug. "I didn't really do much this year."

In retrospect, I had detected her incipient world-weariness back in April 2004, when I told her I also wanted to interview her fellow Queenslander Jodie Moore for my "foreign girls" piece, and her response wasn't exactly sanguine. "We've met and hung out, but she doesn't return phone calls, so I gave up on her as a friend," Monica told me. But she admitted she was envious of Jodie's signing as contract girl to Private North America, an adjunct of the European porn giant Private Media Group. "Lucky girl, hey?" she said to me. "Wish I could've got hooked up like that."

Jodie Moore, however, didn't stay with Private for very long, even though her film *The Scottish Loveknot* won "Best Foreign Feature" at the 2004 *AVN* Awards. By the time I interviewed her in June 2003, she was already gone. She had signed a new contract with Legend Video, based in Chatsworth, and had stayed with Private for just one year. "Private wanted me to be based in Europe, but there's nothing for me in Europe," she told me. "I've made a home here in Los Angeles."

She'd been in the business a mere year and a half but already had a massive publicity machine going. For one thing, she had political ambitions. At the time I was interviewing her, she was running for the position of Lord Mayor of Brisbane in the March 2004 elections. She had previously run for the Australian senate—twice!—and had scored five percent of the vote the first time, slightly less the second try. Cries of "Cicciolina!" abounded, recalling Italian porn star Ilona Staller, who had run successfully for political office back in the 1980s.

But Jodie said something very funny to me. "I don't see myself as a celebrity," she quipped, on her cellphone while driving home on the San Diego Freeway. "Just between you and me, sweetie, this is just porn. I'm just a porn girl. I'm not Julia Roberts."

Was her political drive, though, something deeper than a publicity stunt? It certainly drove traffic to her website (*www. jodiemoore.com*). As David Harris, her webmaster, told me, "When Jodie makes some political statement in Australia, the site really does get hammered. It was overloaded when she appeared on *60 Minutes*. At the peak, we had 10,000 hits a minute." Harris, who uploaded all of Jodie's graphics after she'd chosen them, noted that this created an interesting schism in her fan base. Jodie had both porn fans (mostly in the United States) and political fans (mostly back home in Australia) and so, given the 19-hour time difference between Los Angeles and Brisbane, her site was never short on eyeballs. "One of the advantages of having the site in Australia," Harris told me, "is that the two different fan bases are looking at the site at opposite times, so the load on the server is spread out a little."

Jodie, to me, sounded very passionate about her politics, even if some people thought her downright loony. One of her campaign platforms called for an all-nude Mardi Gras in Brisbane. "Why not? If you get elected Lord Mayor, you can do anything," she told me. "The interest I have in politics comes from my wish to shake up the system and to have my say about the rights of those who like to make their own decisions about adult products. If you don't try, then nothing will change."

She also wanted to start an Australian union for strippers and sex workers (despite having heard all the reasons why this notion has failed everywhere) and was equally effusive about her "celebrity branding" as an Australian. "I think more Americans now want to see Australian stuff," she said. "There are things that make us kind of exotic, like the Australian accent and the fact that we're the only country in the world that eats Vegemite. I got into this business because there are no adult movie stars in Australia. I was a stripper for six years and then, one day someone said to me, 'How come there aren't any porn stars in Australia?' That's when I decided to do films. In Australia, there are production companies but they're only little ones, nothing on the size of Vivid or Wicked. I think that the more I get involved with politics, the more people will get to know about porn stars.

"Now, people are fascinated about us. We have a Sexpo convention in Australia now. When I went there last February, it was so overwhelming because it was held in Brisbane, my hometown, and so many people came out to see me. You have no idea how that made me feel. It felt so warm inside. It made me realize that Australia will always be my home. My fans in Australia usually email me to say things like, 'It's great, what you're doing,' and 'I remember when you were living in Woodridge, I remember when you were just stripping.' I get a lot of emails from girls who

151

say, 'I wish I could be as wild as you.' I'm lost for words when I read that!"

I think a universal emotion was being echoed there. Our search for erotic ecstasy can often become entwined with our capacity of human empathy. The most memorable object lesson for me, in this light, was when I asked Rebecca Lord about the fact that she had been married to the same man for all the time she'd been a porn star.

"I've been married for almost ten years now," she told me, "I think people should remember that marriage is not only about sex. It's a big part of it, but it's not everything. It's also about love. And we don't have much love in the porn industry."

Czeching in at the
Hotel California

For reasons I've never completely understood, all my favorite porn stars hail from the same part of the world, even though they have names that aren't Eastern European at all. Like Monica Sweetheart, Regina Hall, Daniella Rush, Wanda Curtis, Dominica Leoni, and the late Lea De Mae (who died from brain cancer in her native Prague, in December 2004; she'd signed a large poster for me, which I'll never sell on eBay).

But I know of an old Czech proverb that applies: "If the Devil is unable to do a job, he substitutes a woman." Because, of all the women on that chiseled-cheeked firmament, there is one who has always been *the* one: Silvia Saint.

If it's true that you can uncover the mystique of porn stars from simply telling one story, hers is the one to tell.

I first saw Silvia in October 1998, on the cover of American *Penthouse*, after she'd been crowned her native Czech *Penthouse* Pet of the Year in 1997 and won her first *AVN* Award the same year for "Best Tease Performance" (in a film called *Fresh Meat* #4), and also scored the 1997 "People's Choice Adult Award" for "Best Newcomer." By the time I got round to meeting her, she was everywhere, a new media darling, dangerously so. She would come to Los Angeles and find herself booked for three straight weeks. Critics and fans were calling her the new queen of porn, especially after she's sizzled up the screen in director Nic Cramer's *Looker*, his *film noir* porn homage which won the *AVN* "Best Film" award of 1999.

She had only one scene in that film, but what a scene. She played a hooker who services a police detective played by her current beau, the Turkish-German stud Hakan Serbes. I had never seen any girl rock and swivel her hips so sensuously, as the camera held on her open thighs in reverse-cowgirl position, her lusciously pink vaginal lips firmly clamping his erection, and her mouth open in a come-hither, come-quickly half-sneer. But it was the way she rocked and swiveled that blew my mind. I couldn't get that one out of my head for days on end.

"Jack Remy, my cinematographer, said that her scene in *Looker* was the single best sex scene he'd shot in his twenty-year career," Nic gushed. "Silvia Saint is arguably the most beautiful woman I have had the pleasure to aim a camera lens at. She oozes sex. The fact that she's demure, very intelligent, charmingly friendly and always approachable makes her an absolute treasure."

How did I meet her? Nic introduced me to a delightfully chummy English director named Frank Thring. He had directed her first film, *Lee Nover: The Search for the Perfect Breasts*, and then remained her local guide and father confessor, whenever work took her to Southern California. Frank told me she'd be in Los Angeles soon and would set me up with her hotel number and I could take it from there.

"She's extremely beautiful," he told me. "You don't usually walk into castings every day and see girls of that quality willing to do porno, though I wish to God you did. She was fresh and new and willing to take it up the butt. One of the striking things about Silvia is that she's always been very good from day one. She gives a hundred and one percent, and every guy who works with her really feels that this woman, for thirty or forty minutes or what have you, is literally in love with him.

"But she's very professional off-camera. If any of the performers make a pass at her after work, she gets quite offended.

She'll be in bed by nine o'clock at night and read a book instead of going out partying like the other girls. She'll put the light out and go to sleep like a sweet innocent little virgin, and then she'll give you an incredible sex scene the next morning!"

Frank had a theory about Silvia. "Her father dropped out of her life when she was quite young, and she was brought up by her mother. And it's very interesting psychologically, because she actually likes a strong male figure in her life. She likes a boyfriend who can dominate her, she quite likes her bottom smacked during sex, that kind of thing. I think that psychologically, she still yearns for that strong male figure."

I was intrigued by this, since I'd always found dominant women attractive. Silvia never gave me the impression of being submissive at all. Freud could have a field day with us.

I wanted to see how deceptive appearances could be, so I called the number Frank gave me. She was there. She always stayed at the same hotel in Los Angeles, in a US$300-a-night suite. Her voice was a velvety mezzo-soprano burr of Czech consonants, but her English was quite good. We made the appointment.

When I went to the hotel, however, she didn't show up, and I waited two hours before giving up. Later she called, apologizing profusely; she said the shoot had gone late and she hadn't taken my phone number with her. But she said she really wanted to do the interview—it was going to be a profile of her for *Penthouse Variations*, after all, and she was very much part of the *Penthouse* family—so we rescheduled. It was almost midnight, definitely past her innocent-virgin bedtime.

And so came October 5, 1999, auspiciously also the sixty-third birthday of her country's famous quasi-rock star president Vaclav Havel, and she kept her word. I drove her to Yamashiro, an elegant Japanese aerie nestled high in the Hollywood hills, on Sycamore Avenue near the fabled Magic Castle. We chatted for the next few hours, over Pellegrino water and a white Zinfandel from Berenger, since she wanted a California wine.

My first surprise was her admission that she isn't a natural blond. "No, my hair is a little bit darker, like dark honey. I colored it long before I even started in this business in 1996." She weighed 112 pounds, stood five feet six, and before she got into porn she spoke only Czech and Russian. She looked bigger-boned than I'd expected, her complexion a creamy pink-white, her skin smooth to the touch, still the fantasy goddess I had envisioned. She was wearing a new perfume by Jean-Paul Gaultier. The warm late summer breeze caressed her flaxen tresses, worn just past her shoulders.

She had a baby-faced look, with those wide Slavic cheekbones that I'd always been a sucker for. When she smiled, her teeth were immaculately white. I'd seen what her mouth could do, but now she was only talking. "I mean, yes, I love sex. If you didn't you couldn't do it. But I cannot say that I will do everything that any producer likes. I like normal sex, girl/girl or boy/girl, I don't like some of the real hardcore like gangbangs or other nasty things. I have never done a gangbang. I have done it with three boys but not a gangbang, because my agent says it's not good for my image. Now if they ask me, I always say I will do two boys only and no more, nothing nasty. Gangbangs are not my style and I won't do it for any amount of money. Once you start, it's hard to get other jobs."

Yes, Virginia, there is an unspoken hierarchy even in porn. Girls who go the hard and nasty route, performing in gangbangs, tend to stay entrenched in B-grade purgatory and seldom find their careers ascending further (like Annabel Chong, she of the most famous gangbang ever; she'd told me about how hard it was to get work despite her mainstream fame). It's funny to note, of course, and more poignant when I get to hear it from someone like Silvia, who is patently A-list and determined to stay so. Blowjob videos are perfectly fine and very much *de rigueur*, however, even if like Silvia you end up on the cover of a compilation like *California Cocksuckers #5*, in which she is seen on the box cover, looking devilishly seductive with a glint in her eye, in extreme close-up with a very large penis in her mouth. I had my copy of it with me, and showed it to her.

"Oh my God, what is this?!!!" she squealed, giggling in half-embarrassed horror. "My goodness, these pictures!" She obviously hadn't seen it before. I seized the moment and also showed her the latest December 1999 issue of *Genesis* magazine. She was on the cover ("Silvia Saint Cums Wet & Wild!") and the eight-page photo spread inside featured full-color shots of her in fully spread-wide genitalia regalia. We poured through the layout and examined her nakedness, as if we were appraising a Picasso. "Earl Miller shot that. We did that at his house," she recalled.

"Some fans, they bring so many things for me to sign," she sighed. "Some of them make me sign their entire collections of my photos. One man from Japan, I recognize him, he comes every year and brings me so many pictures to sign. Some men bring nasty pictures like close-ups of my pussy, and I sign like this—" She put one palm on the photo of her open vagina to hide it, pantomiming autograph-signing. And giggled again.

I sensed she was comfortable with me. Well, how could one not be? I had already seen her completely naked and in such explicit sleight of posture. However, she was somewhat embarrassed when I gave her some of the new box covers to keep—she pointedly refused to take *California Cocksuckers #5*, with a little wave as if to say, "Uh, thanks but you can keep it." But *Crazy From the Heat*, she wanted to keep that one.

That's the one that ends with her doing a three-way, where she gets thoroughly reamed by Evan Stone and J.J. Michaels, shot once again by Jack Remy and directed by Michael Raven. I tell her it's one of my favorites of hers, along with the opening tryst in another Michael Raven opus, *Dream Master*, a fetish scene in which a young man in leather and chains played by Eric Masterson ravishes her while she's gussied up in a kinky red and black corset. He finishes by ejaculating on her black vinyl boots. "I've worked with that boy before, and I remember he likes the smell of feet," she recalled. "Nothing makes him harder than feet. You see how many types of people are in the business?"

Yes indeed, different strokes for different folks. I would see her again in two more Nic Cramer/Jack Remy films, both made in early 2000—*Skin Deep* (the fictional name of an outcall agency owned and operated by Silvia, who played both madam and escort) and *Sex Deluxe* (in which she had anonymous sex in a movie theatre with two strangers, played by Jay Ashley and Pat Myne, while sitting between the two studs, stroking and blowing and fucking both). She also had no problems appearing in gonzo fare, like the unscripted *Pick Up Lines #40*, where she poses pretty-girl bikini style for "photographer" Jake Steed, a well-hung black stud, before undressing and dominating him completely with a slurpy blowjob before riding him cowgirl and finishing off with anal, literally tiring the poor guy out.

I told her I'd seen him usually in the driver's seat, endlessly working girls over, but in that case he was completely outclassed. "Was I dominant? That was my role," she recalled. "He's such a skinny guy and I guess he was tired. I tried. I've worked with a lot of black guys and it's no different. I think it makes for good contrast." She paused and rubbed her arms, indicating her skin color. "I try to be in control and sometimes I like being dominant. But it's hard because some men don't like it. Many feelings come into it."

She was still very enthusiastic about porn, though, especially after what she considered her crowning achievement, *The Uranus Experiment*, a three-part sci-fi fornication fest (now available in a three-disc box set) produced by Private Media, the European company known for its consistent combination of high-octane sex and lovely continental babes.

The Uranus Experiment, made for US$750,000, featured a crew of American and Russian astronauts on an interstellar mission to "learn how the absence of gravity affects human sexuality, male sperm production and the accompanying female reaction to it." Silvia played cosmonaut Helena Sidorenko and engaged in space hijinks with two foxy Hungarian porn stars, Wanda Curtis (as Helena Vashinski) and Christina Dark (as Dr.

Olga Wiborova), and it also featured Silvia as the lucky recipient of the "first cumshot in zero gravity" (as Private's press release bragged), filmed in a "special aircraft flying at 35,000 feet." In actuality, the plane flew at 11,000 feet and went into a steep dive to create the momentary illusion of weightlessness, enough for actor Nick Lang to do his thing with Silvia.

"I had sex on a plane!" Silvia gushed. "When this boy came, he blew in the air and it was fantastic. It was only a couple of seconds but he came and he really shot it, and it looked like it was all floating in the air. Fantastic! I saw it on DVD!"

Director John Millerman, who also wrote the script, can be seen putting his cast through their paces in the additional behind-the-scenes featurette, *The Making of The Uranus Experiment,* interspersing footage shot at the Kennedy Space Center in Florida and the Johnson Space Center in Housto with sex scenes shot in Barcelona, Budapest, and Lanzarote. Millerman also achieved something most porn directors would die for: mainstream recognition; *The Uranus Experiment Part 2* was actually nominated for a Nebula Award, the science fiction world's highest accolade, for "Best Script" in 2000 alongside other high-profile nominees like *The Matrix* and *The Sixth Sense.*

In an interview with the space technology site *Space.com*, Ann Crispin, vice-president of the nominating association, the SFWA (Science Fiction and Fantasy Writers of America), acknowledged that her board was "not happy" with the choice but its writers "thought it would be 'fun' to put a hardcore porn film on the ballot … Not my idea of a joke, but perhaps I'm humor-impaired."

AVN, in its reviews of the three separate films, disparaged the Private publicity claims as baseless—"the 'zero-g' footage is all earthbound" and "what's left is scene after scene of pretty people having sex on sci-fi-ish sets … the coitus always feels a bit stagy." It did, however, commend the final orgy in *Part 3*, one of my own personal favorite group sex scenes: "You can't beat the concluding cluster fuck for sheer aesthetics—the Continental honeys are all gorgeous, each is vigorously cornholed by a buffed-out Euro-stud or two, and copious cum geysers announce when the scene is through."

Silvia, unfortunately, did not appear in that last scene. But what matter? At last count from her official website (*www.clubsilviasaint.net*), she had been in 416 films (on video and DVD, including compilations and box sets), notwithstanding a period of temporary retirement, during which she switched gears to help her boyfriend and his antiques business. It didn't last, and she returned to porn.

So how did this all happen to a once-shy, 36-24-34 former model, born on February 12, 1976, in Kyjov, in what was then called Czechoslovakia? As we sipped Zinfandel and contemplated the lights of Hollywood below, Silvia took me down her memory lane. Whenever she laughed, she shook her blond tresses but would quickly fix me a hard gaze in the eyes, a knowing look. "I feel nice that I can be sexy for somebody, that I can be an ideal, or a dream, or a fantasy. It makes me feel like a woman."

That was her prevailing thought when she walked into a modeling agency, after having worked as a hotel manager and then a secretary. "When I was growing up, I never thought I would be in this kind of business. My girlfriend introduced me to a photographer in the city where I live, Brno, and I was at first hesitant. I said, 'No, I don't want to try nothing like this.' She said I should do some lingerie and bikini shots, not just nudes. I kept his card and half a year later I called him and he told me to come to his studio for a photo shoot. So I went there and he said, 'I believe you have a nice body. I don't even need to see the test shots. So, come back tomorrow and we'll start work!'

"That's how it started. I worked for him every day and we went to Germany and Austria. I did a lot of calendars. Before this, I had a boyfriend who wanted to shoot me privately, for his own collection, and I did some of those. Posing in the bedroom, little bit naked, it was all very sweet. I was very shy at the time and would never have done anything of the likes of *Penthouse* or videos. But I tried to be professional about it. We would look at magazines like *Penthouse* and I would say, 'Oh, this is nice. This girl is so beautiful,' and he would ask if he could shoot pictures of me like that. So, we did." But it was in Prague where she went to model, that things changed dramatically. "For the first six months, I didn't even do any girl/girl shots, just single girl layouts of just me. Some lingerie and some nudes. But I got to meet other models in Prague and we talked a lot about being in this business. They always told me there was 'something more than this' but they never told me exactly what that 'something' was!

"One day, I went with a girlfriend. We drove to Prague for a casting session for a porn movie. I was so nervous because I had never done it before and I didn't know what to do. I didn't know how to move or how I should come, and I had to learn about lights and cameras. But I knew that I liked sex and I could travel and make a lot of money this way. Now, I've been in the business four years and I've been to a lot of places and met a lot of people. I like it. It's nice."

But what about the mechanics of on-camera sex, with all she's learned about those cameras and lights? "If there are a lot of people there and I know that some of them are just there because they want to see some sex, then it makes me a little nervous. When it's a small crew, and there is a partner I know and I like him, then I enjoy it. When I get a partner I don't like, I do it just to do it. Working with somebody you've never been with before can be strange. If you've met them socially before and we've flirted at a party or something, it's good. And if you've gotten to actually talk with them, it's even better."

We looked again at the *Genesis* layout and not one blush crossed her smooth pink cheeks as she turned the pages. She posed by a pool of water in a rock grotto, completely naked, her body oiled and gleaming, her defiant gaze only conveying one thought: "Do you want to me fuck me?" Two pages over and she has arched her back and spread her thighs, two fingers of one hand purposefully pulling back her vulva. Unlike some models, she said, she made a point of always studying her magazine layouts "to see how I move, how I use certain positions, how my face looks from certain angles. But movies, no. I think it's because I know what went on, from being involved in the production, so I don't need to see the final product. I know there are cuts and there are edits, but I can imagine it. It's enough that I do this work. I don't need to see the movies themselves."

Did she have memories of difficult shoots, the kind that time hasn't quite erased? "Yes, I have shot in the snow," she recalled. "One time, I was in France shooting a movie with the director Christoph Clark and I was playing the part of a spy in a James Bond type of movie. I was outside and I had to have sex in a mini-dress, and that was too much. There was too much snow and it was freezing. He wanted to do take after take and I started to get angry. It always depends on what the producers want, whether you're going to be outside and naked for half a day or just a couple of minutes. That time, I was really shaking. And some directors, they want to do comedy. Like Marc Dorcel. I like him but he likes doing a lot of comedy. We shoot five hours of comedy and one hour of sex! And they want me to speak French! I keep telling him most people who watch it are going to use the remote."

When it comes to sex, there are two areas she excelled in, and her fans never use the remote. "Cocksucking? I only don't like it when the boy comes in my eyes. It's so painful. When it gets on my face or my mouth or on my breasts, I like it. I know it makes for a good effect on video. But sometimes it gets in my hair and ruins my make-up, and I hate it. And then I have to wash it off with the make-up! Sometimes, a boy will go, 'Ha, ha, ha!' and I will say, 'You should try getting this on your face, you don't know what it's like!' One time I said, 'You need a big black man to come on your face, then you'll know how it is!' I try to make it fun. If it's too serious, it's no good."

And the other area? "Sometimes I can say I like anal. It depends on the partner. If I have a partner who is not respectful, it gets very hard sometimes. Usually I will talk with whoever I'm working with, to find out what he likes, what he wants and doesn't

162

want, what is good and not good. I always say to them, 'Be for me nice now, ya, please?' Some of the new guys don't care. They just want to be seen as the best and they don't care if I'm in pain or not. If the guy gets too rough, I will tell him so he will understand. I try to work with people I know who are really professional."

Perhaps it was because we were doing the interview for a *Penthouse* publication in America, but she made a point of telling me she preferred to work here in California. The European way of doing porn is very different because they like to shoot endless amounts of hard sex. I knew an American cinematographer who went to work for Private and he told me they would often shoot sex for six hours straight. The American style puts a lot into preproduction and the editing process, and there are continual breaks in action, lots of stopping and starting again, lot of camera and lighting changes, lots of time to rest. And she gets to go to places like Hawaii, which she said was "the best place to have sex, I was there three years ago and I thought it was fantastic, when you're working and you're being showered by this tropical hot rain. And the smell in the air is so clean, it's like paradise."

She has a longstanding love affair with Los Angeles. "Prague has two million people. Brno has one million people. It's an exhibition city—cars, design, a lot of people come and visit. But it's not like L.A. When I came here, it was like, 'Wow!' It was everything I had heard of, a factory for dreams. And it was my dream come true. I like it here. I like the weather here. I think someday I will move here. When I think of Hollywood, I think of Sharon Stone. But I'm not telling you which Hollywood stars I want to have sex with!"

So I asked her the million-dollar questions we all love to ask porn stars, just because they're the ones who are supposed to know. Is she an expert on sex? And what is the secret to good sex? "No, I'm not an expert," she giggles. "I think I have a lot of fantasies and I like to try everything. Well, not everything. Just the nice things." And the second question? "If I tell you, it's no more a secret," she whispered, winking.

"Sometimes I work with some man and I know he likes it and that's when it's great, when you're not aware of the camera. I can be somewhere else, or be someone else. If you think too much, it doesn't really work because you get too nervous. I like to talk to my partners before a scene. Sometimes if we sleep together and talk about things, I try to remember what these are and I try to use it." Does she have real orgasms? "It depends on the scene and on the partner. When I have sex, I like to close my eyes and feel it. I like to think of things that make me horny."

Well, I told her, I can get horny just hearing her say that, and she cracked up. Like most seasoned veterans of the porn world, she wasn't at all uncomfortable with being seen as a sex object. Being sexually objectified *is* the whole point of what she does, after all. "I don't care what people say. If I did, I wouldn't be here. People can think what they want and I think that usually they are jealous or something."

Silvia is my favorite porn star because she has the entire package—wonderful to watch on film, and wonderful in person. I found myself highly motivated to seize the celebrity photo-op, to uncover things about her private life, especially aspects of her family background which she seldom disclosed in public. Word had traveled, for instance, that she'd had a baby. "Can you believe it?!! I have never had a child!" she exclaimed. "I don't know where they came up with this stuff. One time, I was shooting with a photographer and he was just shooting pussy. So there he was, with his camera aimed right between my legs, shooting my pussy. And he looks up and he says, 'Wow, I can't believe you had a baby!' I looked at him and I said, 'Where did you read *that*?!!!'"

And then there's always that awkward interview question: Do your parents know?

"My mother knows about it," she replied. "We don't talk about this work, other than her saying, 'Where are you staying' and 'Call me when you land.' I know she doesn't want to talk about it. She knows what I do and she respects it and she cares about me. Recently we went to Tunisia together and we rode camels, and we also went to South Africa. It was fun. My mother lives in a city of 15,000 people, a quiet and relaxing place. My mother and father never married. He lives in a different city. I visit him but we are not close. He is fine with what I do. I have two stepsisters. My family isn't poor. All of them have houses, none of them work in factories.

"Right now, I don't have a boyfriend. It's hard for me to find a boyfriend in my country, because of the kind of work I do. Many men there feel it's fine for a woman to be in this business but once you're with them, they want you to stop and just stay home and cook. I think a woman can be strong and also be promiscuous. I remember when I was in school, looking at my fellow students. Out of a class of thirty, twenty-five of them are now married and then divorced, with children. It's so strange. You get a situation when the man works and makes money, and the woman stays home and has no life. I want something for the future, some guarantee, for when I am ready to have a family. I want to have children."

"But I also know people like to talk," she shrugged. "Like they will tell my children, 'Your mother, when she was young, did you know what she used to do for a living?' I have thought about this many times. Sometimes life is so hard, and I am thinking about what is the future."

Which was why I was taken by surprise to hear, a year after our interview, that Silvia was about to officially retire in March 2001. She had called me when she was in L.A., right after our interview appeared in the May 2000 issue of *Penthouse Variations*, to say she had just seen it on the newsstand (she was on the cover too) and had bought herself a copy. I told her I had already saved a copy for her, but she said it was okay, she buys her own magazines whenever she's in them, like any other working model. That was a first for me; I'd never had a porn star tell me she went and bought the actual magazine which had my piece on her inside. It was flattering.

By this time, I had Silvia's cellphone number and we talked

quite frequently whenever she flew in to Los Angeles. She wouldn't tell me herself but my sources said she made US$40,000 each trip, since she was constantly in demand for shoots and movies. (Czechs are sensitive about disclosing income, I was later given to understand when I visited Prague myself, because the tax authorities are big on collecting.) So how could she ever stop? I remember her asking me if I knew anyone who could get her work doing "straight modeling," like bikini and lingerie work. But those gigs, I knew, were *never* going to pay her rates.

"She'll never make the kind of money she's making now with any kind of regular, non-nude modeling," Nic Cramer affirmed, having directed her again in the sequel *Looker 2: Femme Fatale*. "And I doubt she will ever really move here someday, no matter what she says. She will always make more money by coming over to work, however sporadically, since it drives up her market value."

All this surely factored into her decision to leave the business in 2001, though her comeback was imminent and had been heralded by intermittent newsflashes. In November 2004, for instance, a news report on *AVN* noted that some "lost films" of hers had been found online:

> *A trilogy of previously unreleased films featuring porn legend Sylvia Saint will be available on Video-on-Demand (VoD) through AEBN, after being released on DVD exclusively by In-X-Cess in late October. The first film in the Sylvia's Spell trilogy, Sylvia's Spell 1, is currently available in streaming pay-per-view, rental, and download … The films were shot in 2001 but remained shelved till now. Distributor Valley Pro Video's Frank Rizzo said the films were never released due to litigation, but the trilogy is the highest-budget production of the former Penthouse Pet's career and the only one to be shot using film. "As far as the sex in it, you can't beat it," Rizzo said. "As far as we know, she has only done one girl/girl recently. Sylvia Saint gets fucked in the ass in all three of these movies."*

Never mind that they misspelled her name (she herself spelled it Silvia), getting fucked in the ass might be the least polite yet most appropriate way of putting it, given that porn stars never really retire anyway—they're always available on video and on the Internet, and it's for forever. Even in the wake of Silvia's 2001 retirement, a slew of "new" releases issued forth capitalizing on her fame. There was rough-trade gonzo fare like *Dick Lovin' Bitches Volume 3*, as well as the interactive-sex DVD *My Plaything: Silvia Saint* (featuring "dual camera switching, mood control, male/female orgasm control and multi-positional POV sex") and DVDs from a newly established Penthouse/Private joint venture (most notably *Call Girl* and *Dangerous Things*, both directed by Antonio Adamo). In America, features with her on both box covers and titles were swiftly issued (*100% Silvia*, *Dreaming of Silvia*, and *Silvia's Diary*, to cite just a few), almost as if she never went away.

But in May 2005, her comeback was real. She starred in *Private Chateau*, shot on the Costa Brava coast of Spain, a three-part "super-feature" about *Dynasty*-style feuds between families, released by Private Media Group and directed by the award-winning Conrad Son. Silvia wrote to her fans on her website later that same month—from New Zealand, where she was working with Private again on a new film, *Lady of the Rings*, in which she had two lesbian scenes that could probably make Tolkien arise, and not just from the grave.

She also wrote to clarify some nagging issues: "The year was 2000 when I finally stopped making hardcore films, and since then my life has changed quite significantly, but not very dramatically ... I fell in love ... I was not doing anything that would link me with the business in any way ... I made a suggestion to my boyfriend, that I would really like to help with his antiques business ... I immersed myself in his business, I helped him where I could, but soon I found out it was not my cup of tea ... Some time after that, I really wanted to create my own webpage ... which meant that I could get back to doing my own thing, collecting new material for photo shoots and videos ... some interested production company contacted me, and I began working exclusively for them, we shot lesbian scenes and softcore material.

"Then after that I made a new lesbian film for Viv Thomas called *Searching For Silvia* ... During the last two years, I have performed exclusively in these following movies: *Fetish Desires*, *Euro Domination #3*, *Action Girls* ... The New Year 2005 began for me on the flight to *AVN* Erotic Fair held in Las Vegas, USA ... I had the opportunity to work exclusively with the famous Suze Randall."

Suze was the *Penthouse* photographer who'd shot her October 1998 Pet layout, which had first brought Silvia to my attention and so ineffably frazzled my synapses. Full circle, I thought.

I haven't had any contact with her since her previous "retirement" but I have fond memories. Like taking her back to her hotel after our 1999 interview at Yamashiro, and as I bade her goodbye she insisted, "Kiss me the European way," on both cheeks. She was wearing a simple white, short-sleeved t-shirt and white slacks, and told me she was "a little cold." I gently rubbed my palm on her upper left arm, just below the sleeve, and I can still recall the cool touch of her skin, slightly dry yet silky smooth. The Santa Ana winds were blowing. I could fall in love with this woman.

Or was she so adept at the erotic arts that she could conjure pheromones at will, making me the latest in a long line of men so easily infatuated, so drawn to an obvious metaphysical conquest by Czech mate? I still don't know. But I did know I enjoyed talking to her, especially about sex. "No, I don't masturbate a lot," she'd told me. "Because I have so much work, I don't need to do it in real life. Like tomorrow, I have to a do a masturbation video and so I will be masturbating all day. I like it when I can touch myself without the director telling me what to do all the time. I like to masturbate, but sometimes I am so tired from this work that I just want to sleep."

"Here in L.A.," she'd explained, "I just stay in one place and get driven around to shoot layouts and movies. I can stay two months in one place. If you have one scene in a movie, you sit in a car and you're there and you do it and you're done a couple of hours later. In Europe, I am flying always—to France one week, then another country the next week. Sometimes because of one scene, you have to fly to another country. Last year, I shot a film called *Cockzilla*, it was for Private, shot in Hungary. In an old castle, with a lot of costumes, and I played a princess. Nice story, but we shot for two weeks!

"In America, I like Vivid. They make big movies now. They have talked with my agent many times in Las Vegas and I think they want to sign me. But they already have Dasha and Veronica, I think they are both Czech, and I think it's because they take less money. I think for a European girl, I have a higher price."

Hers is an unusual profession, with unusual occupational hazards. I hope she'll always manage to get some sleep.

Part Three

Naked Hollywood

Going, Going, Gonzo!

We live now in an age where almost anything goes, a circumstance perhaps best reflected by things like Jenna Jameson's new Playboy TV reality show (called *Jenna's American Sex Star*) and her free Podcasts for those wishing to download her new Club Jenna movies ("trailers to go," as she herself touts them). How, one might wonder, has the fine line between truth and fiction become blurred?

I was on a set once where a certain male actor overdosed on the infamous "date rape drug" GHB. He ran around the set totally naked and just went beserk. I was out in the hallway at the time, interviewing Nina Hartley, and when we saw this guy running out screaming gibberish, Nina and I gave one another a "What the fuck?" look, for maybe a mere two seconds, before we resumed our interview and ignored the banshee wailing down the corridor.

We had become desensitized to madness on movie sets, though it was a lot less funny when that particular actor had to be replaced since he clearly couldn't work that day and so Kelly Holland, the director, started calling around to find a replacement. Steven St Croix was free that day, and he looked quite smug when he arrived—hey, he was going to be getting some unexpected sex today and get paid for it too—and he was scheduled to do a scene with Inari Vachs, one of my favorite female performers. Inari had never worked with Steven before and told me she was excited about actually doing it with a complete stranger, and the bonus was that he happened to be a living legend, at least in the adult entertainment arena. (Steven told me he had tried to go "mainstream" but appearing in the odd cable movie for the likes of Disney didn't quite pay the rent so he returned to adult, steady work being better than none at all.)

Well, who knew if the original guy had popped Viagra before the shoot, as many of these men sometimes do, and what might that coupled with the GHB have done to his sex-addled brain? The incident reminded me of the many strange sagas that often arose at gonzo shoots, a porn genre which had existed long before today's mainstream reality shows came to our homes, to deviously add one more item to our already bamboozled time-wasting habits.

You see, everyone involved with porn has their favorite gonzo story. And this one, which has never been told before, is mine.

It sounds like a flip thing to say, but the truth is I got into gonzo purely by accident. In May 1999, I received a call from Victoria "V.K." McCarty, my editor at *Penthouse Variations*, assigning me to an interview with Shane. V.K. had mentioned Shane to me when we'd met in her office in New York a few months back, so I wasn't particularly surprised. She had a real jones for Shane, and for the type of porn she specialized in. We call it "gonzo" now, but back then it didn't really have an official name. "Handheld video hardcore" or "travelogue porn" were bandied around, basically anything where all you had was a single cameraman and a bunch of horny people who improvised both dialogue and sex in equally improvised locations.

Porn back then was relatively innocent, if you can even imagine such a thing. Gonzo was the furthest-out that you could go, compared to today. The industry is now flooded with "wall-to-wall" porn, in which there is little or no dialogue at all and it's just one sex scene after another, with every permutation and combination of perversity in between. We have graduated from simple things like choking and fisting to more explicitly graphic

174

fare, like "bukkake" (one girl getting her face splattered with come from a bunch of guys standing around her) and "cream pie" (where the guys will ejaculate inside her, and we then get to see the close-up with come dripping out of her vagina) and there's "anal cream pie" too, of course (where the come drips lovingly out of her anus).

When did all this happen, and how did it happen? Back in early 1999, I certainly didn't know. But I sure was going to find out.

Sure, I told V.K., I'll interview Shane. V.K. was also interested in all the issues surrounding Shane's company, Shane's World, and how she got the whole kit and caboodle going with her paramour and mentor, Seymour Butts. V.K. said she had heard a lot about Seymour, and she considered what he was doing culturally relevant enough to merit inclusion in her magazine. This was going to be my third assignment, for the "Cinema Blue" section of *Penthouse Variations*, which I had started writing, about the wacky world of the San Fernando Valley and its camera-wielding, carnal carnival.

There was just one small problem. I had never dealt with Shane before. Nor had I even seen *any* of her films.

All I knew about her came from reading *AVN* and reviews of her films. And, more crucial to this narrative, I wasn't even in Los Angeles at that time. I was in Singapore, having just returned from a two-year stint in Hong Kong and some months away from moving back to L.A.

But I said yes to V.K., simply because I didn't want to say no. I didn't want to risk losing the gig. I had only penned two pieces for "Cinema Blue" at that point, and felt that I hadn't gained V.K.'s approval yet. I had a sense of foreboding, that while V.K. probably sensed that I was up to the job, this assignment would be the acid test of my competence and, good dominatrix that she is, she wanted to see if I could accordingly rise to the occasion. Was I frightened? Yes, mildly. It was the first time I was going to interview somebody I had not only never met before but whom I actually knew next to nothing about. But I didn't tell V.K. this.

I played along, discussed Shane and Seymour like I was somewhat familiar with them. V.K. told me she had no objection to my interviewing someone by phone or by email, so long as the narrative could cut the expected swath through the morass of sexy details that I was to provide in spades.

Cool beans, I said, let's rock!

I did two things first. I did an Internet search for Shane and located the phone number of her company, with an address in Van Nuys, California (actually a mailbox, I later found out, the actual premises being farther west out in Tarzana). The second thing I did was scour my trusty porn bible, the 1999 *AVN Adult Entertainment Guide*, which I had the foresight to procure (for US$11.95 at *Hustler* Hollywood, back in March 1999, my first actual purchase from that newly opened West Hollywood store). It was a voluminously large compendium of information—large because there were a record 9,000 adult-film titles released in 1998, and it covered everything that was of essential importance in the past year, categorized into genres (Specialty, Amateur, Ethnic, Couples, Cult, Big Boob, Oral, Anal, etc.)—and I was sure that it would have everything I needed to know about what Shane had done. That, coupled with whatever I could trawl over the Internet, would serve as the basis of my research. And I was right. I have this insane belief that if you do the research, it will show in the eventual results somehow, even if you end up not using half of what you've actually read. It took me quite some time to get all the information on Shane that I needed. And then I picked up the phone.

Underwater fibre cables buzzed across the Pacific, from Singapore to Los Angeles. And that's how I "met" someone who would become one of my best friends in the industry, Shane's World owner Jennie Grant.

I explained who I was and what I wanted, and she said sure. Anything to do with *Penthouse* was a really big deal, especially to small companies like hers, and she said she'd be glad to get Shane for me. We could do the interview by email, no problem. Just send her the questions. She would get them to Shane and then send me back the answers.

Now, here was something else I didn't know at the time: Shane had, at that point, decided to retire from the business and had actually sold her company to Jennie. But they didn't want to make a big deal of it in public. Jennie and her husband Brian were now the new owners. The deal was in transition at the time, and so Jennie had decided to not tell me and merely introduce herself as Shane's "publicist."

Shane was now on the other side of the camera, directing the series, and by the time I had made contact with Jennie, they were about to release *Shane's World 19* and several volumes of two spin-offs, *Slumber Party* (an all-girl series) and *Pornological* (a gonzo series in which girls get up to all kinds of spontaneous real-life sex with strangers on the street). They would soon sign, that July, the company's first contract girl, a blond vixen named Sky, who would then leave to sign a contract with Vivid Video, a mere two months later! (Jennie had fired Sky, formerly called Skylar Chase, for being an irresponsible party girl who wouldn't comply with on-set instructions, but Sky would later leave Vivid for much the same reasons, and end up returning to work for Jennie. Weird, but this happened in porn all the time.)

And so, I started preparing a questionnaire for Shane. As with all my "Cinema Blue" columns, I had to keep to V.K.'s brief—concoct a scenario featuring the subject at hand, and then write the interview in Drew McKenzie "cinema verite" style. I decided that I would be "interviewing" Shane in the backyard of a friend's house in the San Fernando Valley, with Shane naked and skinny-dipping in the pool while I made notes and tried to keep my professional decorum despite my obvious erection—thus injecting a sense of comedic interplay. Shane would torture me with sexy stories about her various sexual escapades while filming the *Shane's World* series, for the reader to enjoy.

At the time, I had only done one piece like this before. I'd "interviewed" Asia Carrera on the beach near her home in Malibu, California (also done by email but under very different circumstances, since Asia and I had already known one another for a few years so it was easy as cream pie.) "You write very well," Asia told me later, after she'd read the piece, "and you make it all sound like you were actually there with me on the beach. You manage to make our interview sound so risqué when you weren't even here to do it. I wonder what you'd write if you WERE actually next to me when we did it!"

High praise from Asia (who doesn't ever say anything she doesn't mean) and, bolstered with courage from this morsel of encouragement, I felt ready to take on Shane's World.

Actually, it wasn't all Dutch courage; I had asked Jennie to send me their latest release for my research, and she sent me by snail-mail a VHS copy of *Shane's World 19: Tropical Paradise*, which I watched. In my favorite scene, Cheyenne Silver and Vivian Valentine staged a "spontaneous" *ménage a trois* with Chris Cannon in a tropical Florida rainstorm, very sultry and soulful, like listening to a Sam Cooke song. Wet, wanton and wild at heart; I think I got the idea. (And at least they shot in "tropical" Florida, unlike some of the company's later releases; *Asian Vacation*, made in 2004, was actually shot in Mexico!)

Before I proceed further, let me riff on a wee bit about gonzo. Sure, the genre might've been new to me then but it had already existed for some years, supposedly the brainchild of director John Stagliano, under the auspices of his company Evil Angel. The premise was that porn could be made fast and cheap—with one camera, no script, no clothes, and sometimes even no actual confirmed location—but always shot with spunk and zest, necessity being the motherlode of invention. A typical gonzo costs one-quarter of a typical feature.

Some of those tapes were making serious inroads into the homes of porn-loving pervs who didn't care to fast-forward past all the dialogue found in actual feature movies that had pretty people, picturesque sets and, for crying out loud, an actual *plot*.

This might perhaps be evident to most people only today, since Shane's ex-beau Seymour Butts is now the subject of the 2005 Showtime television series *Family Business* (all about Seymour and his shenanigans, via his extended family), and gonzo porn is now as commonplace as the next mainstream reality show.

Human history abounds with gonzo sex, only the technology to record it had just never been around. The Chinese empress Wu Hu, from the Tang Dynasty, had apparently displayed her power by making all visiting male dignitaries show their respect by pleasuring her orally; her practice was to throw open her robes and her guests would prostrate themselves before her, kneeling down to muff-dive her genitals. (How nice to know that such practices had been part of my own genetic makeup, courtesy of my ancestors.) So what was the big deal? Was there a giant conceptual leap from going down this yellow brick road, enacting sexual rites with or without a camera to record events as they transpired? Truth is, in a sexual context, always stranger than friction. Gonzo was merely the modern-day method of enshrining sexual habits for the viewing pleasure of millions. I had no problem with that.

My starting point was Shane's official bio from her Shane's World website: "As the story goes, one day Shane and her girlfriend were watching a Seymour Butts video and decided that it would be a kick to make a tape of their own, so Shane borrowed her dad's video camera and taped her friend masturbating. Seymour loved it, so when Shane wrote him that she would be visiting L.A., he picked her up from the airport and they promptly moved in together. The Seymour and Shane series was born. They became the porn couple of the 90s. But all good things must come to an end. After a six-month break from the business, Shane decided that it was time to go out on her own."

The *Shane's World* series, also produced and directed by Shane herself (with her starring as well, in the first dozen or so volumes), came about because "she wanted something that would appeal to young people and to women, so she knew that the sex would have to be real ... Shot MTV style, she usually takes along a group of her friends on a trip and keeps a camera rolling the whole time. Also included are segments like 'Shane's Helpful Hints' that teach things like proper pussy eating techniques and how to manicure the pubes."

On porn gossip hound Luke Ford's site (*www.lukeford. com*), Shane was quoted from an interview in *Oui* magazine: "In *Playing With Fire*, I gave a fireman that was on duty a blowjob on the back of his fire truck. I was asking him for directions and I don't know how we got on the whole thing, but somehow all of that ended up happening. It was on *A Current Affair* and it was a big ordeal, especially back East. They were trying to sue us—the fire station—because it was a community-owned firehouse, and I didn't have permission from the community." I made a mental note to ask her about this, and some other less salutary facts from Luke's write-up—"Shane was molested in fifth grade by her stepfather. She dropped out of high school in her freshman year, lost her virginity to a man at age fifteen, and began modeling nude at age eighteen. She sent pictures of herself to various magazines and was surprised to get published. After a year of teaching gymnastics to preschoolers in Sacramento, she became a stripper at age nineteen. At age twenty-one, she did a woman ..."

Now, here's a trade secret I will now disclose: V.K., in assigning me the piece, made it clear that I would have to abide by one cardinal rule—in the world of *Penthouse* publications, porn stars are sex goddesses, with a sanctity that is inviolate. "If they have been sexually abused as children, we don't want to know. If they have drug problems, we don't want to know. If they have anything of questionable taste, we don't want to know. This applies particularly if the girls are *Penthouse* Pets. Bob believes his girls are angels." She said this last bit with a smirk, but made it clear that Bob Guccione's word was law. I was not to write about Shane's childhood molestation and her drug use (since marijuana use was rampant on porn sets, and certainly *de rigeur* on gonzo productions like *Shane's World*). Blah blah blah.

So I did the interview with Shane, and set the scene in as

romantic a way as I could without being too coy. Under the column head "*Cinema Blue*, by Drew McKenzie" ran this subhead (not written by me): "Our man inside the world of adult film chats with Shane, the sex star famous for the hit video series *Shane's World*. They discuss her exciting career as she bares all for our intrepid reporter."

Of course, she would be baring nothing, since I had interviewed her by email and wrote the entire piece while ensconced in a condominium in Robertson Quay, Singapore. (That was the real challenge, for me, but who really wanted to know that?)

Here then are the opening paragraphs of my Shane story, which ran in *Penthouse Variations*, December 1999, with bright cadences worthy of F. Scott Fitzgerald:

Her golden hair cascades down past her shoulders, the summer sun backlights it with a gossamer glow, and she looks every bit the all-American cheerleader you fantasized about. Today, her tank top and blue jeans, her preferred attire when she's clothed, fit her snugly and leave little doubt she's wearing nothing underneath.

"When I first started modeling, back when I was eighteen, I used to be very shy," she says, taking a slow drag on her cigarette. "The first photo shoot I ever did, the guy had to practically pry my clothes off. But the more I did it, the more comfortable I became with it. And the same is true for video. Now I love being naked."

We sit by a swimming pool in the backyard of her friend's house, located in the San Fernando Valley, which is the sprawling home of America's $23-billion-a-year porn industry. She sips her favorite drink, Captain Morgan spiced rum, and I tell her something my friend, the Swedish porn star Linda Thoren, recently said: "If you talk to her, tell her I am a big admirer of hers—the way she

181

does deep-throating is absolutely fantastic. When I look at her, I realize I still have a lot to learn."

"Yes, giving blowjobs is one of my all-time favorite things," the object of such ardor agrees. "There are some things you can do to deep-throat—like practice, practice, practice. Grab your partner and shove his cock down your throat, if you don't gag you're onto something." She pauses and grins. "Just kidding."

I'd gleaned her personal information directly from Jennie, who had told me: "Shane is definitely the Captain Morgan's-drinking, jeans and tank-top type girl. And she does smoke." She wrote this by email, dated June 7, 1999 (I even surfed the Captain Morgan website—*www.rum.com*—owned by Joseph E. Seagram and Sons, Inc, no less, to check on spellings, hence "spiced rum"). The rest, I culled from Internet and *AVN* research; it's really all out there if you know where to look. All you need is a dial-up line, a modem, and a printer.

And that's how I could write in the eventual piece about movies I never even saw, like *Shane's World 6: Slumber Party*, since I had read the review in which it was plainly stated that "Shane wears a 'Girls Rule' knit cap and surfer-boy clothes while zooming around on a go-cart and shopping for sex toys." And then "in *Shane's World 7*, she visited New Zealand and blew a surf-shop clerk. In *Shane's World 3*, she sucks off some roadies from Ministry, the porn-loving rock band known for the come-shot inspired *A Mind is a Terrible Thing to Taste.*" The Ministry tidbit actually came from my own rock-critic, trivia-addled brain. The key was to set the mood with some aptly descriptive details and then intersperse it with quotes that can both enhance the context and make a point.

For instance, when I took Shane back down memory lane, I wrote about her first Shane's World project: "The very first video, shot mostly in an RV careening out of control toward the

Mojave Desert, remains Shane's favorite." Then I followed it with an answer from Shane herself, from our email interview when I asked her to describe her favorite "close encounter" with a fan.

"In *Volume 1*, I went to visit a fan at his job and ended up giving him a blowjob in the elevator," she told me. "That's something that I really love to do, because they're not expecting it. And I know that it'll probably provide them with masturbation material for life!"

I followed that with her reasoning behind the series, in her own voice: "I just like to go out and try to find my own guys, rather than use the guys in the industry. It's not really too exciting for me to book a guy to come over and have sex with me. I'd rather go out and meet someone and tell them I want to give them a blowjob and for it to be in a video. It blows their minds." This was the kind of soundbite that fitted perfectly into the *Penthouse Variations* scheme of things, since it had the kinky edge our magazine prided itself on. I took the interview transcript and looked for things that had these elements, like the way I ended the piece:

> Then, in the spirit of openness, she divulges to me a secret. "Some of the biggest orgies happen in my personal life, when the cameras aren't rolling, when we have big parties at my house and things get crazy. I've never been into the whole gang-bang type thing. I like orgies better." ... She laughs as she climbs out of the pool and flexes her thighs, and I get that funny feeling again between mine. "This is how I like to look," she announces, as if I hadn't known. "It doesn't matter if it's for a photo shoot, video or just when I'm out having fun. When I am featuring, I actually prefer to dance at all-nude clubs." She caresses her light brown patch gently with her palm, parts those famous pink lips for me to see and flashes me that famous cheeky grin. "What a bummer, huh?" she demurs. "I wish I'd brought my video camera with me today."

I still remember typing those very words and then heading out to the corridor outside my condo, overlooking the swimming pool, to re-think that ending. I originally wanted the piece to end with Shane actually giving me a blowjob, but I decided that the piece would end beautifully right there. Brevity is the soul of wit. The reader could be left hanging, to wonder if anything more actually transpired between Shane and myself.

The bit about the video camera, I thought, was truly genius since it represented Shane's career choice, porn (which, of course, can't be done without cameras). I remember feeling quite exhilarated when I knew the piece was done, and felt certain that it was very good, that it didn't matter that the subject was Shane and, more importantly, that I hadn't even met her or even seen her films, but that I had crafted a narrative based entirely on both documented fact and actual quotes from the subject, and fashioned something that was readable and also sexually enticing.

On June 11, 1999, Jennie sent me an email: "I really liked the article. I thought you captured Shane perfectly. I'm glad you left out the blowjob, since she is a married woman now (ha ha)."

Wow, I thought, if only she knew! I've still never told her, to this very day; you can't tell a publicist, much less a company owner, that you wrote a whole piece without ever seeing any of her stuff. The key issue was that I was in Singapore at the time—I would move back to Los Angeles only that coming November -- and so had no access to her films, since all hardcore porn is officially banned in Singapore.

It was my way of beating the system. Honest subversion has its intangible rewards. And I've still never actually met Shane.

V.K., in an email on June 15, 1999, said: "Congratulations on the Shane interview! I do believe you have done it again. You have assembled a lot of data from Shane's actual story, and crafted it in such a way that it works for our magazine. And you have again created the illusion that you are sitting with the celebrity in her sophisticated domestic world, and we the *Variations* readers are eavesdropping on this fascinating situation. And our journalistic reporter, who has managed with his sex-industry jet-set connections to get himself in this situation, while a perfect gentleman, is nevertheless fully awake to the sexual possibilities of the situation ... What you have managed to accomplish for us without moving just amazes me."

I really liked "nevertheless fully awake to the sexual possibilities of the situation." It would set a standard for the months to come, as I crafted similar tales based on the lives of other porn stars, for my "Cinema Blue" column (Shane was followed by such luminaries as Silvia Saint, Shay Sweet, Jill Kelly, Nina Hartley, and Jenna Jameson; Shane, interestingly enough, remains the only one I have still never met in person). I also did long conceptual pieces, like one on the marriage of rock and porn, in which I interviewed Janine Lindemulder (on her part in appearing on Blink-182's CD cover, their hit album *Enema of the State*) and Dyanna Lauren (on her dual career as porn star and rock singer with her band Thousand Year Itch), and some other girls for their participation in a porn-and-rap album called *Deep Porn* with the likes of Kid Rock, Cypress Hill, and George Clinton.

One of the girls in that project was the Vivid contract girl Raylene, a dusky Mexican/Italian/Austrian/Polish beauty, whose very first video was *Shane's World 4: Wet & Wild*, all about horny hijinks on a houseboat, shot in November 1996, right after she'd turned eighteen. In it, Raylene is called Stacey (her real name) and she loses her porn cherry to Mark Davis, getting all giggly after giving him a long, lusty blowjob. "I feel like such a virgin!" she'd giggled, in jest. In the very next scene, she engaged in an enthusiastic lesbo-liaison with Anna Malle, an already outrageous siren who was then in her sexual prime; Anna later died in a car accident in Las Vegas in January 2006 and while I had a connection to her (because she had once been the publisher of *Fox*, a New York hardcore magazine I had written for), I'd never actually met her in person. But I certainly had long admired her skills, as seen in Asia Carrera's best film, *A is For Asia*, and too many gonzo flicks to name offhand. Gonzo was invented for women like Anna, who worked without a net and knew how to fog up the camera lens.

Many famous contract girls started out doing gonzo as a way of learning the ropes. A new contract girl like Krystal Steal, signed to Jenna Jameson's company Club Jenna in early 2005, will typically disclose in an *AVN* interview that "when I first started, I did about fifty gonzos, and I think, in my opinion, that's the best way to go for a new girl. Because that way you get your name out there and you get established, versus being a brand-new girl and getting a contract right away, people aren't going to know who you really are for a while."

Raylene, when I met her in person, a year after my Shane project, equally waxed nostalgic about her own entry via gonzo. Formerly a child actress at age five and later the manager at an L.A. Fitness health club before she became a stripper, she was refreshingly candid about her career. If not for Shane's World and her own youthful enthusiasm for swallowing Mark Davis's cum (as he shot his load right onto her waiting tongue, which she accepted with a huge smile), she might never have eventually become a Vivid girl and an A-list star.

"I met Shane when I was very young, way before I was eighteen, I wasn't even planning on doing movies," she recalled. "But I hung out with Shane and Mark Davis and his ex-girlfriend Yvonne, and decided I wanted to do movies. So I started with my first movie, *Shane's World 4*. If I hadn't signed with Vivid, I might've done more with them. I like doing gonzo, because it's really short and really spur-of-the-moment." She then told me a story of how she recently had sex with a total stranger, a deejay at a club, simply because she had always fantasized about having sex in a men's bathroom. "And so we went and did it, and I haven't spoken to him since," she giggled.

Art imitating life. Happens all the time in gonzo.

However, I'd asked Shane in our interview about being molested as a child, and all she would say was: "You know, that is something that I've gotten past. I like to live in the present, and I try to stay as positive about life as I can." (This quote was, of course, not used in the final draft of that *Penthouse Variations* interview.) Now married to Bobby Hewitt, the drummer of the heavy metal band Orgy, with whom she has two children, Shane still runs across her sets topless but no longer performs any actual sex acts, though in spirit she remained relentless. She told *AVN* reporter Acme Andersson that she recently had her fifth boob job ("I think I have the record for boob surgeries ... Small C's, then DD, then back to small C's, and then fixing and then fixing. I like to trade them in and get new models, just like I do my cars") and also talked about her new series, *Shane TV*: "It's reality porn. You know how I used to go out and blow people unsuspectingly on the street? I miss that the most. So I have Holly Hollywood, she's wearing an earpiece connected to the phone, and I kinda tell her what to do, what to say, who to grab. So I live vicariously through her.

"Like in *Volume 1*, we're driving on PCH (Pacific Coast Highway), saw a surfer, snagged his towel and then we did a U-turn and brought his towel back. Propositioned him. Got him in the back of the car and slurp, gave him a blowjob. I was so in shock. So was he."

Shock value lies at the heart of gonzo. In September 2003, I was in Los Angeles and spoke with Calli Cox, the star of one of my personal favorites, *Shane's World 29: Frat Row Scavenger Hunt 3*. "I feel that gonzo will continue to be the biggest, most watched category," she said. "Sexually speaking, I do think that gonzo is more my kind of thing. I appreciate the beauty of features and the time it takes to make one, but I think gonzo is the best. It's 'realer' sex to me than what you see in a feature." How on earth, I asked, did she learn to give such excellent handjobs and blowjobs? In true-blue gonzo style, she was seen masturbating and fellating young guys she had never met before, particularly college frat dudes who couldn't believe what was happening.

"Funny you should ask," she replied, grinning. "When I started in the business, I felt that I was terrible at oral. I wasn't really comfortable doing it because I didn't feel I did a good job at it. So when I first started, I asked some of the guys in the business who they liked getting HJs and BJs from. What was it that they liked from those girls? Then I watched those particular girls in action, whether on set or on film. I practiced a lot and became pretty good at it!"

Interestingly, at the time that we spoke, she had taken on a new position—as publicist and official spokesperson for Shane's World. A furor had just broken out—*Rolling Stone* magazine did an exposé of gonzo porn featuring Shane's World filming live footage on college campuses. I was in Los Angeles at the time but was due back in Singapore the following week, and only found out about it after I'd landed at Changi and bought a copy of that issue (*Rolling Stone*, September 18, 2003). I immediately emailed Calli, and she was amazed that people in Singapore could now read about her in *Rolling Stone*. (Proof positive, in my mind, that you can't prevent people from knowing about porn even in a country where porn is banned).

The piece discussed how Shane's World had helped bring gonzo into the mainstream, thanks to their latest video *Shane's World 32: College Invasion*, which caused the right-wing television host Bill O'Reilly to admonish this "dorm porn" in his Fox News Channel show, *The O'Reilly Factor*. (O'Reilly alleged that the school in question knew of the shoot but did nothing to stop it.)

The *Rolling Stone* story also carried a sidebar about the woes of one Brian Buck, a student from Arizona State University, who had appeared in *Shane's World 29: Frat Row Scavenger Hunt*. "When footage surfaced of Buck cavorting with two Shane's World pros, the twenty-two year old was expelled from his fraternity, barred from ASU housing and employment, placed on permanent probation and forced to write a twenty-page essay, (entitled "Reflections on Integrity"), complete 100 hours of community service, and resign his post as student-body vice-president. Worse yet, his parents have refused to pay his tuition, and he was offered a measly US$500 from Shane's World for his troubles."

That amount was what the company offered him as

compensation for his unforeseen pain, but he rejected it and insisted that Shane Enterprises pay for his three years of law school. "He got greedy," said Calli, in the *Rolling Stone* story, which also mentioned the company told Buck to "go pound sand."

Buck was then quoted as being in some distress: "I wish I could have my anonymity back ... For years I will have problems, because of a two-minute mistake." But Calli, of course, saw it as a publicity windfall. "The feedback from the article has been pretty positive," she told me. "We received a lot of calls and emails from people who felt that the article was unfair and misrepresented us. We have also gotten a lot of praise from the industry in general for having a four-page article in *Rolling Stone*. I think that overall this mainstream coverage is positive." She defended the gonzo genre from the naysayers, insisting that it's not merely a cheap way to generate massive turnover, even as the industry sales and rental figures showed huge surges in the popularity of gonzos, wall-to-wall and compilation tapes as opposed to the more plot-heavy features.

"Reality porn tends to take a little longer to shoot because a lot of the time it *is* spontaneous, you have to get the right reaction from someone," she told me. "It takes more time because there is more to shoot than just sex. Some performers aren't into this. They simply want to get in and get out. It definitely takes the right cast to shoot a good reality film." Earlier that year, Jennie Grant had told me about the elation they'd all felt at the *AVN* Awards ceremony. "It's funny because I knew winning would feel good, but I didn't know that it would feel THAT good! You should have seen us at the awards show, our table was out of control!!! Plus Calli gave an awesome speech."

Jennie added that she remembered talking to Tricia Devereaux (ex-porn star and wife of famed gonzo director John Stagliano) at the show and congratulating her on the new feature film, *The Fashionistas*, which Tricia co-produced and which had won a staggering ten awards that night. "She said the best thing—she said that 'people always say, oh, they're just porno awards.

But this is our life. If we disregard the award, then we're really disregarding our lives.' I thought that was really cool, since we, Shane's World, put a lot of effort into our company and I know that they do too."

The first eighteen volumes of *Shane's World* were released on DVD in early 2001, and by 2005 the company was investigating transferring all its movies onto the new-fangled contraptions of hand-held mobile technology. Life was good. Neither Jennie nor her husband Brian had ever worked in the adult entertainment industry before they acquired Shane Enterprises, having done mostly documentary films. They simply viewed porn as merely an extension of the same. Gonzo, to some extent, is a quasi-documentary format since it utilizes *camera verite* techniques, unlike features or even "wall-to-wall" porn, where you can catch the cameras panning and zooming, with cutaways for overhead crane shots, and the like.

The closest that gonzo approximated any of that was when the cameraman zoomed in for a close-up of genitalia and then captured the insertion shot and then the obligatory pop shot. "I have a theory that most male porn fans are possibly bisexual or at least bi-curious," Jennie once told me. "Otherwise, why do we always show the guy coming on the girl's face? Why is the pop shot so important?"

Those were valid points. But I also like the fact that gonzo was porn with a sense of humor, particularly when it satirized social conventions. Billy Glide, in the Shane's World off-shoot flick *Pornological 1*, can be seen cooking pasta and talking about how he has to make his girl dinner first in order to warm her up: "You can't just bring them in here, pop on a porno and fuck, you got to go through all the bullshit, bring them dinner, give them some wine, hopefully get them a little tipsy, put in a romantic movie. You might hate it but they'll love it, they'll cry, they'll hold you, and then you're gonna get some. A little bullshit before you get some."

Of course, Billy did get some, with the lovely Claudia Chase, though the scene felt a bit staged. "So, are you horny now?" he asked her, right after she'd just started eating her dinner and complimented him on his pasta—which we all know doesn't ever happen in real life. Claudia made a face, which only underscored the irony. Gonzo humor can be a little too cute for its own good. (Billy and Claudia, of course, cut to sex fairly quickly after dinner—in fact, the dinner pretty much ended right there!—and Claudia talked and giggled too much during the sex, hinting that she'd definitely done Billy before.)

And so we suspend our disbelief, heave a collective sigh, and reflect on our own personal *après-dinner* sex moments. That's the social value of porn, aside from how it gives spanking material to those guys for whom their own past sexual memories can never be evocative enough.

However, one afternoon, I was on yet another set with Kelly Holland, an episode of *Naked Hollywood*, her *Sex & the City* porn-spoof series (winner of the "Best Continuing Video Series" at the 2003 *AVN* Awards), and a bunch of us began a discussion during a shooting break about the limits of permissible porn. Kelly had directed for Vivid for seven years, under the pseudonym Toni English, and she was talking about the gonzo director Max Hardcore, who specialized in testing the limits of acceptability.

I had told her Jill Kelly had recently disclosed to me some edits she had to make to some of her recent films—"Chloe likes to be choked while she's coming, but for cable we had to cut that," Jill said. (Why? In case some folks decided to literally die trying in the privacy of their hotel rooms?) Kelly said one of her favorite things in porn was to have the guy pull out just as he's about to ejaculate and then grab his own cock and spray all over the girl, from every angle and in every direction. "Now, I like that," she said, "but it may not be something everybody will want to see."

"But Max Hardcore will have a girl put an air tube in her mouth, like a straw," she told us, "and insert the other end into her own ass. Max will piss in it and make the sure his urine goes up the tube so she will be drinking it. Now, where do you draw the line with that?

"And why does it happen? It happens because there's always going to be a girl who thinks that US$800 is a lot of money."

The industry term is "scab labor" and such girls are prevalent in the wacky world of gonzo. Exploitation sadly exists, like in any industry, the only difference being that we all make choices based on our economic needs and some just make the wrong ones. Not morally wrong, but economically wrong. Not many of Max Hardcore's girls end up on the adult-biz A-list; most of them end up as hookers in the Nevada desert, if they're lucky to get any work at all, like the gangbang girls who were the bottom-feeders of the porn totem pole, parallel to soap stars in television who never ascended to the big screen and were viewed with a mixture of condescension and pity. It ain't pretty but it's the truth.

In any case, it can seem strange today to look back at Shane's World circa 1996 and realize how her little travelogues, with porn stars reading maps and boarding planes, actually predated current mainstream reality fodder like *The Amazing Race*. One of my all-time favorite scenes in porn featured the blond, bodacious Johnni Black sucking off three guys in the open air, on the houseboat in *Shane's World 4*, shot ten years ago, and it seemed so innocent compared to today's harder-edged gonzo fare.

Because everyone's hellbent now on pushing the envelope, on seeing how far we can go. The production company Elegant Angel, in February 2004, filmed *Gangbang Anals* (the sequel to *Gangbang Angels*): one girl, five guys, all anal. Anarchy Films released "100% Anal, ATM, 120 minutes" flicks ("ATM" is "ass to mouth," any explanation needed?) and there are "all-swallowing gonzos" like Erin Sky's *No Cum Spitting*, shot for Anarchy's Python Pictures, where the girls can be seen swallowing every last lovin' drop.

And then, there's the hardest of the hard edge, like porn's super-nasty gonzo girl Ariana Jollee, who specializes in taking all comers even down to the double-anal (though she won't do the equally scary "double-vag," because, unlike some girls, her vagina is unable to accomodate more than one penis at a time). In May 2005, Jollee, a twenty-one-year-old native of Long Island, New York, journeyed to Prague to star in *50-Man Creampie*, for Devil's Films, in which she had sex with sixty-four Czech men in an exhausting six-hour shoot. "The wronger, the better" was her personal motto. Her work done for the weekend, Jollee then told the *AVN* reporter in Prague that she was booked to do a seven-man gangbang on Monday back in the United States.

However, folks, you ain't seen nothin' till you've seen *Devinn Lane's Guide to Strap-on Sex*, released in April 2006, in which gonzo superstud Kurt Lockwood (last seen in this book in chapter three, "Plot? What Plot?") cheerfully bent over for his first-ever, on-camera strap-on scene—in which two girls, Samantha Ryan and Sandra Romain, took turns banging him up the butt chute. It was produced by none other than Shane's World. "We knew a lot of fans were looking forward to seeing us take the leap into the strap-on niche," quipped the producer, my pal Jennie Grant herself, in an *AVN* news report of April 10, 2006. (Another girl who had worked with Lockwood told me he had been paid a truly obscene amount, something in the five figures, for that scene alone; "I think it's disgusting," she sneered, but didn't explain whether she meant the strap-on method or the massive fee.)

I remember being on the set of a Nic Cramer movie, *Skin Deep*, in which Silvia Saint played an escort agency madam; her dialogue was very much secondary to the sex, limited mostly to picking up the phone to take orders for her girls. But this was a feature film, not a gonzo, so why did I remember being on the *Skin Deep* set? It remained burned into my brain because of one particular scene—between Gina Ryder and Eric Price. I got to see the real spirit of gonzo sex first-hand.

We were on a balcony of a massively impressive house in Bel-Air, shooting Gina going down on Eric like her life depended on it, just as the sun was setting. Nic and his long-time cinematographer Jack Remy called for a break, and they both strolled off to huddle at the far end of the balcony, pointing frantically to the sky. They were trying to determine exactly when the sun was really going to set—so as not to "miss the light," as they say in filmmaking, as the twilight "magic hour" descended. This would never have happened in a real gonzo film, which always eschewed continuity in favor of spontaneity, and I admired them for paying such attention to cinematic detail.

But they were missing out on the real action: Gina and Eric didn't give a damn about the light and they continued their interplay, rutting furiously even with the camera shut off.

"Hey guys," I thought, "you're missing the sex!" Meaning I was the only one who saw them do it, with Gina flushing red from a real orgasm. Naturally, when they decided to resume shooting, she carried on like nothing had happened, and finally took a huge load of Eric's come on her face. "That was really good," I told her later, after she'd washed off and changed into her Gap civilian clothes. White t-shirt, blue jeans. She smiled, thanked me, and grinned, like any working actress savoring a compliment.

I don't think she even realized I was the only one who had seen the unshot scene. And I don't think it mattered. Great sex, even on a movie set, was about losing yourself to the moment, and I'm sure she knew that too. She felt herself coming, and didn't care where she was. How lovely, I thought, when I watched her shudder and quake. Her eyes were both closed during the entire time the cameras were down.

A Dream Called Janine

In the wake of Jenna Jameson's bestselling memoir, evidence abounded that porn had gone mainstream, acquiring the perverse glamour of a pseudo-sport like professional wrestling. Sure, real sports fans deemed the WWF silly, maybe even downright stupid, but what was wrong with that? Silly and stupid was the whole point, after all.

I knew so, because I had been a foot soldier in the cultural endeavour. People were suddenly asking me what I thought of the hoopla surrounding the 35mm release of *Inside Deep Throat*, the 2005 documentary about a legendary porn film that cultural historians now viewed as a watershed event of the 70s and a barometer of social change. Why, it was even shown in Singapore, a country where hardcore pornography remained illegal, under the guise of a truthful documentary worthy of social scrutiny. When I published my most recent book, *Idol to Icon: The Creation of Celebrity Brands*, which tackled the very subject of major-league stardom, many journalists in Singapore were tickled when I told them: "Don't you think it's ironic that Singapore has produced only one international celebrity—Annabel Chong, who happens to be a porn star?"

They all laughed like it was the funniest thing they'd ever heard. What was interesting was that not one person stopped to ask me who Annabel Chong was. They all knew. And not one person stopped to ask if she was still actively involved in the business, because even if she wasn't (and she indeed wasn't), that was besides the point. Thanks to one infamous gangbang video, followed by one equally infamous documentary film made because of the notoriety caused by it, she had become a household name.

In some households, I wondered, did anyone remember Amber Waves? She was the porn star protagonist of the film *Boogie Nights*, played by Julianne Moore, whose brilliant personification of a woman tormented by her calling caught most people by the lump of their throats. Moore spoke about this role when she appeared on television's *Inside the Actor's Studio*; she recalled going to some porn shoots in order to research the role. "The thing I learned," she said, "was that it's positional, not emotional."

Had anyone said anything more profound about porn than that? I think not.

It was the very starting block from which any kind of serious discussion could even take place. The ongoing success of the adult entertainment industry was predicated on one basic premise: people were willing to buy the sizzle, if not the steak, and there were good reasons why so many strippers wanted to be porn stars. Fame was like a beacon lighting up the chrome-pole night, even if many brave exhibitionists were called but few eventually chosen.

I personally met that paradigm head-on when I was assigned to write a feature about the strange confluence of porn stars and rock stars ("Porn Star Rock," by Drew McKenzie and Jamie Selzer, *Penthouse Variations*, February 2001), which enabled me to indulge in a private thrill: I got to interview Janine Lindemulder, about her role best known to the public at large—as the cover girl on the 1999 hit album *Enema of the State* by the band Blink-182, in which she was dressed as a kinky nurse, wearing a sneer and a latex glove, ready for a rectal examination. Janine also appeared in the Blink-182 video for their song "What's My Age Again?" which prompted mainstream attention, thanks to the album selling three million copies.

The mainstream press suddenly wanted to talk to her, but I wasn't just hopping on the bandwagon. It was a huge kick for me because Janine was one of the first women whose onscreen presence (most notably in Andrew Blake's classic film *Hidden Obsessions*) had inspired me to take a real interest in porn. She was the all-American blonde cheerleader who took the genre several steps farther than Debbie had done Dallas. The fact that she had been one of the most popular *Penthouse* Pets gave me direct access to her, thanks to some in-house help from our Pet Promotions department, and so they gave me her number and I simply called her at home.

She lived in La Mirada, a nondescript Southern California hamlet adjacent to Orange Country—not quite the place where porn stars were known to thrive, but such anonymity was naturally a blessing and not at all a curse—and she readily agreed to do the interview. She'd talked about Blink-182 to countless journalists already, but this was special. We were both part of the *Penthouse* family, so she knew I was already in her corner and wasn't going to do a puff piece to merely help hawk the album. It was going to dig deeper, and serve to reexamine her celebrity status, from the inside looking out.

"I did not know the guys in the band," she told me. "I just got a phone call from Vivid one afternoon saying that the project had come about. I was a little hesitant, because I didn't understand it. I think I remember seeing a lot of girls on record covers during the 80s so it seemed like a throwback to an 80s-type gimmick thing.

"But then, when I heard the music and then my son said he was a big Blink-182 fan, I agreed to do it. So, of course, now I'm the coolest mom on the block! Kids come up and want me to sign their CDs, and I get the biggest kick out of that. It has turned out to be one of the biggest highlights of my career."

The album cover idea was midwifed by Vivid's then-publicist Brian Gross, whom I'd known at his previous job; he's been a publicist at Elektra Records, and so used his record company expertise to full advantage. "Fans of Janine want to have everything she does," Gross explained, on VH-1's *Rankin File* show. "When they see her on the cover of a record, they have to have it." Janine's newfound mainstream fame drove a stake into the heart of conservative America and helped pave the way for the casual acceptance of porn today. "Blink-182 made it possible for younger fans to make the connection," Janine told me. "People do look at porn differently now, and I think it has become less taboo."

Or, as Annabel Chong herself told me, "Janine Lindemulder is the new Jimi Hendrix, and porn is the new rock & roll."

It many ways, it was the apex of a trajectory that had begun a long time ago, and it signaled how public knowledge of porn had trickled down through the years. Janine, to begin with, had the right look. She was a brown-eyed blonde born in 1968, all of five feet eight inches and 128 pounds, and a photo-friendly 35-24-36. As a departure from the norm, Janine Lindemulder was actually her real name (she is Dutch-American). While working as a stripper on the bachelor party circuit, she'd posed for *Penthouse* and become the December 1987 Pet of the Month centerfold, which led to her appearing in several *Penthouse* videos—somewhat cheesy, softcore titles like *Ready to Ride* and *Women In and Out of Uniform*, and the Andrew Blake-directed *Satin and Lace*.

With Blake came the vital, fateful connection; in August 1992, she worked with him again on his classic film, *Hidden Obsessions*, which received rave reviews for one particular scene, still talked about to this very day. It starred a winsome threesome: Janine, her regular girl-girl partner Julia Ann, and a dildo made of ice.

"Howard Stern called it Frosty the Penis," Blake had told me, chuckling. "Janine was very business-like and very professional. I picked her because she's very attractive. It's too bad we weren't able to connect more, but that's the way it was." Janine confirmed to me that theirs was an enjoyable relationship, though they certainly went their separate ways after shooting. She told me she was grateful to Blake for helping her get started.

"Well, she did a lot for me too," Blake quipped. It was an

understatement, since *Hidden Obsessions* instantly became a porn classic and got his own career rolling. It won three notable *AVN* Awards, for "Best Cinematography," "1992's Best Selling Tape," and, for that ice dildo sequence, the "Best All-Girl Sex Scene." Janine, additionally, won "Best Actress" at the *Hot D'Or* awards in Cannes. As a direct result of the huge success of *Hidden Obsessions*, Vivid signed her to a contract.

She then teamed up with Julia Ann to dance on the road as a duo, known as Blondage, wreaking havoc in strip clubs across America. They dripped hot wax on each other and performed acts deftly skirting the fine line between permissible raunch and the other kind (the one that gets performers thrown out of clubs). One of their rowdier sequences saw Janine grabbing Julia Ann's hair and dragging her around the floor on all fours. The famous ice dildo scene was immortalized again on video by director Toni English in *Blondage: The Movie*. "The thrill of the cold when we take turns rubbing and probing one another with it is incredible," Janine reminisced in *Club magazine*. "I love the feel of it melting all over our bodies, and using the frozen cock to drip droplets of water onto Julia Ann's pussy, that I naturally just have to lap it up."

However, in March 1998, she came to mainstream attention in a way she hadn't intended. A home video of her having sex with Vince Neil, the lead singer of the band Motley Crue, began circulating on the Internet and then made its way into video stores. *Janine and Vince Neil: Hardcore and Uncensored*, made the news in the footsteps of the more famous Pamela Anderson/Tommy Lee home video. It had been shot while she was vacationing in Hawaii with Neil, and no one claimed responsibility for the leak.

"I don't mind talking about it," she said, after I'd gingerly brought up the subject. This was July 2000, two years later, and she'd come to terms with it. "While it all went down, I was very hurt and bitter. It did come as a shock. I had forgotten about that video. When we walked away from that whole Hawaii vacation, I didn't think twice that that would ever get out and about.

"And it sure did. I'm not one to hold grudges. It was what it was and, at this point, it hasn't affected my life in such a horrible, negative way. It's really no big deal. The only thing is that I feel like I was a little betrayed. It's very possible that Vince is innocent in this whole thing too. There was a time when I was sure he was the one that put it out. But I don't have proof of that. I don't know who did it, or how it got out. I sure would like to know."

The sex itself she had no problems with. "It was a fantastic vacation. People ask who was behind the camera and, most of the time, it was me. Unless I propped it up on the dresser or something. It was myself and one of my best girlfriends and Vince. And Vince can be a real party animal. It was an experience that I look back on fondly. Just like you see in the video, it was fun."

Well, it did set the stage for a certain hotel heiress to claim her fame ticket (The now better-known Paris Hilton home video actually won the "Best Selling DVD" trophy at the 2005 *AVN* Awards). And, more relevent to porn fans, it busted the Janine Lindemulder mythology—for not having sex with men onscreen. I personally liked her for the way she sensually dominated women onscreen and had always accepted that as part of her "branding," but Janine later explained that she was then married to a jealous husband who had insisted on her performing with girls only.

They finally divorced after eight years, and she then married again in 2002—another tragic mistake, this time to the famous custom motorcycle builder Jesse James (who, in 2005, married the squeaky-clean Hollywood actress Sandra Bullock!)—and it was a turn of events that precipitated her new decision to emerge from yet another "retirement" phase with fresh resolve: she would have sex with men on-camera for the first time, starting with the film *Maneater* in 2004, and then the big-budget *Emperor* in 2005. The latter paired her with the Italian male star Rocco Siffredi, in his last role before retiring after eighteen years as a working stud. (The production, shot in Los Angeles and Budapest, did not go well for the two, who fought over Siffredi's refusal to use a condom and Janine's ensuing refusal to do scenes with him.)

However, of all the things I had talked to Janine about in the course of our long interview, two things stood out.

The first was when I asked about her well-known association with rock musicians. The Vince Neil connection was an obvious set-up, the cynics might have postulated, since she had appeared previously in a Motley Crue video. "I've definitely been with my share of musicians," she told me. "But I can't name names. I'm pretty modest when it comes to that stuff. I'm not a kiss-and-tell type of person.

"For a good portion of my twenties, I was a little wild one and I've been on my share of tour buses. But I've never really acted anything out in a gnarly-slut way. It's not fulfilling for me. I've had my *menage a trois* and stuff like that, but they were very spiritual, in a way. I'm not one to get wasted and go do something really gnarly and nasty and forget about it. For me, personally, that would really take a toll on my heart and head."

And that was basically all she'd say about that. I got no good rock groupie stories out of her. Damn. But the second thing I recalled with exceptional fondness from the interview was even better. I did get her to confess to a secret sexual fetish.

It started with my asking her about the nurse uniform idea, the way she appeared in the Blink-182 album package. "That was their thing," she replied. "I think originally I was supposed to be a teacher. They called me and they asked me to dress like a sexy school teacher. Kind of ironic, being that I want to be a teacher. But once I got there for the shoot, they informed me that they wanted me to be a nurse. It was kinky, and fun, for me."

So did she have any sexual fantasies involving the medical profession? "I think I've talked about it more than I've actually lived it out, though it has been a topic of sexual conversation, that's for sure," she admitted. "I do start to sweat every time I go into the gynaecologist." She stopped, and started giggling. "In a good way."

I asked her to explain.

She started blushing.

"Oh my gosh, now you're making me blush! It's just—I must be getting too old because now I blush real easy. I don't know, it's just one of those things—"

She paused again, and I tried to help.

"You mean, like fantasies of being strapped down, onto chairs maybe?"

"A dentist's chair, or anything to do with dental or doctors, I think." She kept giggling, and blushing even more. "I think it's all right up my alley." She disssolved into another giggling fit, and stopped me when I started to get into gynaecological descriptions based on what I'd seen of her own lovely anatomy. "Have mercy!" she cried.

Me, make a porn star blush? That was certainly a first.

Even famous sex workers, I realized, had their deeply held personal demons, usually kept from public scrutiny. And how little her adoring public actually knew.

Janine had actually made inroads into mainstream fame a couple of years back. *GQ* magazine in its August 1997 issue had done a feature on her entitled, "The Sex Worker Next Door." It described her as a "golly-gosh-darn-it Breck girl, a honey-haired, high-cheekboned native Californian who'd look as natural wearing a Laura Ashley sundress and running through a field of high corn as she does with a fifteen-inch dildo, sodomizing one of her pals on a pool table."

That interview was a companion piece to a larger article, "The Porning of America" by GQ senior writer Lucy Kaylin, about porn as a hip-and-happening genre. Jenna Jameson was then only two years in the business (and a whole seven years before her bestselling book) and Janine was already a trailblazer.

Kaylin concluded that "porn is a $10 billion industry deeply embedded in American life" and "a large part of porn's move to the mainstream has involved the prettying up of this historically lurid form of entertainment ... To that end, porn-video companies are strategically marketing their products to better-heeled yuppie couples (an approach that seems to be working: according to

Adult Video News, 665 million hardcore movies were rented last year—up from 75 million a decade before). Vivid Video, for instance, hired an art director and a publicist from outside the business to give the company and its products a 'classier' look. It's also signing porn actresses to exclusive contracts and hooking them up with corporate sponsors ... The plan is to humanize the actresses, make them seem more like happy, responsible stars, as opposed to the drug-addicted meat they were treated as back in porn's outlaw adolescence."

Janine seemed very humanized indeed, and always looked happy. Her biggest contribution to modern pop culture, in my own assessment, lay in enabling the world to see the sparkling visage of the Vivid Girl. Even *The Economist* devoted an article to Vivid (in its August 14, 1999 issue, cleverly entitled "Branded Flesh") which noted that "Vivid Girls command a premium on the stripping circuit, earning anywhere between $5,000 and $20,000 a week ... Every porn girl harbors a secret dream of crossing into the mainstream world; her chances of doing so, though pretty small, are probably higher with Vivid than anywhere else."

I remember the very first time I walked into the offices of Vivid Video. There were no naked women banging away in rooms or corridors, and nothing of the sort that some people outside the business might imagine. No, Vivid reminded me of the corporate offices of *Playboy* and *Penthouse*, both of which I'd already spent much time in, only actually more mundane. Vivid then housed itself in a nondescript red-brick building on a quiet residential street in Van Nuys, a distinctly middle-to-lower class suburb of the San Fernando Valley, so discreetly tucked away that I got lost looking for it the first time.

I even remember the first time I sat in the office of Brad Hirsch, the company's then Director of Marketing (and the younger brother of Vivid boss Steven Hirsch). He had a huge Black Sabbath poster on the wall and hardly anything on his desk except a small stack of work files. No video tapes, no sex toys, nothing even remotely close to controversial. This was just a business like any other business. He spent most of the meeting telling me of his passion for Ozzy Osbourne and Black Sabbath, and we talked about the new projects of the Vivid Girls only at the end of our discussion.

I did run into Micah Levenson, the Operations Manager for Vivid Interactive (overseeing cable, satellite, pay TV, as well as laserdisc, CD-ROM, DVD, and MPEG-compatible media), as he was watching and fast-forwarding through some newly filmed footage, in preparation for a presentation; a lurid errand for some civilians, perhaps, but for him just another day at the office.

Their hard work must have paid off. By 2005, one could buy Vivid condoms with the seductive charms of Vivid Girls like Briana Banks on the box cover (promising "wider shape and longer length for easier fit" and "lubricated for extra comfort"). And for women into porn stars, there was a line of Vivid Girls cosmetics, distributed to salons and boutiques across America, available online (*www.vividgirl-cosmetics.com*). The cosmetics division was headed by Tonia Ryan, a former Lancome executive who had worked "with top chemists to create proprietary formulas for a range of 'luxury lipsticks,' 'super glosses,' blushers, eye products, air brush foundation kits and a variety of other items" (as reported in *AVN*, April 2005). The Vivid girls all made personal appearances to help support such products.

Naturally, they also did so for the Vivid Herbal Supplement line of male and female sexual virility products, with reportedly an upsurge (so to speak) in sales in Asian markets (notably Japan, Hong Kong, Taiwan, and China). Now, how apropos was that? However, the folks in those places weren't as lucky as those in Anaheim, California, where Vivid Girls Monique Alexander and Lexie Marie met with fans at the Natural Products Expo West. The target customers were males aged thirty-five to sevety, a perfect demographic and the same one that Vivid sought when it signed, in June 2005, a licensing deal with MZL LLC of Miami— to market a line of high-end, light-alloy Vivid Wheels, for use on SUVs, pick-up trucks and even luxury cars. The tyres all featured the company's newly designed Vivid "V" logo, available from September 2005 in two designs and in 20-inch, 22-inch, and 24-inch rims.

At the end of 1998, thirty percent of Vivid's total revenue of US$25 million came from DVD and other interactive media (as reported in "Vivid Imagination," yet another piece on the company in *The Economist*, November 21, 1998). It was already releasing 150 new titles a year, though often these were different versions of the same movie (hardcore for video, softcore for cable, penetration without anal or close-ups for hotels, and multi-angle DVDs shot on four cameras—offering angle-switching choices for the more discerning porn fan).

The Vivid Girl concept itself was first introduced in 1984, to impart a sense of glamour to the business (not unlike what 20th Century Fox had done when it famously signed Marilyn Monroe), and the first batch of Vivid Girls from that period—Ginger Lynn, Tori Welles, Hyapatia Lee, Jamie Summers, Julianne James, Nikki Charm, Nikki Randall, and Barbara Dare—were the very first girls I ever saw myself on video. But it was the next batch, from 1988 to 1991—Ashlyn Gere, Deirdre Holland, Racquel Darrian, Janine Lindemulder, Christy Canyon, Heather Hunter, Jennifer Stewart and the incomparable Savannah—who caught my attention.

Truthfully, I wouldn't even be writing this book if I hadn't sat down one night in 1993 with my then girlfriend to watch Ashlyn Gere in Andrew Blake's *Secrets*, even though that wasn't a Vivid film (since the luscious Miss Gere had already left the company). I was completely captivated by her opening scene with Rocco Siffredi. However, by the time the next Vivid Girl class of 1992 to 1995 took over—Asia Carrera, Nikki Dial, Chasey Lain, Dyanna Lauren, Nikki Tyler, Lene Hefner, Celeste, and Jenteal—I had been formally introduced to the industry and realized that the bravest kind of celebrity was that of the porn star. Talk about putting oneself out there, literally, for the scrutiny of millions. But, most of all, I liked the self-effacing humor these girls had. They clearly loved sex but also had the good sense not to take it too seriously.

And my all-time favorite porn wisecrack was uttered by Janine Lindemulder. Asked to explain why she finally decided to forgo her girls-only policy and started having sex with men onscreen, she quipped: "In high school, instead of Janine Lindemulder, my nickname was Janine Weenieholder. And now it all comes together."

I really liked her assertive sassiness, and I was never once surprised when girls new to the industry would tell me that she was the one who had inspired them to do it. (This included some who, unabashedly, admitted to me that they did so in hopes that they would someday have sex with Janine.) She had a mystique beyond words. Two of my favorite films of hers actually emphasized her acting ability: Ralph Parfait's *The Cult,* made in 1999, in which she played the high priestess of a quasi-spiritual sex cult, and Toni English's wry tone poem, *Girl Next Door,* made in 1997 but released in 2001, in which Janine played a car mechanic with a penchant for spontaneous sex, eventually stealing a curvaceous customer (played by the luscious Tia Bella) away from her uncouth boyfriend and rendering new meaning to the automotive term "body shop."

Ah, Janine, what a dream. I never got to check under her hood, certainly not in the literal sense, and I should be satisfied with the fact that I once made her blush.

I kept in touch with her sporadically, once calling her on her cellphone while she was shopping at a supermarket in Sherman Oaks (she'd sold her house in La Mirada and moved), and then met her again some months later, at the 2001 *AVN* Awards.

I was stunned. She had jet-black hair and many new tattoos, including a garish series of flowers and butterflies covering her entire right arm. The sunny blonde cheerleader I once knew had apparently moved on. I had once adored her, but only from afar, and it had been only one version of her. Metamorphosis was a characteristic of the porn star, and I had forgotten that. No longer a Vivid Girl, Janine was now lost to me in the fog of memory.

She would later go on to win the "Best Actress" trophy at the 2006 *AVN* Awards, at the age of 37, a rare achievement in an industry that prized youth beyond reason. But the woman I once knew, or thought I knew, was already gone.

Contractual Obligations

By the time the Vivid Girls of 1996 to 1999 came around—Julia Ann, Kobe Tai, Taylor Hayes, Kira Kener, Lexus Locklear, Raylene, Devon, and Veronica—I was utterly intrigued by the business, and had already begun my own incursion into the adult entertainment ranks. To me, being a porn star was the furthest-out anyone could go in terms of being a celebrity, and I wanted to know everything.

Like, what's a contract girl got to do to stay one? What happens when contracts get broken? Why was it that some girls don't get re-signed? And what's in that damn contract anyway? In general, nobody had a straight answer for that last question. Different companies offered different contracts, and much depended on the girl in question. And on how questionable the contract itself was.

Jenna Jameson, in her autobiography *How to Make Love Like a Porn Star*, actually provided a sample contract for the reader's perusal, stating in an opening caveat that "like most contracts, it is still biased heavily in favor of the production company. If you take the time to read it carefully, you will notice the many ways in which a female performer can get shafted—both literally and metaphorically. When signing a contract, most girls don't add in their own demands."

She learned the hard way herself, given her own less than amicable parting with Wicked Pictures. But the terms of her sample contract provided a useful case study. The document was always an agreement by "the Company" and "the Talent" for a certain duration of time, usually twelve months, with four options of one year each that the company may decide to exercise. It must give "the Talent" sixty days prior notice in writing stating so. The gist of the deal itself was simple and direct: "The Talent will be required to act, play, perform, and take part in rehearsals, acts, roles, and scenes of a sexual hard-core nature over the duration of the contract" and the "scenes may be in the form of any of the following combination (at the discretion of the Company): Girl/Girl, Girl/Girl/Girl, Boy/Girl, and Multiples." Additionally, "involvement in any scenes involving Anal, Interracial, and DP (Double Penetration) is at the sole discretion of the Talent." But the company decided on the number of feature films the girl should star in, usually six a year but it "may increase this number based on marketing." And at least six video/DVD box covers as well; in the United States, box covers were usually shot separately, and the girl on the cover earned extra money.

The girl was expected to work exclusively for "the Company, unless otherwise agreed to in writing by the Company." Any other work done outside, including "dancing (feature or otherwise), bachelor parties, and any and all other services in the entertainment industry must be approved in writing in advance by the Company, not to be unreasonably withheld."

The girl also agreed to "take diligent care of her health, weight, and appearance" and "shall refrain from drug or alcohol abuse and prostitution (including legal prostitution)" and also refrained from anything that could bring her employer "into public disrepute, contempt, scandal or ridicule, or that shocks, insults or offends the community, or that may reflect unfavorably upon the Company." If so, punitive measures would ensue, usually the suspension of residual income, and this often gave the employer room to declare a default of the contract.

Beyond all that, things got complicated. For instance, compensation was agreed upon, but with a "Schedule A" appended for "Additional Compensation" which typically included things like "Same Sex Anal Intercourse (excluding d.p. and Air Tight): US$125 per scene; Opposite Sex Anal Intercourse (excluding DP and Air Tight): US$250 per scene; Opposite Sex Double Penetration (excluding Air Tight): US$400 per scene; Air Tight (three males with three simultaneous penetrations): US$650 per scene; Multiple Partners: US$250 per partner over three."

The Air Tight element, if included in the contract, usually reflected the company owner's insecurity, a deep-seated need to cover his own ass (pardon the mixed metaphors). Most productions never shot such scenes. I'd been to a lot of them, and had never ever seen one. (They shoot them in Europe, though.)

In general, the average income of a porn star in the United States was US$80,000, but some contract girls made only half of that. Vivid, for instance, had often offered a contract girl US$39,000 a year with the assurance of an easier shooting schedule and, as an upside, a longer career. Dancing at the clubs, however, was almost an imperative. A stripper on the circuit armed with a porn company contract immediately raised her rates. The clubs in turn partook of the Vivid promotional machine too, since more patrons would be lured in by the famous names on the marquee.

The girls, in general, did this for one overarching reason— they needed the protective sheen of a self-esteem boost, created by enhanced value. A Vivid Girl was viewed as a glamorous girl, because she was with a glamorous company. Marketers called this "brand parity" and it was a desperately valuable commodity; most girls entered the business to overcome shyness or self-image problems often linked with childhood abuse or parental neglect. The companies, of course, knew this and worked to exploit it, resulting in the current system. It always worked in their favor, because unlike performers in the mainstream film and music businesses, adult stars usually worked for flat fees, earning no royalties or residuals from their movies.

Was this a fair system? Well, like any contractual bond, that depended on whatever the upside was—to the girl signing the contract. "Getting the contract with Vivid helped me a lot, by slowing me down and not having to work as much," Vivid Girl Raylene told me, when I met her to talk about this in February 2000. "I didn't want to be around it all the time, so now I can totally space it out so that I can deal with it. You get bored when you're around it all the time. Doing movies, they usually bunch 'em up into, like, four movies in two months, something like that. And then I'll take a three-month break or four-month break before I do another movie."

"I couldn't really say how many days I work a month, other than being on the road dancing," she cagily disclosed. "Usually five or six days out of the month." She was then in the third year of her tenure, and would go on to win her first-ever *AVN* Award in 2001, for "Best Actress" (in a tie with fellow Vivid Girl Taylor Hayes), before deciding to retire. Six years in the business was long enough for her, and she moved on to a new career— in real estate, at the San Fernando Valley-based brokerage firm Paramount Rodeo Realty, specializing in clients from the adult entertainment world. Since 2003, with her co-broker Staci Mintz, she'd closed over US$13 million in sales, US$4 million of which were porn-related. Porn stars bought houses like anyone else and she'd found herself a new niche.

"You need to go on to bigger and better things," she had told me. "This is a stepping stone, what I'm doing now, and I don't want to be an actress forever. I don't want people to get burned out on me, you know, and I don't want to get burned out on myself." Really? Could her ardent fans burn out on her? "Well, yeah," she replied. "There's new girls all the time." She was smart enough to realize that no one was indispensable in this most fickle of businesses.

I learned about that when I wrote a feature on Sin City contract girl Shay Sweet, and her contract was suddenly terminated just before my piece could go to press. My editor hounded me for clarification, and so I simply called Shay myself and pressed her for the gory details.

"They told me I had to go on the road to dance, and I didn't want to," she explained. Ah, so that decoded the subtle clause in the contract—"dancing (feature or otherwise) ... must be approved in writing in advance by the Company, not to be unreasonably withheld." The operative words were "by the Company"—which meant they had the right to dictate the terms—and "not to be unreasonably withheld," which was a superbly crafted piece of legalese aimed to confound and confuse many an impressionable eighteen-year-old girl with a Valley-girl vocabulary. (Gag me with a spoon, ohmigosh!)

My story eventually ran in the August 2000 issue of *Penthouse Variations* with all mention of Shay's Sin City contract excised. One Sin City staffer told me Shay was fired by the company because she was a total pothead; the company had also hired her as their receptionist, and Shay "couldn't answer the phones half the time because she was stoned." I asked Shay about this and she merely giggled.

Sin City knowingly chose to sign her as one of its contract girls as well as its front-desk receptionist? Only in porn could such a thing happen, with no forethought for consequences. "These girls can't be expected to be brain surgeons," my editor V.K. McCarty sighed. "They're employed because they can fuck. Which is all well and good, but what do we do now?"

She was referring to many of Shay's quotes in my piece, many of which made her sound like an airhead. Well, she was all of twenty years old and three years straight outta Fort Worth, Texas, and had been in 150 videos, none with much compelling dialogue. When I asked her during our interview if she was aware of the sheer amount of noise she made during sex—usually some variation of "Yes, yes, oh my God, oh my God, yes, oh fuck yes, yes, yes, yes!"—she looked up at me, batted her dreamy blue eyes under her bleached-blond hair, and giggled again. "Wow, yeah, I guess I do that, don't I?" she said. "I have to watch my videos more."

I asked another Sin City contract girl about what had

happened with Shay. "Um, I think that they didn't pay her for a while," she whispered. "I'll tell you something, if you won't quote me by name. You know what I was told when I signed? 'Contracts are not for people who do not have any other source of income.' They said they were thinking of signing me as long as I was not depending on them for the money. That was the first year that they signed me. Now, with the amount of money I'm making, I don't have to dance. I just choose to. But the first year, that's what they told me. They came right out, and were like, 'We're not going to support you.'"

At about that juncture, I started to hear rumblings from other quarters. Some of the new Vivid girls were unhappy with their contracts. Cassidey, for instance, was incensed, claiming that her Vivid contract locked her into indentured servitude for three years. Vivid even owned her name, Cassidey. (Methought she should've kept the use of her previous name, Paizley Adams, which I'd always liked better, but alas she'd signed her contract and thereby forfeited it.) Name ownership could be explained by the clause in her contract stating that "the Talent shall cooperate with the Company in connection with any licensing agreements entered by the Company to license, manufacture, and/or distribute adult novelty products or any other product using Talent's name, image or likeness." (In 2002, Cassidey, at age twenty-one, quit the industry; but she returned in March 2006—with a new Vivid contract!)

But not all contract girls were unhappy. Many had signed the forms and accepted the trade-offs. Jessica Drake, for instance, renewed her contract with Sin City for nine more feature films and also scored a provision in the same deal to actively participate in designing her own sex toy line. This was officially announced in *AVN*, in August 2001, but she'd actually told me about it two months earlier, in June. She also told me the craziest thing she'd had to deal with was getting fan mail from prisoners. She lovingly dubbed them her "jail mail."

"It freaked me out and I threw it away," she'd told me, about the first one. "It was the first inmate mail that I had gotten. I opened it up and it was a really, really graphic, explicit letter. I'm reading it and I'm like, 'Oh my God, this criminal is infatuated with me and he's stalking me!' At the end of the letter, he wrote: 'I get out in two years, and I want to come see you!' I didn't think that was very cool."

She'd been in the business for two years when we first met, at the 2001 *AVN* Awards in Las Vegas. Bold as brass and typically Texan, she had moved to Los Angeles from El Paso and called herself a "sex therapist" who ministered to those in need. Getting attention from the incarcerated, however, raised the stakes.

"It creeped me out," she said. "It dawned on me, about this fantasy thing, why I got into this and what I'm accomplishing. I realize I provide a fantasy and I'm fine with that. But it freaks me out to know that they want my stuff and they're smuggling it in. I think that's a little bit odd. I mean, because if you get into trouble for having porn, you can get extra time, you can lose privileges, all kinds of stuff. They're not supposed to have such access to porn anymore. I don't know how they get my stuff.

"Some prisons, some jails and some correctional facilities are different than others, some are more lax with their rules and stuff—I've had prisoners request photos with no nudity," she added. "I've only ever gotten a handful of letters that disgusted me and weirded me out. The majority of them, they're funneling their energy and their fantasy into writing these letters. And they're probably jackin' off while they're writing me these letters. It gives them something to do and it gives them a way to pass the time. And I think it's okay. The problem that I have, to begin with, is how they're finding me when they're supposed to be being punished, you know.

"But I'm okay with it—I don't write them back because I don't want to establish relationships, be it friendships or whatever, and lead them to believe I am being special with them. I take it that some of these people aren't as smart as normal people. And I don't want these people to come looking for me. I don't want a big long line at a convention, of people that are showing me their prison uniforms, asking me to sign it."

She then read me some of her "jail mail." Like this one, a typical masterpiece of purple prose:

"Dear Jessica: Hey baby, how are ya? I was just looking through a stack of fuck books and I had seen you have an address I could write to, so here I am. My name is Ted. I am five-foot-nine, blue eyes, brown hair. I'm 31 years old but I look a little younger. Anyway, I am not sure if you'll be the one reading this but I intend to find out. I hope you will write me back as soon as possible. I would enjoy that very much. You are so sexy. You have a terrific body. I would sure like to have a taste of that pussy of yours. It looks so good. I'd fuck you for hours. I'd especially like to take you from behind. You have a beautiful ass that gets my cock tingling every time. I can tell that you know how to fuck. Right now, I'm in a men's halfway house in Ohio. It sucks. I guarantee if you could know me, you'd probably like me. I am easy-going and not bad-looking. I find women very interesting and I like to pleasure them. I'd like to pleasure you. I'd especially like your lips around my hard cock. I bet you give a hell of a good blowjob. I can feel your tongue going up and down my sacs and all over my shaved balls."

Jessica paused. "I'd like to know where he shaves his balls in prison."

She laughed, and pulled out another letter. "One of the more serious ones," she warned me.

"Dear Jessica: I recently saw your pictures in some magazines and attached was an address to write. I am currently an inmate at Franklin Correctional Facility in Malone, New York. I am serving a long sentence for

racketeering and extortion. I was formerly a union vice-president, and the Manhatten D.A. decided to put me out of circulation for a while. I am somewhat famous in New York City. Not as famous as Gotti, but I came very close. You look quite stunning in your pictures and it's unfortunate we can't be hanging out in Las Vegas at The Bellagio or The Venetian. Are you familiar with John Stagliano from L.A.? He's a porno producer whom I know. If you know him and see him, tell him Gootch from Brooklyn sends his regards. I'm also good friends with Jack Nicholson. Anyway, it sucks being in prison. This place is ten hours from New York and exactly 35 miles from the Canadian border. I guess my days as a bachelor there are over. But I miss all my beautiful girlfriends. I used to have the most beautiful girlfriends, a lot of spending money, good cocaine, and much respect. Now I have canned food, and thirty-five dollars every two weeks. I get to stay in shape and bodybuild, but who cares, where I am? Send some pictures. If you want me to send some money, no problem. If you want to visit, I'll pay for your trip here and give you plenty of spending money. I'm no joke, sweetheart, I'm a man of my word. So write me, let me know what's on your mind. Let me know if you'd be interested in having me take care of you."

Well, that sure was different. Part and parcel, so to speak, of the fun of being a contract girl.

Other guys composed erotic poetry, dedicated to her:

"I love the way your miniskirt displays the beauty of your shapely thighs / Once you step into a room, you'll be the cynosure of all the guys' eyes." And another, even more inventive, one: *"That hourglass figure and that full sensuous mouth is working in your favor / Would you like to give these balls rolling with a different flavor? / If you're*

216

not in the mood for any fucking / You can unzip my fly,
pull it out, pop it in your mouth and start sucking."

Jessica stopped reading and giggled. "I've gotten them from all over the world, let me tell ya. When I started doing porn, I realized that everybody everywhere would be watching me. The more people, the better. But I hope I never have to meet any of these guys. Prisoners are human beings too, but the thing that I have to think about, above anything else, is my safety. My personal safety comes first." At the time of writing, in early 2006, Jessica was still a contract girl but had switched companies, having signed with Wicked Pictures, and she had not come to any bodily harm.

Ah, peace of mind, what a concept! In the world of porn stars, real life is never as simple as it appears and sometimes it can be a real struggle not to lose the plot. I received some insight into this from one of my favorite Vivid girls, Cheyenne Silver, after I'd interviewed her on-set in June 2001. Recent allegations had been posted on the Internet citing her appearance on some escorting websites. Her ex-boyfriend, Gregory Bauman, had given interviews saying he had been the recipient of hate mail telling him: "Your girlfriend is a whore."

He also said he had taken out a restraining order on Cheyenne for stalking him. Now, that was a new one. I didn't know what to make of that but I imagined that some of her fans were clearly more disturbed than he was, by the obvious disconnect: Cheyenne, a fetching brunette of Cherokee, French, and Irish descent, had such a wholesome, all-American look and some of her fans apparently took umbrage with the possibility that their lovely video sweetheart could ever be anything less than perfect. Like, God forbid, a prostitute!

But, I thought, perhaps some of these guys were jealous of Bauman and were projecting it, hence the hate mail. And, in all fairness, there was a conceptual problem here. Did these guys forgot that Cheyenne was a stripper who became a porn star? How could anything be so surprising, or some people be so naive?

Cheyenne had been a model in Florida but failed to make the ranks and so chose to strip in Las Vegas, where she worked under the name of Wildcat, before getting into porn. Her first anal sex scene was in *Cumback Pussy 12*, produced by Elegant Angel, a whole two years before she was enshrined with the gloss of glamour—as a Vivid Girl and then *Penthouse* cover girl and the magazine's Pet of the Month for December 2001.

The less glitzy reality, though, was that she'd had an illegitimate daughter when she was eighteen and had dropped out of college to raise her child. Her mother had become seriously ill, and so porn was the best way she knew of to pay all the bills, since she was supporting both daughter and mother. (Her mother eventually died.) Her daughter did not know what she did for a living and thought mom was just a model. She told me all this herself. "She knows mommy does pictures, I'm going to tell her the truth when she's older," Cheyenne confessed.

She claimed that Vivid had pressured her into getting a boob job, and even disclosed on her website that she cried when she got them done. "They wanted them perked up," she wrote. There were rumors that Vivid had allowed her the luxury of doing only four movies a year and had paid her an additional US$100,000—if and only if she got her implants. I had first seen her pre-boobjob, in *Shane's World 19: Tropical Heat*, a gonzo movie made in June 1999, which she still considered her most enjoyable film to shoot. She told me it was her personal favorite. She probably still had good memories of the business back then.

When I finally met her in person, in June 2001 in North Hollywood, we sat around after a shoot and chatted. She asked me to go to the Roxy to see a band she was helping out. We smoked cigarettes and shared a bottle of mineral water (ah, the closest I'd come to swapping spit with a porn star! I kept the bottle, should anyone aspire to procure it on eBay someday, not that I planned to sell.) Then, sensing she was at ease, I seized the opportunity to ask her about the whole Gregory Bauman business.

No, she shook her head, it was all lies. She said she was sad that a former boyfriend could become such an insane opportunist, grabbing instant fame on the Internet. She asked me to contact the industry gossip columnist Luke Ford, on whose site many of his comments had been reported, and to tell him to set the record straight. I did so, and Ford told me he had been told everything by Bauman himself, had not fabricated any of the details, and the stuff about her working as an escort was actually quite well known.

Hmm, interesting. Maybe Ford was the naive one, if he believed everything Bauman had said. Was there a line that any reporter crossed, even as a gossip columnist, whereby he failed to take responsibility for reporting fiction as fact? Who was really telling the truth here?

I didn't know, but I did know this: I called Cheyenne to tell her about my conversation with Luke Ford. She answered her cellphone, and didn't remember me.

Or the talk we'd had after the shoot.

So much for my being the Good Samaritan.

It kind of ruined Cheyenne for me as a celebrity. In retrospect, I think I had been rationalizing her newfound glamour. Truthfully, I certainly liked her better in *Shane's World 19*, especially the gusto with which she gave a guy a blowjob on a boat out at sea, and her onscreen output after she'd signed to Vivid was gradually less than impressive. Many of the films were quite good (Ren Savant's *Jumping Track* and Ralph Parfait's *End of the World*, in particular) but Cheyenne's sexual self seemed diminished. All she did most of the time was whimper and moan while lying dead still as some stud hammered away. She gave me the impression that it was all just a job to her now. Was a contract such a desirable thing, after all? What had happened to the porn star I once knew and loved, if only from afar?

Maybe I was the one being conned here. Maybe I knew how some of her fans felt now. Maybe it would've been better if I hadn't met her at all. In porn, one always flirted with the fine line between perception and reality. And there are always barriers one shouldn't have crossed.

It made me think about all the stuff that happened to porn people and their psychic baggage. There was always a darker side to the glamour game, and often the forces of commerce conspired to usher in hard reality checks.

Or sometimes, it could even be hard yet poignant. Of all the big *Playboy* interviews the magazine was famous for, my all-time favorite was the one in the issue of December 1998, with actor David Duchovny of *The X-Files* fame. He actually went on record to discuss his own favorite porn-viewing habits and disclosed that his favorite porn star was Alicia Monet. "If anything good can come from this interview, it's that Alicia Monet would contact me and we could have lunch," he told interviewer Lawrence Grobel. "God, if she only knew how many lonely periods she got me through. I don't think porn stars know how weirdly important they are in people's lives."

Weirdly important—was there a more *X-Files* way to put it? "The truth is out there," as the show's slogan read. Several porn stars I'd met preferred to play down their social significance, with the right ounce of self-effacement. Occasionally, if they played it up, there was a good-humored levity to it that I always found charming. Sometimes, even disconcertingly so, as in the case of Belladonna, who remains one of my favorite adult performers.

Belladonna had performed the very first double-penetration I ever saw (on the set of the Michael Zen/Jill Kelly film, *Perfect Pick 7: Sink the Pink*) and, a few years later, I got to behold her bounteous assets again in a movie customized for her, *Belladonna's Fuck Me*, directed by the European auteur Garry Gazzman and produced by the British company Harmony Films (distributed in the US through Evil Angel).

In the opening scene she took on three guys; the film's finale featured three guys doing six girls (including Belladonna). In the interview segment, she talked about her experiences in the industry. "Once you do anal, that's all they want you for," she revealed, and how well she would know. In May 2003, at age twenty-two, following three years in the business resulting in some 250 films, she had decided to quit performing and started directing, mentored by Evil Angel boss John Stagliano (for whom she'd starred in his multiple-award winning film *The Fashionistas*, a disturbingly dark sex-and-fetish romp that was possibly her film to top all films). Her reason for quitting? She had contracted gonorrhea and chlamydia a couple times each and had endured several other infections.

"I don't want to put up with any STDs ever again," she told *AVN*. "That shit is what ruins my desire to fuck anymore. It really does. If I would have sex every day and walk away without any diseases, I would do it forever. There's a lot of shit that goes around and it's not good, especially as a female. You can lose your chance in life to have children. It's draining on your body when you have to go to the hospital every fucking day and it's not your fault."

Two months earlier, she's signed a five-year directing deal with the company Sineplex. The deal did not require her to appear in any of her films and she quickly shot three episodes for the first line, *Bella's Perversions*, and then began talks with John Stagliano to direct some new movies for Evil Angel. (The Sineplex contract was clearly non-exclusive.) She had won four *AVN* Awards that year, including "Best Supporting Actress" and "Best Oral Sex Scene," and was on her way towards retrofitting her career.

At the 2005 *AVN* Awards, her latest film *The Connoisseur* (produced by her new company Belladonna Entertainment in conjunction with Evil Angel), won the "Best All-Girl Feature" award, though that wasn't the only all-girl event in her life. She'd also just delivered a healthy six-pound-seven-ounce baby girl named Myla, and her baby shower held a month before was actually filmed and shown on *Family Business,* the Showtime reality series about the porn business. Surely that was more important than all the awards in the world. How many porn stars could claim to breaking into the mainstream with their baby shower?

Still, I will always treasure the autograph she gave me on the *Perfect Pink 7* set, just before doing her double-penetration scene. She handed me the latest issue of *Hustler*'s new magazine *Barely Legal Hardcore* (Volume 1, Number 2), in which she was featured in a sixteen-page spread as well as the centerfold. Aptly, she was seen being double-penetrated. She gave me the magazine and signed it "Licks and kisses forever"—a more sincere sentiment, I thought, rather than the usual syrupy "Love always" or some such—on a page which showed her in deep concentration, one penis in her mouth and another in her hand.

There was such a fresh-faced innocence to her, aged nineteen in those photos. Perhaps it was no coincidence that she came from Utah. I liked edgy, sexy people hailing from conservative places, because they were my kindred spirits. After all, I came from a famously ultra-conservative place, Singapore, and I certainly related to that sense of outlaw spirit. ("To live outside the law, you must be honest," Bob Dylan once sang, a line that had reverberated in my head since my teens.) Years after that meeting, I was curious to see if Belladonna still had that same wild-eyed spark in the Harmony video, released in 2004, and to my surprise she still did. But there was something else too. A glint in her eyes, much deeper than the steely stare she'd beheld me with back in 2001, something that spoke of self-acceptance, or self-awareness, only intermittently present before.

Maybe a directing contract and a baby girl could do that to you. Maybe the best kind of deal was the kind you could give yourself, that suggested your self-worth hadn't been lost amid the contract negotiations and the flesh carnival. Porn was effectively a surrogate drug, enabling a girl to use her body to hold the pain of the material world, and often the pain of her own past, at bay.

I hadn't been appraised of Belladonna's past but I didn't need to. I could easily guess. She'd been a neglected child who needed attention, and pulled all stops to get it with an adult career in her adulthood. So, really, who needed a contract anyway? Everybody, in the end, as they say, really wanted to direct.

Death and Taxes

One sunny afternoon I was hanging out with Asia Carrera at her house in Woodland Hills, when a car pulled into her driveway, and out stepped a director she had recently shot with, making a pit stop to deliver some videotapes.

We chatted amiably and shot the breeze. I had not met this particular director before, but knew of his work and was familiar with the company that had produced his movies. Suddenly, his cellphone rang and he excused himself to take the call, turning his back to us before stepping outside.

"How is this? Any good?" I quietly asked Asia, pointing to one of the videotapes. We were then still in the good old days of VHS, and it was the latest film she had made with the director. The copies were for her to sell to her fans on her website.

"Piece of shit," she whispered back, winking.

We both laughed. When the director finished his call and asked us what was funny, we both said: "Uh, nothing. Private joke."

This little episode resurrected itself in my head now and then, whenever I reflected on my years covering the adult film industry. Anything made to be sold as entertainment was subject to interpretation, but porn was a field begging to be mocked and scorned—not always deservedly so, but sometimes; there sure was a whole lot of really bad crap out there.

Why was this? Because people in porn often forgot that not

everyone accepted sport-fucking as a spectator sport, to be slickly packaged for home consumption. But then again, it all depended on your perspective. Those of us old enough to remember the mid-80s can still recall one of the biggest hot-button topics in American publishing—the so-called "pubic wars" being fought between *Playboy, Penthouse,* and *Hustler.* To me, that was the cultural watershed of the American sexual revolution, when lines were suddenly drawn in the sand. Those were the early days of modern print-porn, when genital penetration was *verboten* but wide-open vaginal close-ups were *de rigeur*, and people took sides according to their personal views and their visual perception.

One bought *Penthouse* if one wanted hardcore that (mind the metaphor) straddled the fence. When I moved to Los Angeles in 1984, I was confronted by that cultural divide and constantly amazed by it. One of my graduate-school classmates bought *Penthouse* openly and she told me she liked it for the "microscopic" pictorials—I suspected she was a lesbian, though she never admitted it, but she enjoyed looking at naked women in spread-eagled splendor—and I realized that one of the great things about America was that, for all its inherent democratic foibles, it did at least offer such freedom of choice. I had grown up in Singapore, where reading material was either overtly or covertly restricted by government edict, so nobody was supposed to think too much about having too many choices.

Ignorance was supposedly bliss, but not to me. I was interested in having questions answered, and living in Singapore was, of course, never going to allow that to happen except in the most vicarious of ways, which was much too obtuse for me. Porn offered me a new window to the outside world, to be pondered anew. At what point, I mused, did an inquiring mind turn into a skeptical one? Why did some people get so worked up over poses and positions, at how photographers specializing in erotica depicted the display of human genitalia? It might've all been skin-deep, but what was really going on under the surface?

I remember discussing that very topic with George Kenton,

who was the first American art director of *Penthouse* (he had helped Bob Guccione take his fledgling publication from its humble beginnings in London over to its eventual power base in New York), and he told me a fascinating anecdote.

At one point in his career, George was the art director at *Playboy*'s sister publication, *Oui*, and had been courted by Larry Flynt's super-hardcore magazine, *Hustler*. He instinctively decided against it. "Then, I was talking to a buddy of mine, back in Pennsylvania, when I was visiting there," George told me. "He was a working as a pipe fitter, and I had known him all my life. I told him about this offer I had to work for *Hustler*. They were going to pay me twice what I was making at *Oui*, with a brand-new car, any car I wanted. But I didn't even interview for it. He said, 'You asshole!' I said, 'Why?' And he said, 'You could be working for the best magazine in America!' I said, '*Hustler*?' He says, 'Yeah. I'm a pipe fitter. I don't see women like that, like the ones in *Playboy* or *Oui*. Women like that don't even look at me. The women I like are the kind that like me, and they're the kind that you see in *Hustler*.'"

George smiled sagely. "Cheap, bad-looking women—those were the kinds of women that he had access to. That was his idea of sex. Whereas people who read *Playboy* were people like doctors and lawyers."

He had thought about this kind of thing often, when designing layouts in *Penthouse*. "More realism in sex," George chuckled, "is kind of interesting, you know."

The only question, then, was this: How realistic did your pornography have to be? In the course of my own exploration of this most misunderstood of pop-culture genres, I was always confronted with that timeless question, and my own final answer was seriously simple: It only needed to be as realistic as you wanted it to be. Because it had to work in tandem with the kinds of sexual fantasies you most enjoyed.

As Sheryl Crow and Liz Phair sang (in Crow's song "Soak Up the Sun"): "It's not having what you want, it's wanting what you've got."

What was the point otherwise?

For instance, I enjoyed meeting Juli Ashton back in 1995, and I had met her at an opportune juncture, too—I was working for *Spice* and had only started exploring the business professionally— but my interest was truly piqued when I started researching her background on the Internet and discovered that she had been a schoolteacher in Colorado before entering porn and that she had begun expressing her sexuality in the most flagrantly carefree of ways while in college—she openly admitted that she had screwed half the guys in her dorm.

Now, that truly excited me: Juli Ashton, the sex-positive slut, doing something usually associated with most frat boys, her bragging rights instantly trangressing social mores. Young women weren't supposed to be proud of their sexual conquests, but she was. And this immediately elevated her standing in my eyes. I would never look at her autograph the same way again; "Gerrie—Lick me all over!!" she'd signed on the 8 x 10 glossy that proclaimed: "Introducing JULI ASHTON, Starring in *New Wave Hookers 4* and *Butt Detective* from VCA PLATINUM". Not long after, she became a mainstream celebrity as the host of the *Playboy* cable channel's *Night Calls* program, and then signed a record US$25,000-a-movie contract with VCA Pictures.

Her glamorous sheen aside, though, Juli was a role model of sorts for me, since she reflected my own sexual pedagogy; I was very *sympatico* with women who enjoyed that kind of psychic gender-bending. I'd once had a girlfriend who liked me to call her "Slut!" while we were in *flagrante delicto*; she got a real kick out of it, and she also liked receiving "facials." It wasn't something one only saw in porn movies—she actually told me she believed that sperm all over her skin was responsible for her good complexion. Small wonder that I took to porn like a duck to water. More realism in sex was, to quote George Kenton, interesting indeed.

However, in any serious contemplation over porn, two overarching issues needed due consideration: prostitution and obscenity. Most people outside the business wondered the same things whenever they encountered porn. Were these real working girls as opposed to merely actresses being paid to enact sex acts? Was there a clear demarcation between the two? And, finally, when was something unequivocally obscene?

Easy answers did not exist and shades of gray abounded. People had fought countless court battles over pandering and obscenity. Philip D. Harvey, the founder and chief executive of Adam & Eve, told the story of his own misadventures with the United States government in his amazing book *The Government Vs Erotica: The Siege of Adam & Eve* (published by Prometheus Books, 2001), summarizing the long saga of obscenity prosecutions in the country. How far had we come from the landmark case *Miller Vs California*, in which pornography was deemed obscene only if it violated certain "community standards"? Or from the time of Supreme Court Judge Donald W. Stevens, who famously said he didn't know what pornography was but "knew it when he saw it"?

In point of fact, then, how did one know a slut or a whore, or a morally-questionable woman, whenever one saw one? Whatever did that mean? And was it a meaningful distinction anyway? The political philosophy major in me (as was my undergrad field) wrestled with that one gleefully.

Historically, pornography had been defined as "the visual or literary depiction of whores," and the whole mess should be blamed on the Ancient Greeks, and then the early Christians. As the cognitive scientist Nicholas Kelman pointed out in his fascinating book *Girls* (one of the most thought-provoking treatises on the male outlook on love and sex today, in my opinion), the Ancient Greeks had no word for romantic love. A man related to a woman only in terms of being "owned" or "valued highly" or "had sex with," and they would also use "mingle" to mean "copulate."

Kelman added that Aphrodite was not, as school children were taught in elementary mythology, the goddess of love. She was actually the goddess of sex. And she was also the patron saint of prostitutes. Her son Eros, from whom was derived the word "erotic," was the god of passion. The Greeks also created a system of classification for working girls, with the *heterae* at the top (the ancient world equivalent of today's escorts and call girls), the *peripatetae* in the middle (akin to today's freelance street walkers) and then, at the bottom of the food chain, the *porne* (the garden-variety, menial-task brothel workers, from which was derived the tellingly debasing word "pornography").

The Greeks, like some other ancient cultures, also had a system of temple prostitutes. This was not a culture that associated the human body and its natural desires with shame and scoffing (unlike Christianity, which proclaimed exactly that) and sex was deemed a sacred thing that could even be practised in places of worship as ritualized sanctity. And then, as the feminist scholar Riane Eisler first made me become so very shockingly aware (with her trailblazing book *The Chalice and the Blade*), the self-righteous Christians came along and wiped out all that.

Placing a premium on chastity, naturally, had its undeniable downside—as exemplified by Catholic priests molesting altar boys and, more hilariously, televangelists caught literally with their pants down in places of ill repute—but that still didn't resolve the problem of why the place of the slut or the whore was socially derided. I never saw that issue in its proper light until I was entrenched in the porn industry, where one encountered it countless unsuspecting ways.

Nobody, for instance, knew for sure how many *bona fide* porn stars were really part-time hookers (or the other way around, in the case of girls starting out in the business) but everyone told me the numbers were high. I saw the ads for the infamous Moonlite Bunnyranch in Carson City, Nevada, the legal brothel where famous porn stars fled to winter away their post-contract days. The names of some of my own favorites from the days of yore often came up ("Samantha Strong! Wow, so that's where she ended up!") but, beyond such surprises, I paid the issue scant heed. Until early 2001, in the midst of a phone conversation, when Andrew

Blake told me he wasn't going to be working with Regina Hall anymore, because she had "visa problems."

It looked like she was about to be deported back to her homeland, the Czech Republic. Reports circulated on the Internet, in February 2001, that Regina had just been busted for being a madam, for bringing in high-priced hookers into the United States from Eastern Europe. A Fox News special in Los Angeles stated that she was under house arrest and also cited the blond Czech glamour model Teresa Benesova as one of the girls procured by Regina for her American clients.

That was, to me, more heart-stopping than the more famous Heidi Fleiss scandal, simply because I really adored Regina Hall. Her opening solo masturbation rhapsody in Andrew Blake's *Secret Paris*, shot in a sensually brooding sepia tone, was one of my all-time favorite scenes. Her pictorial layouts, most notably by Richard Kern (in *Cheri*) and Robert Gordon (in *Penthouse*), remained among my favorites in the still photo category. She had been part of my own personal porn ecology, and now she had been arrested for prostitution and pandering.

How was I supposed to respond to that? The American government had chosen to label her an undesirable entity, to be expunged from these shores, but where did that leave her in my own eyes?

I responded in the most direct and obvious of ways, as only I knew how. The diligent, obsessive reporter in me confirmed it with my sources (including my contacts in the Czech Republic) and then the porn fan in me went straight to my archives. I watched *Secret Paris* again and looked at the Richard Kern and Robert Gordon photographs. And I found Regina as enchanting and enthralling as ever. To me, she had that luminous quality that separated real sex goddesses from mere damsels in undress. None of her lustre had been lost, despite new information wherein real life suddenly intruded on fantasy.

In short, it wasn't a problem for me. Even if she was a prostitute and a madam, Regina did not lend herself to real-world attachment; I wasn't even going to seek her out, to try to meet her when I visited Prague for the first time in the summer of 2005, though we were a few degrees of separation apart and I could easily have. (Besides, I was traveling with my girlfriend and wasn't about to kid myself). I had friends who mixed sex tourism with their porn fantasies, but for me erotic imagery just didn't work that way. Some things were always best left in the realm of fantasy. It kept any hot-blooded porn fan safe and sane. Masturbation was still the safest sex anyone could have.

I discussed that very subject with porn veteran Nina Hartley, then in her seventeenth year as a porn star, on the set of a Toni English *Naked Hollywood* episode (aptly enough, shot in a studio in Hollywood, off Santa Monica Boulevard). I told her I enjoyed her scene in Bud Lee's film *La Femme Chameleon*, in which she picked up a hitchhiker and seduced him. Nina laughed and said she remembered that scene, even though the film had been made in 1999, a whole two years previously. Picking up a hitchhiker was a popular saxual fantasy, re-enacted *ad nauseum* in porn, but it was especially fun when the woman wasn't the one standing by the road with the proverbial thumb out but rather the one in the driver's seat, initiating the seduction.

"I think a lot of people should understand," she told me, "that porno movies are live-action sex cartoons. Just because a person likes a certain kind of pornography doesn't mean he actually lives it out. Also remember that porn is, by nature, very transgressive. It takes society's norms, like monogamy and heterosexuality, and subverts them. Interracial sex! Toy sex! Anal sex! Group sex! You watch movies to see things you would never do in person."

The person who didn't understand that was the person who didn't understand porn. It was really as simple as that.

And that was also, in essence, why most pandering busts in the porn business usually came to naught. Police harrassment and eventual prosecution took place regularly but defendents were usually acquitted. All good American constitutional lawyers have affirmed the scenario, which in the simplest terms ran something like this: Under the law, prostitution meant person A paying person B to perform sexual acts upon his or her own person. Porn, however, entailed person C paying person A to have sex with person B.

In other words, it involved payment by a third party (usually the movie studio or production company or an agent of some sort), whose representative did not take part at all in the sexual activity so assigned. And so, it followed, porn and prostitution were legally not the same thing.

And that, boys and girls, was why porn remained legal in most of the United States (with the exception of certain states in the Bible-belt south, which regulated mail-order purchase and engaged in other similarly restrictive scare tactics). It was sheltered by a conceptual framework, one so simple that it actually boggled the mind.

It also paved the way for women in the industry to inject some zany humor that pushed the public boundaries, like one of my absolute favorites—from Lauren Phoenix, a feisty twenty-four-year-old Canadian who won the 2005 *AVN* Awards "Best New Starlet" trophy, who was asked in an *AVN* interview about a snippet of dialogue from her film *Hellcats 2* in which she said, "I am a raging whore!"

"Thanks. I *am* a raging whore," she sassily replied. "Yeah, I am. My sex drive is massive. I don't know where it came from, but I've always been incredibly sexual. It's pretty normal for me."

Such statements once had shock value but, by 2005, porn had become such a commonplace thing in American culture that only the most ignorant could be surprised. Popular porn stars like Brittany Andrews and Olivia Del Rio openly advertised their escorting services (with prices clearly displayed) on their personal websites. And then, there were porn stars like Chloe, the VCA contract girl, who unleashed her sexual energy like a heat-seeking missile in every film she made and minced no words about her profession. "In the end, we're really all whores," she told the eminent English novelist Martin Amis, who then quoted her in a *Talk* magazine article about porn stars, smugly entitled "To Millions of American Men, These Women are Movie Stars."

Amis had earlier been credited with an observation I'd always liked, about the difference between fashion models and glamour models—fashion models looked like you could do whatever you liked to them, but glamour models looked like they could do whatever *they* liked to you. Most porn stars, of course, worked as glamour models too (posing nude or at least semi-nude), and I also thought it especially intriguing that it would be Chloe who would make such a frank admission, since she was one of the most pro-active performers in the business, a girl known for pushing the edges of all sexual boundaries. I'd seen her enact orgasms so earth-shattering that you knew it was definitely the real thing, and she particularly enjoyed choking and fisting. There was an incipient violence to her kind of porn, truly not stuff for the faint-hearted.

"We're prostitutes," Chloe had told Amis. "There are differences. You can choose your partners and they're tested for AIDS. You won't get your john to do that. But we're prostitutes. We exchange sex for money. I looked it up in the dictionary and that's what it says."

I'd only met Chloe once, an all-too-brief meeting in a very crowded backstage area, so we'd never really talked. I had no time to tell her how much I admired her scene with Raylene in the elevator and then with the massively endowed Lexington Steele, both in Michael Zen's film *Peckers* (about a female photographer who liked shooting the male organ in its turgid state), or that I admired her for her abundantly sex-positive perspective. Being called a whore was actually a perfectly acceptable state of mind? Well, at age twenty-nine, an elder statesperson by American porn standards, Chloe was unrepentently unconventional. She was small-breasted—unlike most porn stars, she'd refused to get a boob job—and she had trained as a ballerina for eleven years before getting hooked on speed and cocaine at seventeen, which explained much of her wild-eyed, wanton sexual frenzy.

Maybe one needed to break on through to the other side, to quote Jim Morrison quoting Aldous Huxley, to pass through the doors of perception. (Chloe's ongoing ambition by 2005, however, was sobriety; the drugs and drinking had taken their toll, she told reporters, and she wanted to stay alive.) At any rate, she reminded me of porn's highly democratic nature—it was a very fluid genre, one that accomodated all tastes and broke all barriers (excepting snuff films and kiddie porn, which I found hideous).

To be sure, most men preferred their porn stars classically built, like the Vivid girl Briana Banks. I was stopped dead in my tracks when I first met her. She was runway-model tall, impossibly thin, with huge breasts, and so resembled a human blow-up doll. But hey, that was obviously what her many fans wanted to see. I actually preferred the more notorious Marilyn Star, the Canadian porn star sentenced in 2002 to three months' prison for aiding and abetting her stockbroker boyfriend in insider trading.

The first time I ever saw her was when she posed with the rock star Marilyn Manson in *New Rave* magazine, April 1996, an outrageous fetish/bondage layout that was one of my first porn epiphanies ("How," I thought, "could I even like this? Could there be something wrong with me?"). My *AVN* colleague Mark Kernes lambasted her for lies and deceit, after she'd claimed to the *New York Times* that she was "raped and abused" and had used her insider tips to "save money and get out of the abusive pornographic film industry." But I was glad she got her fifteen minutes. Her layouts still turned me on, so what did I care about her real life? And, honestly, what would porn be without wacky kooks like her?

I felt the same way when the news broke in May 2005 that Joy Marquart, formerly known as the porn star Farrah, had stolen more than US$40,000 from six banks in New Jersey, and was accordingly arrested by police, who alleged that she was a frontwoman for a New York City based crime ring. Utilizing her glamorous physique and thespian skills, she had apparently used a series of fake driver's licenses, fake bank checks and fake debit cards to pilfer some real customers' bank accounts. ("She was very well-dressed, she didn't need a lot of make-up," a police detective noted.) Farrah was one of the forever-blond porn stars of the 90s who somehow never quite made it to Jenna Jameson status, but to me her saga contributed to the colorful quilt that made American porn so fascinating.

Sure, she was trading on her past glories—she had peaked, and her career never quite recovered, after some of her best films made for Vivid circa 1998—and now she was sadly slouching toward a second act. But the curtain had closed down on her, echoing F. Scott Fitzgerald's famous dictum that there were "no second acts in American lives." It lent a certain pathos to the whole picture, adding to the litany of celebrity death by metaphor—robbing banks, after all, meant stealing money one didn't have, and sometimes the fleeting nature of fame could be desperately painful. For some, the porn persona was never quite enough.

"There is no wrong thought, only wrong action," to quote Nina Hartley, who had talked about porn with more zest and zing than anyone I'd ever met. "Sex is a wonderful, joyous, positive, transformative, healing, hot, horny gift of evolution. Its immense power demands respect. As adults, we decide for ourselves what sex means to us … Shame over our desire is useless, alienating us from love and connection. Mindless chasing of desire is equally destructive … Ten honest seconds can change a life."

Yes, indeed. I was, in my guise as a cultural observer, a collector of life-changing acts. I remembered a discussion with the director Nic Cramer, done as part of a long piece I was writing on Asia Carrera for *Penthouse Variations*. Nic told me how much he had enjoyed working with her and gave me a copy of his film *Intimate Strangers*, which he considered his best film with her. "She's an example of how to do it right," Nic said. "Asia and Jill Kelly, to me, embody the savvy businesswoman, the modern feminist, who says: 'I'm a feminist, I like my orgasms, I like my body, I'm not ashamed of showing it and I don't mind profiting off it, I see nothing wrong with it, and I deserve to get rich by it.'

"I think that's cool. If I could get rich off my penis, I would. Or my naked body. I'd probably do it." He laughed. "Are you going to quote me on that?"

Asia, in turn, had over the years made me laugh quite a lot too, as both comrade and friend. I remembered her closing lines at the end of *Malibu Hookers 1* (which was slightly better than the sequel, *Malibu Hookers 2*, but not by much), in which she played a madam working her girls out of her beachside house. Her own house in Malibu was used in the film (I only know so because I'd been there many times and recognized the rooms onscreen) and, in the final scene, she was seen strolling contentedly alongside the lapping waves and hovering seagulls.

"They say there are two things in life you can count on: death and taxes," she said, in voiceover. "Well, I've found two things I can count on: sex and money."

Everything in the American porn industry, of course, really revolved around those two things, metaphorically represented by a set of jiggling 34Cs and some perfectly shaved pubic topiary. There was something both amusing and true about that. And while some may scoff, I had never met a more unequivocally honest and more morally courageous class of people that I did while reporting on the porn industry.

Perhaps there was something about the genre itself, perhaps best represented by the "real sex" metaphor—what you see is very often really what you get, and unlike mainstream Hollywood nobody uses body doubles or socks covering genitalia, which means nobody gets to hide very much for long. With or without Viagra. And if you get stabbed in the back, you'll get it with your eyes open.

I'd talked about this a great deal with Kelly Holland, known to most porn fans as the Vivid director Toni English, who afforded me perspectives aplenty about the role of porn in society. As a female director in a business selling mostly to men, she possessed a unique stance, and I recall a formal interview I did with Kelly at her house in October 2001 in which I asked her if she felt any different being a woman behind the camera. Her answer was so startlingly profound that I haven't forgotten it.

"I don't put a lot of weight on being a female director, as opposed to a male director in this business," she said. "Only because I have to answer to the marketplace. I have to put facial cumshots in. I have to put tight hardcore in. I have to put insert shots in. So anything I may or may not find appealing is overridden by my necessity to answer to what drives the market."

Was she a realist disguised as a romantic? Kelly had come into porn straight from a career directing mainstream documentaries. She had shot riotous soccer matches and incendiary military *coups d'etat* in Latin America. She knew about organized chaos, so group sex was a walk in the park.

"I think what affects me more than being a woman is just my background, as a mainstream film person that came out of television and my background as an actress that came out of theatre," she added. "It's my background as an actress that, I think, moves me to try to always justify action in the script. I hate dumb shit, you know. I hate stuff that happens out of the blue for no reason, and characters that have these huge shifts in the middle of the story, where all of a sudden they discover that they're lesbians within twelve seconds because the scene necessitates it. I can't stand stuff like that.

"But that's not, I don't think, because I'm a woman. I think that's because I spent a long time in college and then as an actress in theatre and television and then directing theatre. I'm always looking for what motivates characters. How do they move, how do they change. So it's more my artistic background that dictates the way I make films, much more than I'm a woman."

I realized there and then that while one's personal leanings often informed one's professional aspirations, the stakes were always raised in the sex industry. The personal and the professional always merged, and that explained why I was so attracted to it. These people had put their lives on the line. It was a vocation to them. Work was not a lacy bra and garters one merely wore and discarded after a shoot. It was a whole way of life.

That was why I'd always liked Alexus Winston, one of my favorite *Penthouse* Pets, who didn't do hardcore movies and preferred to struggle with the vagaries of mainstream television and the occasional Pinnacle Horny Goatweed print ad. In every pictorial I'd seen her in, particularly those shot by the great Suze Randall, she looked a hundred percent the sexually voracious vixen and never failed to entice me with her confident, come-hither stares. And when my colleague Tripp Daniels interviewed her for *AVN Online* and asked her what kind of underwear she was wearing, she replied: "I don't wear underwear. That's absolutely a fact. And anyone close to me knows that's true."

"I've noticed that working with *Penthouse,*" she added. "Pets don't wear panties. I swear to God. Pets don't wear panties. It's like a rule of thumb."

Ah, *la dolce vita*, sans underwear, that was her way of life. And that was my kind of rule of thumb, since exhibitionism was my particular favorite turn-on. Certain body parts never lied, and in the end we all relied on what we saw and heard and, more emphatically, on what we entrusted to imagination.

A whole industry, in fact, turned itself on because of four words, filched neatly from the familiar American greenback that was its very reason for being. That, in the end, was how I saw it: In lust we trust.

Acknowledgments

I would like to express my heartfelt thanks to Wei Hui, who personally gave me permission to quote from her novel *Marrying Buddha*, for the opening epigraph. And to Asia Carrera, for allowing me to quote from her personal journals.

I am also indebted to Darcey Steinke, the first writer I met, back in 1992, who openly expressed to me her fascination with pornography. I loved the sex scenes in her novel *Suicide Blonde*, which compelled my own investigations into the shadowy realms of sex culture. Karl Taro Greenfeld also inspired me with both his own memoir, *Standard Deviations*, and one particular dinner conversation during which he shared his own experiences of covering the American porn industry and discussed with me the metaphysics of sex and memory.

Portions of this book have appeared elsewhere in other forms, in the United States (*AVN Online*, *Fox*, *Penthouse Variations* and *The Wall Street Journal*), Singapore (*BigO*) and Sweden (*Guld Rapport*). Salutations, then, to my colleagues at *Penthouse Variations*, past and present: Lori Applebaum, V.K. McCarty, Barbara Pizio, and Jamie Selzer. And at *AVN Online*, also past and present: Tripp Daniels, Tom Hymes, Erik McFarland, and Ken Michaels. And at our irascible mother ship *AVN*: Nikki Fritz and Mark Kernes. I would like to thank all parties for permissions to quote from my published text.

Special thanks to Dottie Meyer, Director of Pet Promotions at

Penthouse magazine, for having facilitated so many of my more memorable interviews, particularly those with Janine Lindemulder, Dyanna Lauren, and Silvia Saint.

I'm also grateful in so many ways to the following people, for keeping contact and talking shop over the years: Wayne Akiyama, Halli Aston, Helen Boyd, Asia Carrera, Kyla Cole, Nic Cramer, Adrian Daskalov, Jessica Drake, Tomas Edberg, Luke Ford, Christine Fugate, Jennie Grant, Brian Gross, Kelly Holland, Jake Jacobs, Jill Kelly, Ginger Lynn, Monica Mayhem, Melissa Monet, Grace Quek, Devan Sapphire, and Brenda Scofield. And also, of special note, Cecilia Tan, who shared with me her experiences of working with Jenna Jameson.

None of this would have been possible, however, without the unwitting participation of three amazing women: Katie Elliott and Stephanie Smiley, who in 1994 first introduced me to Traci Lords (in person, not on video), and then Lily Burana, that same year, who as the then editor of *Future Sex* magazine encouraged me to interview Traci and then elevated the game with her own brilliant book *Strip City*.

For reading chapters and offering comments, thanks to: Sandy Cheah, Pamela Fahey, Anna Span, and Trevor Wingert.

Major thanks to Ming Pang and Collin Patrick for their excellent art direction and cover design. And, as always, salutations to Dana Duncan Seil, from Art Center College of Design in Pasadena, California.

And to Karen Green, wherever you are now.

I would finally like to, most of all, thank my most significant other, P.H., for her longstanding tolerance of my ongoing madness, particularly since she has absolutely no interest in the wacky world of porn. Her trust and confidence in me is precious and rare, and immeasurably appreciated.

Everything in this book attempts to echo the words of the late, great New York photographer Diane Arbus: "A photograph is a secret about a secret. The more it tells you, the less you know."

Recommended Reading

In the process of writing this book, I found the following useful as both research resources and inspirational touchstones, many of them having been my traveling companions over the years:

Anderson, Dan, and Maggie Berman, with the Vivid Girls. *How to Have a XXX Sex Life: The Ultimate Vivid Guide*. New York: Regan Books, 2005.

Bentley, Toni. *The Surrender: An Erotic Memoir*. New York: ReganBooks/HarperCollins, 2004.

Bogdanovich, Peter. *The Killing of the Unicorn: Dorothy Stratten (1960-1980)*. New York: William Morrow, 1994.

Boyd, Helen. *My Husband Betty. Love, Sex and Life with a Crossdresser*. New York: Thunder's Mouth Press, 2003.

Burana, Lily. *Strip City: A Stripper's Farewell Journey Across America*. New York: Talk Miramax/Hyperion, 2001.

Carre, Didier. *Stainless Ladies*. Zurich, Switzerland: Edition Skylight, 2005.

Coren, Victoria, and Charlie Skelton. *Once More, With Feeling: How We Tried to Make the Greatest Porn Film Ever.* London: Fourth Estate, 2002.

Field, Genevieve, and Rufus Griscom. (editors) *Nerve: Literate Smut.* New York, Broadway Books, 1998.

Flint, David. *Babylon Blue: An Illustrated History of Adult Cinema.* London: Creation Books, 1998.

Ford, Luke, *A History of X.* Amherst, New York: Prometheus Books, 1999.

Gitler, Ian. *Pornstar.* New York: Simon and Schuster, 1999.

Greenfeld, Karl Taro. *Standard Deviations: Growing Up and Coming Down in the New Asia.* New York: Villard Books, 2002.

Greenfield-Sanders, Timothy. *XXX: 30 Porn-Star Portraits.* New York: Bullfinch Press, 2004.

Harvey, Philip D. *The Government Vs. Erotica: The Siege of Adam & Eve.* New York: Prometheus Books, 2001.

Jameson, Jenna, with Neil Strauss. *How to Make Love Like a Porn Star: A Cautionary Tale.* New York: Regan Books, 2004.

Jenkins, Emily. *Tongue First: Adventures in Physical Culture.* New York: Henry Holt, 1998.

Kelman, Nic. *Girls.* New York: Back Bay Books, 2004.

Lim, Gerrie. *Invisible Trade: High-class sex for sale in Singapore.* Singapore: Monsoon Books, 2004.

Lords, Traci Elizabeth. *Traci Lords: Underneath It All*. New York: HarperCollins, 2003.

Merritt, Natacha. *Digital Diaries*. Koln, Germany: Taschen, 2000.

McNeil, Legs, and Jennifer Osborne. *The Other Hollywood: The Uncensored Oral History of the Porn Film Industry*. New York: ReganBooks/HarperCollins, 2005.

Millet, Catherine. (Translated by Adriana Hunter) *The Sexual Life of Catherine M*. New York: Grove Press, 2002.

O'Toole, Laurence. *Pornocopia: Porn, Sex, Technology and Desire*. London: Serpent's Tail. 1998.

Orloff, Erica, and JoAnn Baker. *Dirty Little Secrets: True Tales and Twisted Trivia About Sex*. New York: St Martin's Griffin, 2001.

Palac, Lisa. *The Edge of the Bed: How Dirty Pictures Changed My Life*. Boston: Litte, Brown, 1998.

Serpieri, Paolo Eleuteri. *Serpieri Sketchbook*. New York: Heavy Metal, 1995.

Taormino, Tristan. *Tristan Taormino's True Lust: Adventures in Sex, Porn and Perversion*. San Francisco: Cleis Press, 2002.

Tan, Cecilia. *Black Feathers: Erotic Dreams*. New York: HarperPerennial/HarperCollins, 1998.

Tisdale, Sallie. *Talk Dirty to Me: An Intimate Philosophy of Sex*. New York: Doubleday, 1994.